CHESTER LIBRARY

D0321897

CHANGING
ORGANIZATIONS

Other titles in the
Systemic Thinking and Practice Series
edited by David Campbell & Ros Draper
published and distributed by Karnac Books

Credit Card orders, Tel: 0171-584-3303; Fax: 0171-823-7743; Email: books@karnacbooks.com

CHANGING ORGANIZATIONS

Clinicians as Agents of Change

Edited by

Alan Cooklin

Foreword by

Sir Brian Wolfson

Systemic Thinking and Practice Series
Work with Organizations

Series Editors
David Campbell & Ros Draper

London & New York
KARNAC BOOKS

First published in 1999 by
H. Karnac (Books) Ltd.
58 Gloucester Road
London SW7 4QY

Coventry University

Arrangement, Introduction, & chapter 1 © 1999 Alan Cooklin; Foreword ©
1999 Sir Brian Wolfson; chapter 2 © 1999 Carlos E. Sluzki; chapter 3 © 1999
David Campbell; chapter 4 © 1999 Gianfranco Cecchin & Alan Cooklin;
chapter 5 © 1999 Suman Fernando; chapter 6 © 1999 Lennox Thomas; chapter
7 © 1999 Harlene Anderson & J. Paul Burney; chapter 8 © 1999 Yoel Elizur;
chapter 9 © 1999 Howard M. Weiss.

The rights of the editor and contributors to be identified as the authors of
this work have been asserted in accordance with §§ 77 and 78 of the
Copyright Design and Patents Act 1988.

The material in this book was originally published
in a slightly different form in *Human Systems:
The Journal of Systemic Consultation and Management*

All rights reserved. No part of this publication may be reproduced, stored in
a retrieval system, or transmitted, in any form or by any means, electronic,
mechanical, photocopying, recording, or otherwise, without the prior written
permission of the publisher.

British Library Cataloguing in Publication Data

A C.I.P for this book is available from the British Library

ISBN 1 85575 218 2

10 9 8 7 6 5 4 3 2 1

Edited, designed, and produced by Communication Crafts

Printed in Great Britain by Polestar Wheatons Ltd, Exeter

CONTENTS

EDITORS' FOREWORD

The publication of this book broadens the horizon of the Systemic Thinking and Practice Series. Because there is relatively little written about work in oganizations from the systemic perspective, we felt we should bring these examples of organizational consultation to the attention of readers who might have missed them when they were first printed in a special edition of the *Human Systems* journal a few years ago. We are also pleased to collaborate with Alan Cooklin, a consultant in his own right, who edited that special edition and prepared this book for publication in our Series.

There is enormous diversity among the projects undertaken in this volume, and while some of the contributing consultants would not describe themselves as systemic practitioners, there is nonetheless a common thread uniting the contributions. That is, compared to other approaches, these authors relate organizational problems and dilemmas to meaning structures, and they clearly describe the ways their client agencies interact with the broader context of other agencies and socio-cultural values. We have found that this book provides a rich mine of ideas that stimulate thought and challenge us to transfer the techniques from one context to another.

David Campbell
Ros Draper
London
October 1999

ABOUT THE AUTHORS

Harlene Anderson, Ph.D., has an international reputation for her innovations in the philosophy and practice of collaborative relationships and conversational processes with human systems. She is a founding member of the Houston Galveston Institute and the Taos Institute. Her work is explicated in her book, *Conversations, Language, and Possibilities: A Postmodern Approach to Therapy* (1997).

J. Paul Burney, Ph.D., is a frequent presenter at conferences on working collaboratively with individuals, groups, and organizations. He is a faculty member of the Houston Galveston Institute and an associate of the Taos Institute. Together with Harlene Anderson, he founded Collaborative Consultations.

David Campbell is a clinical psychologist dividing his time between clinical work as a family therapist and supervisor at the Tavistock Clinic, a National Health Service training centre, and freelance work as a consultant to organizations in both the public and the private sector. He has adapted systemic thinking to create a model for consultation which he teaches and practices in the United Kingdom and other European countries. He is the co-editor, with Ros Draper, of the current series, *Systemic Thinking and Practice*, which also includes *Work with Organizations*. He lives in London with his wife, who is a modern languages teacher, and their two teenage children.

Gianfranco Cecchin, M.D., is Co-Director, with Dr. Luigi Boscolo, of the Milan Centre of Family Therapy, Italy, a training centre where groups of 12–13 students spend two days a month discussing cases and theoretical issues and see families under supervision. Whilst his major contribution to systems thinking has been through his teaching activities at the Milan Centre and worldwide, he has always retained an interest and a concern in applying his ideas in organizational consultation.

Alan Cooklin has for over 20 years been concerned to integrate the approaches and services for children and adults both as individuals and in family contexts. For this reason the title of his post in the National Health Service was designated as Consultant in Family Psychiatry. As the Director of the Marlborough Family Service, of The Institute of Family Therapy, and as Consultant and Hon. Senior Lecturer at University College and Middlesex Hospitals, and finally as Clinical Director in the North West London Mental Health NHS Trust, he has frequently been active in organizational change, as a participant, as a manager, or as an invited consultant. For some ten years he has also acted as organizational consultant for "change" programmes commissioned by a number of multi-national companies.

Yoel Elizur, Ph.D., who has been a supervisor in psychotherapy and family therapy, developed his work as systems consultant with an emphasis on institutional change following the publication of *Institutionalizing Madness: Families, Therapy, and Society* (1989), which he co-authored with Salvador Minutia; the book highlights the effects of the institutional context on the course of therapy. Since then he has been developing family-oriented work in various institutions in Israel, has published a model for ecosystemic training and organizational development, has done research, and has been doing workshops in Israel, Europe, and North and South America.

Suman Fernando was a Consultant Psychiatrist at Chase Farm Hospital, Enfield, Middlesex, for 23 years until July 1993. Also, he served as a member of the Mental Health Act Commission from 1986 until October 1995. He is now a part-time Senior Lecturer at the Tizard Centre, University of Canterbury, and Chairman of the Board of Directors of NAFSIYAT (Intercultural Therapy Centre), London. He has had a long-standing interest in transcultural psychiatry, in particular institutional racism within systems that constitute the mental health services. He has written two books, *Race and Culture in Psychiatry* (1988) and *Mental Health, Race and Culture* (1991), and edited another, *Mental Health in a Multiethnic Society* (1995).

Carlos E. Sluzki, M.D., is Director of Psychiatric Services, Santa Barbara Cottage Hospital, Santa Barbara, and Clinical Professor of Psychiatry, University of California Los Angeles. He was formerly Chairman of the Department of Psychiatry at the Berkshire Medical Centre. Whilst there, he was also Editor of *Family Process*. Prior to that he was Director of the Mental Research Institute in Palo Alto. Throughout his career he has remained a prolific thinker and writer.

Lennox Thomas came to consultancy work with organizations after many years of working in residential child care, hospital social work, and probation during which he undertook training in family therapy and psychoanalytic psychotherapy. His interest in organizational consultancy developed alongside the Brunel University Masters Programme in Social Policy and Social Administration, which he began in 1988. As a black manager in the Social Services, he was often consulted by related services on equalities issues. He is now employed as the Clinical Director of NAFSIYAT, a therapeutic service for families and individuals from black and ethnic minorities, as well as consultancy and training, in London.

Howard M. Weiss, Ph.D., a clinical social psychologist, is the founder and director of the Ackerman Institute's Center for

Family–School Collaboration. He also serves as the Director of Research and Clinical Projects at the Ackerman Institute for the Family, where he has worked as a faculty member since 1980. He is a licensed psychologist in New York State, practising individual, marital, and family therapy.

Sir Brian Wolfson started work at 16 trying to save the family engineering business after his father died. Failing the first time, he started from scratch again at 19 and sold out at 22. After a hard-fought business career, he put a consortium together to take over Wembley Stadium in Autumn 1985, becoming chairman in 1986. He describes his achievement there as turning the world's biggest toilet into the world's number one sports and entertainment venue, succesfully increasing profits until bitten by 1980s-itis—making acquisitions for cash/debt. He now holds directorships in a number of companies, and throughout his career he has served on the boards of numerous professional and public bodies. His long-standing interests in the management of human resources and in management education is reflected in, among many others, appointments as Governor, Ashridge Management College; Chairman, British Institute of Management, 1986–1988; and founder Chairman of the National Training Task Force, 1988–1993, which was established, among other things, to set up the TEC movement. In 1994 he founded the Investors in People programme and became its Chairman, a position he still holds.

FOREWORD

Sir Brian Wolfson

When a group of clinicians, trained in understanding individuals and families, take on the task of consulting to different kinds of organizations, one needs to be clear to whom they are talking. The Editor has been clear that the primary target audience for this volume is the growing group of clinicians who try to use their clinical skills in organizational contexts. This is important because whilst the practices described would in many cases hold good in the commercial marketplace, the theories may not. However, the implied truth in this—that ideas are never effective, only their execution—holds true for most management change and management consultancy, or for that matter for most of life. After all, a lousy idea well executed murdered six million people, whilst a good idea badly executed won't pull the skin off a rice pudding. If any idea that we capture or try to capture is going to be effective, it is going to be effective through the doing of it rather than through its originality. It is by the way that an idea is *done* that will make or break whatever system change or personal change we seek to bring about.

In this volume, I see a common denominator running through all those contributions that I would define as "doing" chapters—

those that describe programmes and change, where someone has said "I need to take it from here to here, and I'm going to try and do it". This common denominator is best summed up by the word "ownership". Nothing ever succeeds unless enough of the key people have ownership. Without ownership by the key members of an organization, any change initiative is dead, and in fact to me the various techniques described here, even though they are not labelled as such, are techniques of trying to establish ownership to generate the foundation of whatever is then going to follow.

Of course, there is always an overall concept or idea, but the power of the machine to *do* is always greater than the power of the machine to *create*. Consider, for example, one of the so-called great differences between East and West in decision making. In the West, I get up in the morning, go into the company, and have decided on the way from home to the office how I am going to change A, B, C, and D. So I call my managing director and say, we are going to do so and so. He puts the 'phone down and promptly forgets about it if it does not happen to be on his agenda. He's busy anyway, and he's got other priorities and that's that. So, what I've actually done is that I've *taken* a decision before I've *made* a decision—and nothing will happen. Things don't happen that way everywhere. In Japan, for example, it is common for all the people who may or may not be involved in a concept and in its execution to discuss and discuss and discuss and eventually, after three, four, five, six, seven weeks of discussion, they have *made* the decision. After that, when somebody *takes* the decision it goes into action across a broad church of people who are involved in its execution. That's a difference between East and West when you talk about the effect of doing. This is not in conflict with, for example, the great respect for authority which is expected in Japan. Rather, it is that a Japanese company moves very much to the rhythm of one drum in terms of where it is going, because every person who has subsequently become part of that broad "doing" area has had his or her involvement in the debate and argument process of what is going to be done. In Britain, there are now some examples of something similar. One of the first things we do when we are checking out a company to see if it reaches the Investors in People standard [a government-endorsed standard for organizations and companies, of which Sir Brian is Chairman—*Ed.*] is to look at the business plan for the company. We want to know that every individual in the company knows about the business plan and knows what his or her role in relationship to it is expected to be.

Thus the use of authority is not hierarchical or authoritarian. Rather, it is very focused, and open to modification by different levels in the organization. For example, the Japanese company Komatsu, which makes earth-moving machinery, made a strategic plan to beat Caterpillar, the American construction-machinery company. It was no big deal to beat Caterpillar, but that was their purpose in life and that focused the whole organization very simply: "That's what our goal is, and every action we take under that umbrella will reinforce that goal." In the process of this, the different levels of the hierarchy *would* have the right to challenge their superiors' views on how to achieve that goal, but it wouldn't come down as their superiors' views; it would come down as being thought that it might be good for the company to do A, B, C, and D. That document would then circle the various committees and people and executives involved. The president would have the leading role in the discussion groups, and then everybody would sign off the document, stating that they had talked about it and that they were all in support after it had had the following amendments and so on. And that document would go back up the organization before it got the final seal of approval.

Within the cultural constraints of difference, some of this is beginning to happen in the United Kingdom. Firstly, most of the pace-makers in the United Kingdom today have been led by foreign companies. Britain itself may have been rotten in the world league of creativity in this sort of thinking, but if you take Sony in Bridgend, or Nissan in the North East, or IBM at Greenock, all those factories are out-producing the other factories of those companies across the world. With the right management applied to British people, we can do it, we can deliver, and we are delivering, and those techniques do work—but it is summed up by the word "ownership". John Neal, who is Chief Executive of Unipart, actually established a university within the company to teach people to open windows on their thoughts, to teach them whatever they want to know, and to get them hooked on the general prospect of learning, so that they would be more effective no matter what they wanted to do.

In this volume, I see the objective of many of the change processes illustrated in terms of ways to engage the members of an organization in ownership of that process—that is, ownership by the people who are trying to carry out change or who can be effective in carrying out the task.

The recent developments in the British National Health Service illustrate some aspects of this. Everybody was seized with the idea that the NHS could be better managed—everybody, that is, except the people within the service! To bring it about, so-called competent and effective managers were plucked from the business world and elsewhere and made into chief executives or chairmen of health bodies. They died; they got ripped to pieces, because the culture tore them up. The changes were not owned by the clinicians in the service, and you can't do a job like that alone. It had been a health service that was entirely run by clinicians and internal health service bureaucrats, and both these groups had such strong cultural mutual support for each other, despite their differences, that they ate any individual who came in to try to change them. As a result, most of the "new" managers from industry have become part of the culture that already existed, although the odd one stands out. This is an example of what happens when you (1) don't have ownership of change by the people in an organization and (2) *"take"* decisions rather than *"make"* them. This was the government taking a decision without really making it.

Comments on individual chapters

Alan Cooklin's introductory chapter, "Frameworks for the Organization and for the Agent of Change", sets the scene in two main ways. First, it considers why people join organizations; second, it examines the kinds of roles from which people try to change organizations. However, it is the descriptions of attempts at implementation of change which most interest me. Coming from a world where management techniques come in as flavour of the month—where we rush from "total quality management" to "descaling", "down-sizing", "re-engineering", where buzz words just pour out—I believe that in practice there are some enduring qualities of those managers who are effective and successful today. The consistent theme in the best of these ideas is to push the point of decision making down the ladder, to de-centralize it and get it as near to the customer as you possibly can. The sole purpose of having a business is to serve the customer. This does not mean abrogating responsibility at the top, but it does mean that feedback to and from the top must be quick and effective. In semi-formal cascaded systems, the difference in time between what goes down and what comes back up again should be a matter of days or weeks, nothing longer. We used to say that when one was running a business you only had to watch the four Cs: the costs, the cash, the competitors, and the customers. But there's an important word missing from this list of common denominators: that word, which comes up again and again, is *communication*, which must be equal and flowing in both directions.

This chapter also illuminated for me some issues about the nature of organizations, and particularly the persistent effort needed to bring about change in organizations. This is particularly demonstrated in the account of trying to bring about changes in a mental health service over a period of time. That seven-year crusade highlighted for me the dominant requirements of persistence and determination, which is true of everything that worked that I have ever done in my own life or seen other people do. As Calvin Coolidge put it: "Nothing in the world can take the place of persistence: talent will not; nothing is more common than unsuccessful men with talent. Genius will not; genius is almost a proverb. Education will not; the world is full of educated failures. Persistence and determination are omnipotent."

The other issue the chapter illustrates is that an individual cannot change things alone: one either goes in with a team that has total commitment and support for what one is trying to do, or one has to create a team upon arrival that is equally committed to what one is trying to do. The most important thing in a new managerial role is to create a team that has people on it from inside the organization, people who know the ropes and the back alleys.

Carlos Sluzki's chapter, "Language, Practices, and Record-Keeping: A Reflective Consultation and Some Institutional Changes That Resulted from It", was fascinating to me and again brought Coolidge to mind, particularly the description of being in the role of the junior member of staff changing childbirth practices in Buenos Aires. He managed to get ownership from the people whom he impressed by what he had achieved. He was determined to see that it worked, and that the others were too, and even after the bureaucracy came and undermined him, the good that he left behind, the corn that he had sown, was able to flourish.

This is also one of the chapters where for me the clearly described case studies conquered the difficulty of some of the language—all specialities and cultures have their own buzz words and shorthand way of communicating to others in the same field. Overall, I think that what is described in the case study in the prologue is a classic management situation. When the ideas and action were coming from the bottom of the organization they got away with it, until somebody higher up discovered what was happening. Even though it was working it was against the culture, and against the system, so he tried to "can" it. From a management perspective, the second example seems to me to be a classic example of dysfunctional management: decisions were being made altering people's perceptions of what they were supposed to do, and so one half of the organization didn't know what the other half was doing.

In David Campbell's very matter-of-fact and down-to-earth chapter, "Connecting Personal Experience to the Primary Task: A Model for Consulting to Organizations", I particularly like the part where he very simply sets out in a list what he wants to do. To me, you could take that and use it in virtually any company or organization; it would be an operating plan that is simple and to the point. I also like the way he talks about "creating a climate for working together". Quite simplistically, one could define the job of a manager as creating an atmosphere in which people will give of their best. As Campbell is in the role of the consultant, he has the luxury of being able to do just that, side-stepping reality by saying that in an ideal world this is what we should and shouldn't do. Having said that, he sets his stall out very well. The question of formulating and "implementing the mission statement with a strategic plan" is of course fundamental: "Where are we now, where do we want to get to, and what do we have to do to get there?" In an ideal world, strategic plans would be designed by the people who are going to carry them out, because they are the people who know most. However, given the resources with which he was working, he had to adopt a more positive posture to get his message across, because the organization he was consulting to needed certain things that they were not going to get from within.

The chapter by Gianfranco Cecchin, "The Feelings of the Consultant as Indicators of Problems and Solutions", in discussion with Alan Cooklin, continues to illustrate the headline issues that I have already identified—ownership, persistence, determination, bottom-up and top-down communication, and the speed with which information moves in either direction. Cecchin, who comes across as a very sensitive and reflective individual, describes how all these factors operate in an Italian setting, with a small team of people working from the bottom up who were trying to achieve something. However, having failed to do business in Italy myself, I see what he describes as a classic Italian situation!

The chapter by Suman Fernando, "Black People Working in 'White Institutions': Lessons from Personal Experience ", leads, I believe, to an essentially pragmatic conclusion about how racial equality issues should be handled in an institution such as the one he was describing, and I support his conclusion. It is important to go to the key people involved and say "this is the problem, let's agree our perception of the issues and let's agree how we are going to work together to solve it." Of course, they might not agree, and one might have to say "If we don't agree, then I wish you to understand that this is the position from which I am coming and will continue to come until things move in that direction", although that is not the best way of bringing about change. When we set up the National Training Task Force (NTTF), we made sure that ethnic minorities were represented on its board. When we set up the Training Enterprise Councils, we insisted that every Training Enterprise Council (LEC in Scotland) also had ethnic minority representation on its board. That itself doesn't say anything except that the representation was there: one realizes, therefore, that some further skill is required. What I did as chairman of the NTTF was to invite a black businessman with strong equal-opportunities credentials to be my mentor in guiding us to maintain our stance on racial equality. He had open access to me at all times, and he was there to tell me at any time when he thought I was treading the wrong water or going in the wrong direction. As a result of that, we made a great deal of progress. We didn't solve every problem and crack every issue, but we made substantially more progress than we would have done otherwise.

Lennox Thomas's chapter, "Organizational Change in the Probation Service", interests me greatly, partly because of my lack of knowledge about the subject. I was unaware that there had been a shift in the service from people who came in with training but no basic knowledge of what was going on and then made a career within the service, to people who are qualified in "life" and have then given their second careers to the probation service. That was an interesting and educational distinction of which I had never been aware.

My second point about this chapter is that I think he was able to make substantial progress with "Midshire" by using what I see as a classic management approach of the best sort—an approach aimed at creating ownership. Again, I am back to one of the common denominators in bringing about change that I have already identified. He achieved this by using the point of view of an outside consultant to put history into perspective and then ask "How do we bring about change for the better in this context?"

The chapter by Harlene Anderson and Paul Burney ("Collaborative Inquiry: A Post-Modern Approach to Organizational Consultation") for me illustrates through a case study the use of a simple idea that obviously worked. I have already acknowledged that different specialisms have their own languages, and this for me was an example where I would have appreciated it more had the language been more accessible. That apart, what makes their approach special for me is that they decided to try to crack the assignment in a day, which is unusual. Cracking it in a day made the whole thing worthwhile. Another point worth making is that again the dominant themes of ownership and teams come through very strongly.

The chapter by Yoel Elizur, "'Inside' Consultation through Self-Differentiation: Stimulating Organizational Development in the IDF's Care of Intractable, War-Related, Traumatic Disorders", is fascinating, and my reaction to it was "wow!". This chapter deals with a unique situation originally and thoughtfully. In an entirely coherent manner, he describes the issue, he describes the problems, and he describes his relationships within the situation.

The chapter by Howard Weiss, "Family–School Collaboration: Consultation to Achieve Change ", is very satisfying to read. He describes problems, says what makes a model unique, describes relations with children, and goes to the questions that were posed. He captured my attention as a layman because I can relate to what they were trying to do, I can relate to the managerial approach. Furthermore, the project he described had a dramatic knock-on effect. Again, the thing that stood out for me was the importance of communication. When he talks about the Baron de Hirsch Institute in Montreal and what he was doing there, communication turns out to be the critical feature. By communication, I mean telling somebody something and then spending the time to have the dialogue with them subsequently that makes sure they understand it.

INTRODUCTION

Most clinicians in the mental health and human relations fields began their professional lives with the task of understanding the inner world, or at least the distress, of individuals. What then leads such clinicians to believe that they should or could generate positive change in institutions or organizations? If they do seek to achieve such changes, do they have relevant skills? If so, what are these skills, and how do they operate? How do different clinicians see themselves as implementing their clinical "wisdom" in the organizational rather than the individual domain?

When the goal of change is to improve the efficacy of an organization or institution whose explicit task is to treat the mental health problems of their clients/patients, then it may seem logical that clinicians should have developed skills to improve the instruments of their own trade. However, within the field of systemic thinking the shift of focus from the individual's inner world to the context of intimate social relationships has often been expected to progress logically to the social organizations within which people work or in relation to which they live. This assumption—that what has been learnt in a clinical setting is necessarily applicable to an environment of non-intimate social relations—may contain a number of fallacies, and it has been strongly challenged by a number of workers familiar with both the systemic and organizational development fields (Borwick, 1986; Hirschorn & Gilmore, 1980; Merkel & Carpenter, 1987).

The terms "organization" and "institution" often describe distinct entities, although they may also share a number of significant properties. In this volume, they are deliberately referred to as though interchangeable, in order to focus on the common dimensions of the forces for relevant change in relation to the forces opposing such change. The *Shorter Oxford English Dictionary* (1973) defines an institution as an "establishment, organization, or association, instituted for the promotion of some object, esp. one of public utility, religious, charitable, educational etc. The name is often popularly applied to the building appropriated to the work of a benevolent or educational institution". This definition focuses on the goal and on the "establishment" or premises of an institution. In this volume, the term is less likely to be used in relation to a building but, rather, relates to the kind of social structures that have evolved in relation to a key task of the organization, and the particular relationship between those social structures and the task.

Health, "functionality", or "virtue" in families has often been defined as antithetic to "homeostasis", "rigidity", or other definitions of an opposition to change. Institutions have often been considered as, by definition, antithetic to growth, vitality, or change. Given that the "family therapy approach", and the later "systemic" approaches in their various waves, were all essentially crusades for change, it is not surprising that institutions, with their implications of restriction and "closure", have often been perceived as the target enemy of many such crusades. Family therapists have sometimes been placed in a quandary about how then to apply their thinking to these "alien" contexts. This idea of institutions as being in "opposition" to change is close to what in some earlier systemic formulations was described as "homeostasis", as though defining some inherent pathological property of institutions. Alternatively, the forces against change can be understood in terms of the disparity between the social structures set up to carry out a task and the human needs that may be provoked by an organization and that, of course, in turn may have themselves provoked the form of the organization that was set up. In quite different ways I think this "opposition" to change is particularly illustrated in the chapter by Harlene Anderson and Paul Burney on the one hand (chapter 7), and in Yoel Elizur's chapter on the other (chapter 8). In the former, the goal was profit and success of the business, whilst in the latter it was to maintain the military "health" of the army. From a different perspective, this process was most compellingly described in the classic study by Menzies, "The Functioning of Social Systems as a Defence against Anxiety" (1970). In this, she described her intervention in a major London teaching hospital in which there had been a breakdown in the arrangements for nurses' allocation to the various departments and wards, as well as in the arrangements for the nurses' training. She showed that the various sub-groups in the organization had become separate "institutions" which were being maintained more for their own membership rather than to promote the task of the organization. What they had constructed was some kind of icon or monument to themselves. Menzies formulation arose from Kleinian psychoanalytic theory of the individual being applied to organizations. The descriptions did indeed present a picture of an almost inherent resistance to change, akin in many ways to the early descriptions of homeostasis. On the other hand, chapters 7 and 8, as well as those of Campbell (chapter 2) and Sluzki (chapter 3), seem to me to illustrate that what in a bird's-eye view might be variously described as "resistance to change", "rigidity", or "homeostasis" is in fact made up of a complex series of interlocking human dilemmas. When the participants in the consultations are helped to discover new resolutions to their dilemmas, they show no reluctance to adopt new solutions.

Historically, at least in industrialized Europe, institutions were associated with buildings, if only because benevolence and charity were so intimately connected with property. But the promotion of social systems for "public utility, religious, charitable, educational etc. . . ." in other cultures may be associated less with property and more with various explicit forms of representation of social structure and order (Cooklin & Gorell Barnes, 1991). In fact it may be that "Western" institutions do fulfil some function of support for the dominant social order in a way that is provided less divisively by natural/family systems of kinship in the tribe, village, and so on, in non-industrial societies. In many sophisticated and older societies, such as the "old villages" of Bali (Ramseyer, 1977), there are complex "societies" that young men, and separately young women, join as part of a complex initiation process. They then graduate to similar but different societies as they progress through young unmarried adulthood, married life, married with children, and so forth. These versions of "institutions" act as a primary organ of socialization of the culture but in a manner that does not alienate the members from the rest of at least that mini-society. This view of an "institution" then only becomes problematic when the form of socialization becomes focused on "removing" negative attributes, as appears to be the case with many "Western" institutions, without offering any formal pathway or ritual to introduce positive and new changes, or rites of passage (Fried & Fried, 1980; Gennep, 1969; La Fontaine, 1985; Lewis, 1980; Richards, 1956). It is then that an institution, usually set up in the "West" to perform some explicit task—such as healing or care—can become more a source of permanence than of function (see discussion of the Tower of Babel, in chapter 1).

Thus, many family therapists may express an implicit antipathy towards institutions, at least in the tone in which they refer to such human structures (institutions), if not by direct criticism or rejection. Given that "institutions" of various kinds so often are created in many cultures in response to some human need (see chapter 1), the antipathy to these organizations must be based on a different set of principles or philosophy, or at least on a different set of ideas about how such human needs should be met. Furthermore, those who try to "change" institutions may be organized by the different tasks they are asked to carry out, by the different roles from which they perceive the organization and/or try to implement change; but they will also be organized by the different philosophy they espouse. It was for this reason that I constructed a questionnaire to which the contributors to this volume were invited and/or asked to respond. The questionnaire was designed to try to tap the authors' thinking about how each perceived his or her role, including the position from which he or she was invited, or chose, to try to change the organization; the kind of thinking he or she had about the structure of the organization in the first place, the kind of thinking that he or she had about how the organization could or should be; and the ideas about how he or she attempted to promote, elicit, or "facilitate" that change.

Questionnaire

1. Think of one or two contexts in which you have been involved in changing an institution/organization in one of the following three roles:

   a. Invited consultant to either the organization or to a specific task.

   b. As a member of an organization either at the top or in some middle-ranking role.

   c. As a leader or explicit manager of an organization.

2. Consider the structure of that organization, its objectives, and its ways of functioning and define these briefly. In what ways do you believe the dominant culture or other cultural or ethnic factors have organized the structure and/or goals of that organization?

3. Define the overall and specific tasks that are the *raison d'être* of that organization or institution. In what ways do you think that the particular "human structures" (variously called Institutions and Organizations) developed as responses to the particular human tasks: child care, education, mental health care, social order (police, defence, forces etc.), social/ community provisions, manufacturing and marketing, financial services, group and professional identities?

   To what extent to you think that the particular "human structures" developed in response to factors other than the primary human tasks of that organization (political/economic factors, survival of the identity of a particular organization, philosophical/religious or "power" factors, etc.)?

4. Give a hypothesis about why that particular structure of organization might be the response to those particular needs or tasks. Include in your hypothesis the relevant cultural and

ethnic influences that you believe may have organized that institution to be structured and operate in that particular way. What do you believe was the kind of thinking or "logic" that was inherent in the choice of each particular structure as a response to that particular task, and the forces that prescribed that choice in the face of alternatives?

5. On reflection, could you think of better or more rational (in your own terms) structures or ways of operating such an organization, or can you define a totally different organization that you think would have been more appropriate?

6. What is your hypothesis about why the current structure of the organization developed rather than the one you had subsequently proposed? (Some of this may be a repeat of part of the answer to Question 3. If this is the case, choose under which heading you wish this point to be made.)

7. If one wanted to move from the current organization to the structure that you proposed, what ideas do you have about what would be needed to happen for that to be achieved?

THE ROLE OF THE AGENT OF CHANGE IN AN ORGANIZATION

8. In which of the three above roles (invited consultant, member, or manager/leader) were you in, in the work you have described? If you were in a role that is not covered by these definitions, can you define it? What do you believe principally activated you to take on your particular role as an agent of change: interest, altruism, money, power, belief systems, etc.?

9. If you were there as an invited consultant, who authorized you to act, and how would you define that person's level of power/influence/authority in relation to that organization or the people to whom it is responsible? If you were there as a manager, how would you define the freedom of action that you had, and how does that relate to way the organization was set up (a personal business set up by yourself, a charity, a state agency, etc.)? If you are in the role of a staff member, what do you see as the "medium" for you in attempting to achieve change: e.g. as "activator" within the organization to convince the man-

agement; as somebody given a specific task which, if carried out successfully, might lead to change; as somebody who had specific responsibility for changing organizational arrangements, or as somebody "at the bottom of the pile"?

10. [*I would recommend that you answer the following question after you have written your case description.*] On reflection how would you define the role, task, and goals that you had set yourself in this piece of work (change, consultation, etc.). In what ways are your answers organized by your own cultural/ethnic influences?

11. What were the forces acting on you that led you to choose this course of action and to define yourself in this way (your own skill base, beliefs, ethical position, financial reward, cultural influences; pressure from managers, bosses, colleagues, allegiances, etc.; or particular ambitions of success, fame, etc.)?

12. If you reflect on the components of this piece of work that were successful or those that were failures, how would you link those forces with those successes or failures? Specifically, what influences from your own current and past experiences, both personal and professional, have affected how those choices were made?

* * *

When I designed the questionnaire, it seemed a good and simple idea ... at the time. But the reader might wonder whether the authors actually used it. Some did, some didn't, some used parts of the questionnaire in innovative ways, some were put off from contributing to the volume by it. I had not—although perhaps I should have—predicted such a complex response. It seemed that the questionnaire had itself become a kind of metaphorical institution—it defined a way and form of thinking. It provoked its respondents to take a position of compliance or defiance in relation to it, although, as I said, some chose to ignore it, and some not to "enter" it at all. Thus it appeared to me on reflection, that this volume had to include some considerations on the process as well as the content of the contributions. This is initiated here in the Foreword by Brian Wolfson. In addition, the "discussion" that takes place between Gianfranco Cecchin and myself in chapter 4 is explicitly about the process of thinking behind the chapter as well as the content presented. I suspect that the readers will also include this in their assessment of and response to the chapters.

The volume contains chapters with a considerable range of topics and approaches, along several different dimensions:

a.   *Variations in the size of group consulted to*

The size varies from the six or eight participants in the group worked with by Gianfranco Cecchin on the one hand, to the medical services of the Israeli Army worked with by Yoel Elizur, or the educational systems of New York and Montreal worked with by Howard Weiss on the other.

b.   *The goal/ task of the group consulted to*

In four out of the nine chapters, the consultee groups were concerned with some form of human care or therapeutic service. However, even within these there is great disparity, between the goal or task of the "Midshire" Probation Service described by Lennox Thomas, the Mental Health Commission described by Suman Fernando, and the teams described by David Campbell or Gianfranco Cecchin. Almost the complete spectrum between social control on the one hand and personal therapeutic services on the other is represented here.

c.   *The degree to which the consultant is explicitly aiming to encourage the consultee group to adopt and/or become sensitive to particular issues or beliefs*

This is again a dimension within which both extremes could be said to be represented. On the one hand, the consultations by Harlene Anderson and Paul Burney or by David Campbell explicitly set out not to engender, encourage, or impose a particular belief system or set of practices. On the other, in the case of Suman Fernando (chapter 5) and Lennox Thomas (chapter 6) it is clear that they at least were explicitly aiming to generate sensitivity to racial issues and to encourage the development of anti-racist policies and practices in the organizations that they were consulting to. There is probably a variation even among their chapters in the degree to which the organizations were explicitly inviting them to take on this aspect of the consultant role. The work described by Howard Weiss (chapter 9), however, was explicitly commissioned to make the changes that he espoused within the educational services.

d. *The roles within which the different "consultants" were invited into the consultee organizations*

Although I have in general used the terms "consultant" and "consultee", these are not technically correct descriptions in the case of Yoel Elizur's and Suman Fernando's chapters. Both of them took on a consultative role within their strategic aims to generate change within the organizations of which they were a part, but they were not, at least initially, explicitly invited in in that role.

* * *

What has been collected here is a broad range of approaches to changing organizations, demonstrated through actual consultations within business, the educational services, probation, and so on. Sir Brian Wolfson's Foreword provides a commentary from the perspective of commerce and industry.

There has been a definite intention of not aiming to draw conclusions on "how to do it". The concern is to expose the various dimensions (explicit and implicit) in the "consultant" and "consultee" groups when clinicians attempt and/or are invited to promote organizational change. Clinicians as well as others concerned with organizational change should find that this volume offers a useful framework of thinking in mapping their own contributions and roles.

Alan Cooklin

CHANGING
ORGANIZATIONS

CHAPTER ONE

Frameworks for the organization and for the agent of change

Alan Cooklin

T his chapter first outlines some frameworks for considering the nature of different organizations and institutions using a number of dimensions. These dimensions are principally:

1. the relationship between the way in which the human needs of the members of the organization are expressed in relation to the primary task;

2. the relationship between a person, his or her role, and the system of which he or she is a part within the organization;

3. the dimensions of flexibility versus rigidity, compliance to authority versus encouragement of initiative, intimacy versus isolation, and other dimensions of the ways that dimensions (1) and (2) above function.

The chapter then considers a number of roles within which individuals may commonly attempt to achieve change within institutions and organizations. The principle roles defined are:

*   The outside "Invited Consultant".
*   The "inmate" who attempts to initiate change—"The Irreverent Inmate".

• The "Line Manager" who tries to effect change from within the management role.

Such change is usually geared to moving the organization towards focusing on its primary task. Alternatively, or in addition, the aim may be to achieve a change in the ethos or belief systems represented by an organization, or to improve the working environment of the members of the organization.

Institutions/organizations, the "human need", and the "work or task" need

In Western industrialized culture, the work setting has become divorced from the social context. In fact, we explicitly define maintaining "boundaries" between social life and work as a virtue. When this is achieved, the social intercourse that is often part of the work life of less industrialized cultures is unavailable, and work is more likely to be associated with boredom and disconnection from pleasure. Miller and Rice (1967) distinguished work groups from "sentient" groups; they defined the latter as organized to promote the security and comfort of the members. It may therefore be that the failure of many Western institutions to recognize and acknowledge their social functions plays a major part in the constraint and dehumanization that we often associate with institutionalization. But this failure may in no way reduce the need for the "security" that is promised by the collective nature of organizations. Whilst Attachment theory (Bowlby, 1969, 1973, 1980; Ainsworth, Blehar, Waters, & Wall, 1978) has provided an elegant set of proposals to explain the behaviour of humans in "two-person" relationships, it has been of limited use in the thinking about human groups. Psychoanalytic thinking has also been limited to explanations of the meaning of behaviour in groups, rather than the human need expressed in the formation of such groups. The function of group collective formation and function has tended to be examined more by organizational psychologists (Ackoff, 1960; Emery & Trist, 1965; Katz & Kahn, 1966), and there has remained a gap in the thinking between this and individual psychology.

For the purposes of this chapter, I shall assume that the following "sentient" human needs are sought to be met from becoming a member of an institution:

1. To gain a sense of collective security or invulnerability, based mainly on the principle of "safety in numbers".

2. To find a "low-cost" (i.e. demanding little personal intimate investment or risk) context of comfort and intimacy.

3. To achieve mutual validation of the task of the group. This is of particular importance when the task is one that may be criticized or even proscribed in the dominant culture (e.g. a particular religion or cult).

4. To develop a shared and mutually confirming identity.

The Old Testament legend of the Tower of Babel described a group of people who thought that they would construct a monument or an icon for themselves, and then had the illusion (building the tower up to heaven) of belonging to a permanent group and borrowing some elements of immortality from the size of the thing that they were going to create. The ambitious tendency of some institutions for self-promotion and the expansion or multiplication of themselves seems set towards a similar goal, as may the institutions or even the books or ideas we leave behind us. The problematic aspect of that tendency is in relation to its effect on the processes of development. The individuals in an institution may develop, they may "grow", their thinking may change, but the institution that was set up in the service of their original idea may not change, either with them or with the development of the original idea. It is then that the membership—the reason that people go on belonging to that organization—may become reified, turned into "a thing", and maintained for its own sake rather than for the needs of the task for which the institution was set up.

The sentient needs, and the search for a sense of permanence through the institution, are often represented by special rituals (particularly in relation to eating habits in residential organizations such as schools, colleges, etc.) or special words or language. The latter are, of course, criteria that could also be applied to family therapy associations, conferences, and journals. An interesting example is illustrated in the rules imposed in an institution that institutionalizes "not being an institution". In this case, a psychiatric hospital that was set up as a "therapeutic community" (Jones, 1968) in the 1960s espoused the virtues of "democracy, openness, and informality". Whilst these may have been laudable goals, their institutionalization was based on the myth that the patients were really being allowed to share in the government of the hospital—a belief for which there was ample evidence to the contrary. One junior psychiatrist expressed his protest against what he saw as the falseness in this arrangement by insisting on referring to staff and patients by their formal titles and second names. His action was treated by the director of the hospital, who insisted on the informal use of first names throughout, as insubordination, for which he reported the junior to the hospital board. This was an unusual and perhaps extreme example of pressure within psychiatric institutions to adopt particular rituals and language, but within the mental health field in particular many such "languages" and practices, whose rationale is rarely explicit, still abound. To the "uninducted" observer they are often rife within the "ward rounds", "ward groups", and particularly the arrangements for overnight or weekend "leave of absence".

All organizations concerned with social control or change, particularly because they are usually paid for and commissioned by governments in some form or other, have to develop their own closed idea of themselves (Goffman, 1959). Ironically, mental health workers in particular, and family therapists especially, may have been seen by their other (medical in the former and psychiatric in the latter case) colleagues as revolutionaries, as "strange" people, people who do not really fit in. But in the construction of our institutions, whether mental health institutions or learned associations, many of us have developed our own languages that other people do not understand, and such "private" languages are also to be found throughout all work organizations. Gorell Barnes (1990; Cooklin & Gorell Barnes, 1988) has described the confirmation of self which can similarly emanate from the intense team camaraderie and rituals common in the executive groups of many companies and financial institutions.

Most of us associated with the systemic movement are also "iconoclasts"; in my case a lapsed Jew, doctor, in some ways psy-

choanalyst, psychiatrist, and perhaps even a lapsed family therapist (even though I see a great many families). But as one grows
older the "lapsing" can go full circle. In my case, this has meant
reconnecting with at least some of the Judaic culture (the religion
more than the rituals), I feel more of a doctor now than I used to, I
have taken on some psychoanalytic ideas and found them useful
again having given them up, and I find myself strangely being
accepted nowadays by my psychiatric colleagues. I have been
asked to chair committees that I used never to get involved in, and
to take on management roles. Discovering that one can "leave" an
institution or an institutionalized role or set of practices and later
find value in the practices or ideas that were embedded in that
institution supports one's capacity to see the positive elements
potentially available in that institution. To enter an institution with
some sort of brief to effect change requires that one respects the
human need for "permanence" and stability at the same time as
finding ways to challenge those aspects of the institution which
lead to constraint or "dehumanization". Respecting the "need"
may mean temporarily joining with, and using the language of,
that institution whilst at the same time challenging the reverence
in which it may be held. For the "agent" of change, this could be
experienced as an ethical dilemma. How can one remain true to
oneself at the same time as joining with an institution that may be
part of a process of constraint and "dehumanization" or in other
situations represent some ethos of which one does not approve?

The agent of change therefore needs to operate in a way that
allows respect for the institution at the same time as irreverence for
the forces that promote "institutionalization" and such practices
that act against the development of the individuals or the creative
aspects of the primary task.

A model for the functioning of organizations in relation to the primary task

John Cleese (1991)—comedian but also author and producer of
many training videos about management skills—summarized four
components of "successful" businesses:

1. "Excellent" companies—defined as those that are consistently successful in the long term—treat people more positively.
2. Good companies trust their employees, and only 5% of employees ever take advantage of this trust.
3. Effective selling has become a cooperative activity between sales person and potential customer, in which the sale is the result of effective problem solving.
4. Separateness of teams and individuals—or at least enough autonomy to allow entrepreneurial creativity—are the life-blood of a successful company.

In the past twenty years, management training programmes and manuals have increasingly stressed the correlation between these sorts of principles and effective business planning and marketing. Thus, what would more commonly be represented as humane and ethical treatment of employees has a new and added validation from profitability. Therefore, to reflect on, or intervene in, organizations, the agent of change needs a framework of function which as much as possible brings together his or her beliefs about a "humane" organization with the need for the organization to be productively effective.

The development of ideas represented in this chapter originated from a number of sources:

1. Main's classic paper "The Ailment" (1957), which described how hospital units could become organized around certain "special" patients, with apparent "secrets" being held by, but not shared by, different groups of staff. Each staff member (or group) was sworn to secrecy. The "special" patients then became the central focus of the whole organization, complained about but also revered.
2. Menzies' "The Functioning of Social Systems as a Defence against Anxiety" (1970), described in the introduction.

Both Main and Menzies, at that time, conceptualized their ideas about the organizations in terms of the psychopathological states or processes in the individuals organizing the behaviour of the organization.

3.   The work of Trist and Sofer (1959), and of Miller and Rice (1967) who although basing much of their original thinking on psycho-analytic principles, particularly those of Bion (1961), eventually moved beyond individual and group psychology to a model that included primitive unconscious processes in an organizational framework. The work of these groups led to the useful distinction between the "primary" task of a work group and the "covert" task, and between "work" groups and "basic assumption" or "sentient" groups.

4.   The attempts to apply the principles derived from structural family therapy (Hirschorn & Gilmore, 1980), which added a systemic dimension. The latter placed the arrangement of roles within the organization as the primary frame of reference.

5.   The work of Irving Borwick (1986), coming from a background in organizational development, who for a time joined forces with members of the Milan associates (first Boscolo and Cecchin, and later Boscolo) to try to apply the principles of their systemic model in the consultation to large business organizations.

Borwick's own framework focused on the relation between the Person, the Role, and the System (Figure 1.1). This is an interesting systemic framework if only because clearly the Person is still a

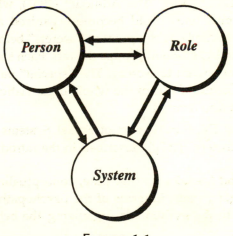

FIGURE 1.1

person in the differing roles he or she may fill, the person in role makes up the system (or at least plays a major part in organizing its internal structure), and the system organizes the roles that the person fills. Non-biological "intimate" human systems will be organized by their size, their task, their philosophy (or religion), and the power differentials between the leaders and the led. For example, a dictatorship or non-constitutional monarchy assumes a considerable power differential between the leaders and the "led". The survival of such an organization in that form will depend on its size, on its relationships with other such organizations and their proximity, and on the political cultural and "power" environment surrounding it. Such an organization may or may not be dependent on a particular ethic or philosophy. If it is, it is likely to be some such notion as "The Divine Right of Kings", the "mature and strong" knowing "what is best" for the "immature and weak", or a variant of these. A democratic structure assumes certain ethics, such as "everyone equally deserves a voice", "the strong should care for the weak or disadvantaged", and so forth. Business organizations will also be organized by size and by power differentials, but they may be equally organized by the need to generate profit against the background of these other variables. Figure 1.2 represents a framework I have found useful in considering the interaction of the person, in his or her role, in some form of "managed" work organization. The formal structure of the organization is represented in the bottom line of the "system" box ("line" management, "dual" management, or "complex" management). Simple line management is that which would apply in a small family business, or in any organization that has only one chain of command. Larger organizations commonly employ dual reporting structures: the individual manager has overall "line" responsibility to his or her immediate superior but is commonly dependent on separate chains of command for different functions such as personnel or human resources, financial control, or purchasing. Whilst this more complex structure allows for some sharing of tasks and responsibility and provides some checks and oversight in the larger organization, it can also be the source of greater inefficiency or of increased stress in the manager. The structure of nearly all organizations poses a dilemma for the leaders. On the one hand, authoritarian rigidity kills enthusiasm and generates

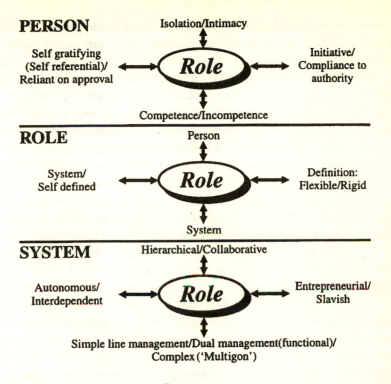

PERSON Isolation/Intimacy

Self gratifying (Self referential)/ Reliant on approval ← *Role* → Initiative/ Compliance to authority

Competence/Incompetence

ROLE Person

System/ Self defined ← *Role* → Definition: Flexible/Rigid

System

SYSTEM Hierarchical/Collaborative

Autonomous/ Interdependent ← *Role* → Entrepreneurial/ Slavish

Simple line management/Dual management(functional)/ Complex ('Multigon')

FIGURE 1.2

bitterness or rebellion, whilst weak leadership is often associated with low productivity, chaotic organization, and low efficiency. Highly authoritarian structures, coupled with high levels of ambiguity, lead to maximum stress in the members of an organization. Borwick (1978) described this structure being taken several stages further in a number of multinational companies, and in a case report he looked at the workings of senior management of ITT. In what he called the "Multigon", the top of the "pyramidal" structure was lost, leaving the senior managers not only with multiple reporting but also potentially in immediate competition with each other. Whilst this might potentially lead to increased productivity, it also meant that these personnel were working in an environment of maximum stress. In that case, it was probably a deliberate strategy to keep the management at high levels of stress.

How do staff in "stressful" organizations commonly respond to such dilemmas? The responses that one most commonly obtains from people in the lower or middle ranges of management are the following:

1. To seek and develop "informal" alliances to combat their sense of loneliness and powerlessness. These alliances are usually an attempt to bypass, and often to try to deny the existence of, the power of the formal authority structures (the "old lags" group in some factories, which often includes workers, supervisors, and sometimes junior managers, and which sometimes fulfil an informal deciding role).

2. To develop "sentient" or comfort relationships, so that more of the organization's time and energy goes in to comforting social contacts, with lowering of productivity and increase in inefficiency ("gossip groups" or "cosy" meetings that tend to complain and avoid taking effective action).

3. To hold back the development of new skills and competencies, partly in an attempt to avoid redundancies, and partly to promote a shared belief that "nothing can change".

4. To engage in conflictual relationships that promote blame of others (the "fight/flight" response).

5. To increase absence through sickness.

Organizational consultancy, on the other hand, often tends to promote the converse—namely, to increase the participation of senior management, by pushing conflict "upwards" and by increasing the focus on, and definition of, the formal hierarchy. The former combats a common management strategy of devolving decisions to the lowest possible level in the organization. Whilst this strategy may be explicitly aimed at maximizing a sense of responsibility and commitment at the lowest levels of management, it is often combined with a process in which "information" filters rapidly down the hierarchy and only slowly or incompletely upwards. The result is often that the "devolvement" of decisions fulfils more the function of protecting senior management than that of "activating" or "empowering" junior management. Increasing the definition of the formal lines of responsibility and accountability is one way to clarify what is real delegation as opposed to abrogation of responsibility.

What roles exist for the agent of change in organizations?

How have these principles organized the thinking, techniques, or actions that family therapists have contributed to organizational change?

Many family therapists have tried to use their "systemic wisdom" to improve the environment of, or working of, various institutions. Often this has been by offering "training" or some sort of supervision (in institutions concerned with personal change or care), or, when a powerful enough member recognizes that there is a problem and asks for consultation, by consulting directly to the organization. The degree of power held by the "applicant" (the one who asks for help, if such has in fact happened) is usually the key factor in the potential for change. That person has to recognize a problem, ask for help to change, and be senior enough to be able effect change.

A wide variety of approaches of family therapists adapting their skills in working with families so that these can be applied to institutions of various kinds are summarized in *Systems Consultation* by Wynne, McDaniel, and Weber (1986).

Family therapists have tended to take one of a number of common stances:

1. To try to ensure (and/or convince themselves or others) that their treatment was so effective that institutions were irrelevant.

2. To restrict themselves to clients whose problems would never invoke an institutional response.

3. To treat institutions as the "patient" and achieve a role that is called "meta" to them.

4. To work with organizations, such as family businesses, in which there is much overlap between the intimate family dynamics with which the family therapist may feel familiar and the task of the organization.

5. To try to apply their consultative skills, developed in relation to intimate relationships, in relation to larger and less intimate organizations.

Family therapists may have inherited a legacy from Gregory Bateson's (1972) proposition that one could not be "meta" (or an outside observer at a "higher" level of abstraction) to a system of which one is a part. The implication of this thinking was that one could not achieve an overall perspective with which to intervene in a system of which one was an active participant. But Bateson was also a proponent of the view that the observer must also be part of the field of observation. This view has been rediscovered in the ideas about Second-order cybernetics (Howe & Von Foerster, 1974). Despite both of these developments, it usually seems as though family therapists were much more comfortable when consulting from outside (or at least on) the boundary of an organization. At the same time, we have nearly all created or become part of some form of institution. Borwick (1986) has offered some useful distinctions both between the structure of organizational systems in comparison with family systems, and between the roles of organizational consultants in comparison with family therapists (Figure 1.3).

Characteristics of Family and Organisational Systems		
Item	*Family System*	*Organisational System*
Boundary	Defined by relations	Defined by task
Task	To be family member	Achieve organisation task
	Survival	Survival
Role	Individual taken up by role	Role taken up by individual
Authority	Based upon relations	Derives from task
Power	Anarchic when used without authority	Revolutionary when used without authority

Systems Relations of Therapists and Organisational Consultants		
	Therapists	*Organisational Consultants*
Goal	Member-system welfare	Organization functioning
Tactics	Person	Role
Results	Symptom resolution	Role resolution
Strategy	System-person relations	Role-system relations

FIGURE 1.3

In the remainder of this chapter, I review some case vignettes to illustrate organizational intervention from the three perspectives outlined earlier:

- The "Invited Consultant"
- The "Irreverent Inmate"
- The "Line Manager"

The "Invited Consultant"

The role of the "Invited Consultant" requires, as I have already stressed, that one is invited to intervene by someone in a sufficient position of power. Selvini (Selvini Palazzoli, Boscolo, Cecchin, & Prata, 1980) has suggested that this person is usually one who is "losing the game".

EXAMPLE 1

The Clinical Director for Paediatrics in a teaching hospital outside London consulted me about a problem. Clinical directors are senior doctors who have been given the responsibility to decide on the strategic objectives of a particular service, usually have one or two managers to work for them, and the rest of the time do their usual clinical work. From the senior management point of view they are there to give the services clinical direction, but they are often used covertly to protect the senior management from the wrath of the "powerful" doctors. This clinical director had been forced to contract two wards into one, one of which worked mainly with paediatric urology (i.e. with the surgery and long-term developmental follow-up of children born with genital or urinary malformations) and the other with paediatric oncology (cancer) and paediatric endocrinology (mostly growth problems and diabetes). In arranging the merger, he had to choose between the two senior nurses running the wards and was forced by the senior management to accept a particular ward space (and one that was highly unsuitable) as replacement. He asked me if I would talk to the nurses, who had "a whole lot of interpersonal problems", adding that the ward had ceased to function properly, sickness rates were high, the atmosphere was tense, and some parents had complained about the way senior nurses publicly criticized less senior nurses. Also, the ward was inefficient, was often not able to meet its targets, and frequently required extra "agency" nurses.

I politely said that I would not meet the nurses but would be happy to meet the whole staff team of nurses, teachers, play specialists, physiotherapists, junior doctors, and so on, provided that he and the senior nurses were present. I met with a group of about twenty staff. The atmosphere was tense—"Why had this shrink been brought in?" I made some speech about whose agent I was, succeeded in preventing the senior nurses from talking all the time, and added that all I knew was that there had maybe been some problems. The response I got was a tense silence, everyone trying not to meet the gaze of anyone else. Eventually, a black nurse—and I wondered what the significance could be that a black member of staff had spoken up first—said that the "constant destructive criticism from senior staff was unbearable" and that they did not recognize their skills and training. When I managed to block one of the senior nurses and the clinical director from immediately responding, more and more staff contributed. I learnt that twenty-five different medical staff at times used the ward because the hospital had a policy that all children must only be treated in a specialized paediatric ward. Architecturally, the ward was in two wings, so it was continuing as though two wards, but they had lost one very senior nurse. The senior nurse who had attempted to respond (the one who had not been chosen to run the combined ward) was black and was perceived by her loyal team as the more competent of the two. So I wondered (to myself) if this made sense of the fact that a black nurse had spoken first—representing at least an unspoken accusation of racism in the selection process. This senior nurse let it be known that she felt highly criticized by the clinical director but had never before articulated this belief.

I began to see the wings of the ward, the surgeons and paediatricians, and the doctors and nurses, as well as the victorious and vanquished senior nurses, as representing divisions at many levels. In turn, I wondered what possible function so many divisions, at so many levels, might fulfil. Might these "divisions" fit snugly with a successful strategy of "divide and rule" by the senior management?

The outcome of these explorations and "recognitions" was that the staff group set up a series of six working parties to analyse six different aspects of the problem, to propose solutions, and to consider how to tackle senior management. In fact, this process was relatively easy for them to achieve at that time, because the clinical director had identified the problem and had much personal investment in finding a solution. Later it confronted all of them, including eventually the senior management, with the more fundamental divisions that had to be faced.

This example illustrates a fairly common mode in which systemic therapists may from time to time be invited to act as agents of organizational change. The invitation was clear, and the "host" was of sufficient seniority and power to be authorized to effect the changes.

EXAMPLE 2

For some seven years I worked intermittently as a management consultant with various subsidiaries of multinational companies. Borwick was my original mentor and introduced me to the work. Coming from a background concerned with change and care, the philosophical shift that I encountered in organizations concerned with productivity and profit confronted me with what I perceived as ethical dilemmas. Of course, they were only really ethical issues as long as one held on to the notion that one was in some way acting as a healer. Borwick (1986) strongly challenges the notion of family therapists applying their wares in business organizations when still adopting this latter role. The focus has to be on the companies' success in the marketplace.

In consultations that were undertaken at the request of the president of a group of companies that marketed a similar information service in each of seven European countries, this focus was pursued in the context of examining the interactional factors that may have inhibited the success of a group of companies in a changing environment. Although the environment for each company was different in each of their respective countries of origin, it was apparent to the president and board of this multinational company that they were similar in their vulnerability to the impacts of new information technology. The changes were thus imposed by a combination of new technical developments, political change, changing market requirements, and increased local competition. It was apparent that this new environment required these companies to pool certain resources (which might of course mean the loss of some tiers of the management structure, and the possibility of management redundancies) and allow greater influence from the research and development (R&D) departments. This would have meant the amalgamation of departments into a "super" R&D department and the consequent giving up of the competition between the current departments, leading to a greater possibility that the rapid introduction of new technologies would seriously cut down the manpower requirements of each company. Thus the resistance to change was based on the effects of a "traditional" view of business expertise and conflict between the power and influence of line management versus functional management, especially staff functions, R&D, and financial control, all in turn exacerbated by the increased pressure to change, threat of redundancies, and so forth, leading in turn to increased resistance to change.

The context of the consultations was a powerful incentive for change. They took place in a structured programme attended by representatives of at least three levels of senior management from each of the seven companies. The four-day programme, held in an attractive residential conference setting, was organized into a combination of didactic "educational" presentations about the dilemmas facing successful organizations that wish to change: "role analysis sessions", "systems group exercises", "strategic planning sessions", and "reflective" plenary sessions.

Role analysis sessions are close to a format developed by Borwick (1986). Participants sign up to explore specific problems of work "role" in response to a volunteered "problem". The leader first interviews the presenter whilst requiring that all questions from the group are preceded by a hypothesis about the "answer". After the first demonstration interview, the leader "supervises" other group members in interviewing other members who have presented problems of "role".

Systems Group exercises involve the whole conference group of participants and consultants. The explicit goal is to use "any method" to study the process of the conference as it relates to the specific goal of organizational change in response to the challenges of the changing marketplace. The consultants and each sub-group of the participants attempt to form hypotheses, and then they share and debate these as part of the plenary sessions.

Strategic planning sessions are held in relation to each component company, as well as in relation to the overall goals of the parent company. The task is to formulate, "on the assumption that what has been learnt in the conference could be of direct relevance to the back-home workplace", strategies of change on the bases of the hypotheses formed during the conference.

The effects of these interventions in this context were as follows:

1. Each group could begin to see the common factors in each of their separate companies.

2. The presidents and vice-presidents could be encouraged to take more active responsibility for the changes needed and for their consequences, rather than pushing all the responsibility downwards.

3. The information chain was reversed, so that information travelled up the hierarchy of management more rapidly than, or at least as rapidly as, it travelled down from "on high".

4. As a result of the increased flexibility of thinking, the companies could develop a greater diversity of products and therefore increased marketing opportunities, resulting in a diminution of the pressures previously forcing the changes in the face of resistance.

Comment.   This vignette outlines a complex structure for the consultations, with a perhaps unusually "attentive" set of managers, given that they were all in the same business and all facing, in different countries, market pressures that demanded urgent change if they were to survive. The role of the consultants was in general that of the outside/inside observer who offers a methodology and way of thinking, rather than specific solutions. That is, the consultants designed a programme that attempted to promote creative problem-solving behaviour in the participants, without prescribing particular solutions. The degree of anxiety in the participant companies, the residential setting, and the relative strangeness of the tasks being offered in the consultation conference did inevitably excite a heightened expectation of leadership from the consultants.

The "Irreverent Inmate"

Many inmates and staff of institutions and other organizations will attempt to initiate organizational changes that represent their philosophy—commonly one that they see as more humane, fair, or egalitarian than the current dominating ethos. It is most commonly in these situations that the person who seeks one's help is less likely to be in a position of power, and that one has to find a way to join the institution while maintaining one's own humanity and sense of humour. I suggest that this can be approached through "irreverence" (using the term in a way similar to Cecchin, Lane, & Ray, 1993, although applied here only to certain aspects of institutional behaviour) for the institution's "sacred cows". Thus one becomes a supporter of the people in the institution, and perhaps of the aims (depending on what they are), but a saboteur to some of the rituals of the institution and, through this, a questioner of some of its beliefs. To achieve this, one's tasks are to be able to "join" (metaphorically rather than literally) the institution, and preferably be paid to do so, at the same time as finding an acceptable way to express this "irreverence". For example, in therapeutic institutions one may need to start with the "private" language of therapy—what I call "therapspeak". A whole series of common phrases need to be questioned, by asking innocently what they mean: phrases such as, "It seems to me . . .", "What I'm hearing is . . .", "I'm wondering if . . . ", and so on. Also, words like "therapy"—especially "family therapy", "family problems", "personal problems of my own", "being disturbed", and so on—have to be questioned "innocently" too. "Joining" the institution holds the danger that one becomes lulled into beginning to "think" in the language of the institution and, as a result, begins to believe that one understands this language. I do not mean to imply that all language used in an institution is incomprehensible, but rather that one must retain the freedom to question the meaning ascribed by the institution to its commonly used terms. So, if it is common for staff in a particular unit to describe patients as "brittle", then it is crucial to ask them to explain exactly what they mean by this term. One may receive a reply such as, "Oh, well it means she's very vulnerable . . . you know can't cope, or hold herself together". Again, one needs to know what "vulnerable", "coping", "holding together", and so on mean, and what are the assumptions about what will happen if she "fails to cope" or if what is brittle "fractures". "Family therapy" is itself a most seductive term, as it is likely to be the one that therapists are most likely to fall into the trap of believing that they know the meaning of.

EXAMPLE 3

Some eight years ago a job as a general psychiatrist had become vacant, and I was encouraged by one senior family therapist to apply for it—"Because all you family therapists who are psychiatrists avoid the real problems of changing psychiatric hospitals. It's time some of you bit the bullet, and did it." Whilst I did not accept the advice, it was perhaps a factor in my accepting an invitation to act as consultant to a small but innovative project. The psychiatrist who was appointed to run the unit had been part of the original team with Julian Leff that had carried out the expressed emotion research (Leff, Kuipers, et al., 1982; Leff, Berkowitz, et al., 1990). This psychiatrist had become interested in whether this work could be applied outside major research departments. He set up the Family Project at University College Hospital, working only half a day per week, and asked me to be its consultant on family therapy. The idea we had was to try to change the ward climate so that nurses could think about the patients in relation to their "natural" relationships, rather than in relation to themselves as nurses, counsellors, therapists, and at the same time to invite the nurses to join the project and work with some families under supervision.

After a crusade of some seven years, this project became an integral part of the mental health services providing for a population of about 250,000. For us, the importance of the project was reflected in the time needed for its acceptance—seven years—as well as the fact that it could at last be recognized. How did it happen? This acceptance was not achieved through any carefully thought-out strategy, although persistence and a belief that we could make a real change kept us going. For two years, there were four of us meeting once a week for about three and a half hours seeing families on the ward. Various nurses and medical students came from time to time to look, and usually went away again. Then we thought that the project needed some full-time staff. We applied for many grants and finally came second out of 200 applicants for a major grant of £250,000. Fortunately, the head of this very influential grant-giving body telephoned the head of the health service and told him, "You really should be doing this work, but why should we pay for it?", but he did offer a small grant on condition that the health service matched it. Finally, through other grants we raised enough money for some staff, but only for two years. So we started trying to train the nurses . . . but they did not come, which was surprising as many had asked if they could join us. Our "systemic" explorations uncovered the fact that a change in staff structure would mean that any nurse who attended might be challenged by his or her colleagues for doing "non-essential" work and showing disloyalty to the other nurses who were facing job cuts. So we talked to Julian Leff, who suggested that the only way to get nurses to come regularly to training in which they will learn new and difficult skills is to provide a course that has a qualification at the end. So we got two qualifications, one from the university and one from the Nursing Board for the same course. Then we had to convince the new head of the new trust that now owned these services that we had something that he could not refuse. Two things came to our rescue:

1. Expressed emotion research—which has conclusively demonstrated that certain kinds of interventions in the families of patients with schizophrenia can very significantly lower the relapse rates after a first acute episode—was now known

throughout psychiatry, and it had been shown that relapse rates could potentially be reduced from around 85% to 15%. The research had respectability in established psychiatric circles, but no one knew what to do with it.

2.   The trust was under heavy pressure to reduce the number of beds available for psychiatry. So we did a calculation that if we trained 10 nurses per year, we could expect to lose 3 per year to other jobs, but by the time (after five years) we had trained 50 nurses we could predict a reduction in the number of beds required of at least 20%. This was central London, with a large migrant population and an escalating use of in-patient resources, so if this was achieved it would have been a significant intervention.

What is more important about the project is that its thinking is now beginning to get into the "bones" of ward life, at least on some of the in-patient wards. In at least six of the ten wards in the trust, we have nurses who are thinking about how to apply the principles, even if this involves just one senior nurse initiated to do genograms (a study of family relations using family trees) on all the patients admitted. The main symbol of having become part of the established—although you might say ethically subversive—order was when we were given nice offices with video, mirrors, and so on. And although the two years of our funding ended several years ago, we became an "offer that cannot now be refused", and the validity of the organization required that they continue to fund us.

Working in the Family Project and becoming more intimately familiar with the aspirations and frustrations experienced by the nurses led me to rethink some of my ideas about institutions. It helped me to shift from a perspective that perceived institutions in terms of a pernicious "homeostatic" conspiracy to one that respected the "human" needs, whilst not espousing the "revered" practices. As described above, I began to rethink many institutions as a form of substitute for the absence of organized kinship structures in Western industrial and post-industrial society. And this fitted the way I have seen many individuals and families become attached to institutions and then return to them in times of turmoil, regardless of whether or not the people they originally saw are still there. They say "it's good to know the 'place' is still there".

Comment.   If it is not to lead to "revolution" or rejection by the organization, the role of the "irreverent inmate" can only be successful if a number of criteria are satisfied. These are commonly:

1.   That the "initiator" must have and must promote an idea that is at least tacitly accepted by the philosophy of the organization.

2.   That he or she must be of sufficient seniority or influence, or be openly "sponsored" by one who is, to maintain the impetus for change.

3.   That he or she needs a reference group who can also be challenging about the strategy of implementation of change.

4.   That he or she (or "they") may need to be persistent for very prolonged periods.

All these points were both present and highly relevant in this example. Within the organization, a tacitly accepted, although totally unacted upon, belief about "supporting relatives of the severely mentally ill" was combined with the ingredients (2) to (4) until the ideas became part of the everyday expectation of first a few and later increasing numbers of the units within the larger organization of the trust.

The "Line Manager":
taking management on

Management consultants often seem to share with family therapists a kind of antipathy towards engaging in the power operations of large organizations. With few exceptions, family therapists have avoided taking on senior management roles in large institutions and other large public organizations. Those who have have sometimes been coy about presenting the systemic aspects of their work in their own organizations, as though the "purity" of their systemic principles were in some way compromised by being in a role of power in a large organization.

EXAMPLE 4

Until a few years ago, I was mainly employed by one of the NHS trusts that provides only mental health services. As well as general out-patient and in-patient psychiatry, it provides old-age psychiatry services, six child and family psychiatry clinics including an academic department with a professor and her team, three psychotherapy clinics, and a special in-patient service for mothers who have "broken down" soon after giving birth, to be admitted with their babies. The Trust has to earn from the purchasers about £25,000,000 per year to pay its way.

I was telephoned one night by a senior manager to ask if I would agree to act as Clinical Director of six child and family clinics, the psychotherapy services, and the mother-and-baby in-patient unit. I thanked her but declined. Then I was approached by the chairman of the board of the Trust; various "helpful" colleagues in my own team also pointed out what their fate might be if an alternative clinician were to become clinical director. While I was recoiling from these conflicting pressures, I realized that I could limit the job to only two to three years, and maybe, just maybe, I could do something on a larger scale along the lines of the comprehensive adult and child family mental health service that we had developed at the Marlborough Family Service, where I have been director for 20 years. So, with some misgivings on the part of both myself and those staff in my directorate who feared that I would try to replicate The Marlborough in all the clinics, I agreed to take the job for two and a half years on two days a week.

There is not space here to describe the various stories that could be told about the experiences of setting up a management team with a business and operations manager, the suspicion and fears of fellow clinicians when one of their number takes on a powerful leadership role, or the battles about "change" that were had with each component of the organization on behalf of the organization as a whole as well as on behalf of a different philosophy of care and treatment. I had several specific strategic goals of my own:

1. To try to integrate the child and family services with the psychotherapy and mother and baby services. Whilst it may seem logical that they should function synergistically, they had all

tended to function in autonomous and some might say "discon-nected" ways. This was compounded by the fact that they all operated on the basis of very different premises or philoso-phies. The child and family services varied with different mix-tures of systemic, psychoanalytic, and academic "psychiatric" influences. The adult psychotherapy services were almost ex-clusively psychoanalytic; whilst the mother and baby unit was based on traditional adult psychiatric hospital practice. My aim was to allow mutual influence to occur between the models and clinics, to make them more answerable to their "communities" and to their clients and their families. This meant challenging a whole range of well-embedded practices.

2.   Partly in the service of the above, to encourage the whole direc-torate to become a consultative resource for the Trust as a whole.

3.   To use systemic skills in the service of achieving both the above.

4.   To generate an increased awareness of, and sensitivity to, eth-nicity and cultural difference.

I think I was well aware that these goals would not be fully realized within two to three years, but they seemed reasonable objectives within which one could measure what could be achieved within that time frame. In reality, I found that it was possible to:

1.   begin to integrate the child psychiatry with the psychoanalytic psychotherapists (who are themselves beginning to change), and eventually with the in-patient mother and baby unit (this has been helped by being able to appoint some senior systemi-cally trained child psychiatrists and adult psychotherapists, as fortuitously some others left);

2.   to begin to employ systemically trained psychiatrists in the senior posts in the psychotherapy clinics;

3.   to create a multi-age service that is beginning to be recognized as a potential source of philosophical leadership by the clinical director of general psychiatry.

This represented an achievement of about a third or a half of the goals I had set myself. One could argue that there were many variables in both the organization I was working with and within, as well as in my own strategy and personal approach, which could account for this level of achievement—low or high, depending on one's expectations of organizational change. There were two main things I learnt from this experience:

1. The changes were significant along the dimensions represented by my original goals. Therefore, I felt I had challenged to my own satisfaction the belief that a management role mitigated against the initiation of organizational changes within a systemic perspective.

2. I believe that my capacity to initiate change was significantly enhanced by my knowledge that the commitment was specifically time-limited to a maximum of three years.

The freedom to use one's power in this way confronts one with an ethical question based particularly on the limits of one's freedom. There is a real danger that in the interests of the survival of the institution one could feel forced to compromise the ethos one stands for, which is the old problem on which institutionalization is based. It is in such circumstances that "irreverent" questioning and teasing of the commonly "grave" issues discussed in trust board meetings can be a protection of one's own "self confirmation" and allow one to continue to represent a stance that allows personal and interpersonal change to remain the dominant goal. When terms such as "quality control" or "activity data" or (the worst) "cost-improvement schemes" (which means financial cuts) are heard, one has to remember to muse about, for example, "the nature of quality?", "the activity in stillness?", or "the connection between good money and improved costs", to remember to be what Cecchin, Lane, and Ray (1993) have called "the fool".

Conclusions

Whilst the "Invited Consultant" role is not the only position from which change can be effected, agents of change—other than revolutionaries—need to have a view of the organization as a system, with its connections to wider systems, at the same time as being an active participant as subordinate, peer, or supervisor. To achieve this systemic perspective often requires the formation of some sort of reference group that can plan change-enhancing interventions, whilst being open to the observation of feedback, and help to maintain a readiness to adapt one's activities in response to feedback. Such a reference group, however, needs to find some way for the organization to recognize its validity if it is not to be perceived as a revolutionary threat and, as a result, excluded, marginalized, or neutralized.

The goal of this chapter has been to offer some frameworks for conceptualizing the functioning of organizations and to suggest some roles within which one may successfully act as an agent of change. A secondary goal of this chapter, as of this volume, has been to encourage practitioners in the systemic field to examine ways in which they may act as agents of organizational change, so that the skills can be defined and refined to a level comparable to those expected from approved trainings in family therapy.

CHAPTER TWO

Language, practices, and record-keeping: a reflective consultation and some institutional changes that resulted from it

Carlos E. Sluzki

Prologue: a personal anecdote

A long time ago, in 1956, when I was still in medical school, I was assigned to do a clerkship in emergency medicine at a neighbourhood public hospital in Buenos Aires. It was a small facility with only two in- and out-patient sectors, namely, emergency medicine and maternity. One day, as I was passing by one of the delivery-rooms, I heard what sounded like a major brawl and shouting match. Out of curiosity I entered the room and witnessed a free-for-all wrestling match between an extremely agitated, violent, terrified woman well in the midst of the process of childbirth, and a nurse midwife and two aides trying to contain her on the delivery gurney. Now, it happened that, out of professional curiosity, a couple of evenings before this event I had attended a conference on "fearless/painless childbirth", introducing to the audience the by-then pioneering work of Lamaze and of Reed. On the basis of that information alone, and with the omnipotence fitting a soon-to-be-physician, I jumped into the scene and improvised a form of intra-delivery mini-Lamaze preparation: during the free intervals between contractions, I talked soothingly to the lady, educating her about the whole process of delivery (drawings included!) of which she was totally ignorant, and inviting her to become an active participant in the process by teaching her to pant-breathe and later to push, explaining to her how that would help her in terms of analgesia and the baby in terms of oxygenation. I also reassured her that I would accompany her and coach her on those tasks until the end of the delivery. In a short half hour, and to the amazement of the midwife and nurses—and, indeed, to my own marvel—this woman, until then totally wild, became a collaborative, friendly participant, wholly concentrated on making the best of the experience and extremely grateful when it finished successfully with the reward of a beautiful baby.

After it was all over, the midwife and nurses, rather excited by what they had witnessed, managed to pump my imagination with the idea that that type of service should be offered at the hospital on a regular basis. Following the saying "In the kingdom of the blind, the one-eyed is king", I took it as a call. I proceeded to read whatever I could find on "fearless childbirth" (by then there were, I remember, a total of three books on the subject, of which only one was translated into Spanish), I designed a blueprint of a painless childbirth program, I invited a couple of fellow medical students and friends to join me in the endeavour, and, a week later, I presented the idea to the chair of the obstetrics service, requesting his authorization to offer, off-hours, a voluntary "Fearless Childbirth" program for pregnant women and their mates. After examining our protocol, he accepted, "as long as it didn't interfere with the regular activities of the Service". I then organized a presentation of this project to the whole contingent of midwives and nurses and affixed a small notice in the out-patient clinic inviting parents-to-be to join the programme. Within three months we were conducting four staggered groups in training, with a total of some thirty couples. One of the three of us was always on call and ready to cross town towards the hospital on our scooters whenever one of the women from our programme arrived at the hospital to deliver, in order to coach them during the process. Thus opened the first "Fearless Childbirth" programme in a public hospital in Buenos Aires, and probably in Latin America. The experience was glorious—enlightening for the staff, a blessing for the parents-to-be, and enormously gratifying for me and my team, not only authors of this successful endeavour but officiants in the never-ending miracle of natural birth.

Six months later, however, there was a change in the leadership of that Department of Obstetrics, and the new chair informed me that he would no longer authorize our programme, "as we were not yet physicians, and therefore our activities were not endorsable". Needless to say, we were crushed, our patients/trainees were crushed, and so were the midwives and nurses, who had seen their work transformed by our programme. But, fortunately, through those six months, midwives and nurses had shared our work and had learned the new ethics, the new language, and the new practices and procedures. A qualitative change had taken place in their way of conceiving of their professional identity and in the way they conducted their daily work. In their own words, "they couldn't picture a maternity service the way it was before". As a result, they not only coached the pregnant women, but they themselves, as insiders, within a few months requested authorization from the new chair to develop a(nother) "Fearless Childbirth" programme, following the pattern of the one that we had created, and permission was granted. That programme is still being offered today. So, not only did the staff experience a transformation, the institution as a whole was qualitatively transformed by a process that was serendipitously initiated (my having passed by the delivery-room while that brawl was taking place, my having attended a presentation on "fearless childbirth" two days before, and, even more important, my having had the audacity of putting into action knowledge held till then with pins) yet shifted the role of the staff, the role of the women in their own delivery, as well as the role of the physicians. The result was an epistemological shift that started almost subversively (change frequently does), shifting the balance of power by and in the circulation of new knowledge and new ways of speaking.

Introduction

Health agencies, mental health agencies, and institutions in general are systems in permanent change. Change may take place so slowly as to seem non-existent, or it may take a rapid, revolutionary pace. It may be generated by the institution's own developmental needs (a growth or a downsizing), by the pressures and needs of the context in which the institution operates (be it changes in the community, the political situation, or the overall economy), or by sheer chance. Indeed, most institutional changes occur by a combination of all those undercurrents, a prime example in practice of the principles of Chaos Theory (cf., for example, Gleick, 1987).

However, one cannot wait for those ingredients simply to appear. More specifically, one of those ingredients—serendipity—by definition cannot be orchestrated. There are, however, consultative methodologies that foster creative thinking, collective responsibility, and qualitative changes in the participants and, frequently, in the institutions of which they are a part. This chapter illustrates the effect of one of those methodologies, namely, *reflective conversations*.

The 1990s has been an era of reduction of access to public services and a shrinking of what in the United States is known as entitlement funds—that is, public funds for the payment of health services provided at non-public institutions for the poor and the disenfranchised. In that climate, in which public and private non-profit organizations compete and fight for survival just as a private corporation would, mergers and consolidations are a not infrequent strategy for not-for-profit health and mental health agencies, as they allow for a reduction in the duplication of managerial positions and of overall support services and increase what, in the new lingo, is known as "control of the market share". Those periods of consolidation—an unsteady period for all the staff, as it is perceived as threatening the security of their jobs—are ideal for the introduction of changes "from the top down" (changes feared but expected by everybody when the sign "Now Under New Management" is posted). And those changes generally start with the institutionalization of new procedures and the reorganization of personnel. But unless the management is very savvy and generates opportunities for a safe grass-roots expression of ideas, initiatives, and needs, it is a bad time for any changes attempted "from the bottom up". The latter have a greater chance of success if they are initiated during a non-crisis period, and definitely when they are packaged as being non-critical to the management—paranoia freezes any managerial goodwill and disposition even to consider change.

Most institutional transformations, as most evolutionary processes, take place discontinuously, in bursts, alternating with periods of steady state. Change is frequently preceded by crisis—that is, by an increasing tension between the morphogenetic (shape-generating) and morphostatic (shape-retaining) tendencies that escalates until it upsets the unsteady equilibrium between them. But change may also take place during non-critical, calm periods, when it may not be perceived as mandatory or as threatening. Regardless of how change is initiated, qualitative transformations that affect a whole institution will always be systemic in nature and include change in institutional goals (i.e. in the very mission and objectives of the institution), a change in a given institutional practice (i.e. in the way procedures are carried on), a change in language (i.e. in the way participants talk about goals and practices), and a change in protocols or record-keeping formats (i.e. in the way events are registered).

An example of a *change in goal* could be a shift in the mission definition from "improve patients towards an early discharge" to "helping the patient to reach his/her own potentials, regardless of discharge". An example of a *change in practice* in an in-patient unit is to begin to include patients in their own treatment planning or discharge-planning conferences, or a decision to place experienced clinicians in charge of responding to initial telephone calls from prospective patients, with the goal of redefining the motive of the consultation from *symptoms* to *problems* (from intra- to inter-personal) before the first face-to-face consultation. An example of a *shift in language* would be the introduction of solution-oriented, strength-based rhetoric in lieu of (or as a second language in addition to) symptom-based, problem-oriented rhetoric. And an example of a *change in protocols/record keeping* may be the replacement of symptom-based admission sheets for ones that may guide the interviewer to explore (more) centrally situational–contextual variables. Change in any one of these dimensions will favour change in others. Once the process of change has been triggered and resonates at another level, a cascade effect takes place by which these levels reciprocally impact on each other. Changes may start at one level in the system (sometimes almost serendipitously, as was the case of the introductory anecdote), but, through rever-berations and ripple effects characteristic of complex systems/processes, they may affect other levels and be affected by their change in turn, reconstituting and consolidating each other at an-other equilibrium point of the system. Hence, at a given moment it may become impossible or at least only arbitrary to pinpoint the original trigger of the change. But because organizations are living systems, morphostatic processes all too often block those ripples, reconstituting the previous knowledge/power relationships.

Unless a change at a given level reverberates and is comple-mented by changes at another level, the transformative process will in all likelihood stall. It can be ground to a halt by lack of resonance at other levels, poor timing, ideological incongruency, or vested interests in the status quo. For instance, one may introduce a change in the institution's rhetoric (e.g. in its "mission" or "vi-sion" statement), but unless this change is supported by simultane-ous changes in the institution's daily practices and/or modalities of record-keeping, the likelihood that that shift in language will result in a qualitative change at the level of the whole institution is rather remote. Qualitative change is a culture change, a shift in the discourse and practices that glue together interaction and relation-ships. Instantiation of new discourses/practices requires a learning that, in turn, depends upon the possibility of reflective conversa-tion.

The clinical consultation discussed below contributed to the triggering of reflective conversation leading to qualitative changes in a mental health agency, changes that permeated goals, lan-guages, practices, and record-keeping. That institutional shift happened in this case not by design but as a spontaneous, if not unavoidable, process following a series of clinical consultations that were themselves reflective conversations. Guided by systemic principles, these consultations were carried on following a con-sultative style that empowered the consultees and enhanced their own resourcefulness. Rather than preached, the systemic view was (co-)constructed and enacted with the participants, generating the proposal for a shift in some institutional goals and a change in some practices: "things happened"—that is, a qualitative change took place—anchored by a felicitous change in record-keeping that demanded daily practices that, in turn, replicated (and reminded the staff of) the newly spelt-out goals.

A clinical consultation with the staff of an agency

The director of a residential agency invited me to conduct monthly two-hour consultations for his staff.* This facility provided evening and night structured living care for ten chronic psychiatric patients who, during the day, were engaged in other community activities; most of them participated in therapeutic programmes for chronic psychiatric patients, some of them worked, some just wandered around town. This residential (therapeutic) facility was part of a medium-sized not-for-profit private agency contracted to provide those services by the regional department of mental health. Two years ago, the residential agency expanded to include a nearby day hospital that served the same population.

During one of those consultations, the consulting group—five enthusiastic and dedicated staff members, including the director of the evening facility, all with abundant front-line experience but with a low level of formal training—began to discuss their frustration with one of their residents, a 48-year-old man named Bruno. Bruno had a loaded history as a chronic psychiatric patient, starting in late adolescence. He had spent some ten years in a psychiatric hospital, followed by many cycles in a revolving door between community and psychiatric hospitalizations. For the past year and a half he had enjoyed a rather steady-state, living in town in a protected environment that included chiefly both this residential facility and the day hospital. The essence of the staff's frustration was that Bruno's social behaviour would consistently improve in the course of several months, during which he would conduct himself in an increasingly pleasant, responsible, and col-

*This consultation has also been discussed in chapter III of Sluzki (1996), where, subtitled "There's Nothing Like Home", it exemplifies the key role played by the staff of mental health institutions as inhabitants of the personal social network of psychiatric patients.

laborative fashion, but quite suddenly and unexpectedly he would shift to antisocial and irresponsible behaviours that baffled everybody.

Examples of those behaviours went from the sublime to the ridiculous: Bruno would, for instance, sneak into the pantry of communal supplies and steal boxes of candies or pastries to gorge himself, a behaviour that not only exasperated the staff because of the bad example it provided to other members of the facility but also placed him at risk, since Bruno was a diabetic and required a rather strict diet. In addition—and this was one of the main sources of vexation for the staff—Bruno would, rather unprovoked and unexpectedly, escalate into diatribes filled with profanities and offensive behaviour toward the staff (i.e. defiantly baring his behind to indicate contempt or displeasure), which took place during what was usually perceived by everybody else as low-intensity interactions. The staff could not figure out what triggered those episodes, nor were they able to obtain a cogent explanation from Bruno himself.

I began by exploring what the consequence of those outbursts would be. The staff explained that this would involve reconsideration of his status at the house in terms of duties and privileges, a demotion of sorts that would relieve him of some of his communal responsibilities and, indeed, delayed the plans for his "graduation" into a less restricted, more independent living environment, which had been defined as the agreed-upon goal. I requested more details of these discharge plans and was told that the personnel were guided by the reasonable criteria that patients should progress and that an improvement in the patient's social skills would signal that he was ready to undertake the challenge of moving into a less structured facility—namely, community-based housing in which he would enjoy less control and more autonomy. I explored who else was involved in Bruno's care and was informed that during the daytime he, as most of the other residents, participated in the day hospital, a programme that included therapeutic and educational groups and various recreational activities. That day hospital (which I heard about for the first time in a rather casual way during this conversation) had been, as mentioned above, incorporated two years earlier into the overall administrative and fiscal structure of the agency that now managed both. I explored whether Bruno had any relatives and was informed that he had had no contact with his family for over twenty years and that, in terms of his personal social network, his only relationships of consequence were the inhabitants of the residence and the staff and patients of the affiliated day programme.

At the end of this consultation, I suggested that we should invite some staff members from the day hospital to our next consultation, with the intent of facilitating a conjoint conversation centred on the puzzle of Bruno. After some hesitation (which was smoothed away by assuring them that the consultation series would still be defined as "theirs"), the staff accepted this idea. One of the participants was designated to convey the invitation, and a tentative appointment was made for two weeks later.

Eight staff members attended the next consultation, equally divided between personnel from each of the two programmes (the residence and the day hospital). Following a round of introductions and a general reminder of the clinical focus of the consultation, I explored with the personnel of the day hospital what difficulties, if any, they had with Bruno. They answered that, from their perspective, this patient did not present any problem. When I asked them what their goals and expectations for him were, they stated that their hope was to help him maintain the level of socialization he had achieved already, which they considered a satisfactory plateau reached as a result of important progress made by him since he joined the programmes. I asked whether they assumed that Bruno could "graduate" from the residence, and, much to the surprise of the staff of that house, they labelled the idea of Bruno's graduation as wishful thinking: they saw him as a psychiatric patient heavily impaired by his chronicity, and therefore their goal was only to maintain his current status.

I redefined "wishful thinking" as an important and sometimes necessary virtue to be able to keep on working with difficult populations such as the one represented by this patient, and I explored with the residence team what would happen if Bruno were not released and, more specifically, whether there was any institutional regulation that precluded the possibility of a patient remaining in the residence for an indefinite period of time. After an animated debate among them, they answered that "graduation" was a programmatic goal but, as far as they knew, there was no institutional regulation that mandated a graduation or punished the lack of it with expulsion. The collective discussion that followed crystallized the realization that Bruno may have been trapped between contradictory expectations and hence contradictory messages conveyed explicitly or implicitly by both teams. As a first reaction to their own formulation, both teams voiced the complaint that their agency's administration has been ineffective in terms of circulation of information and that, as a case in point, the two teams did not meet on a regular basis to discuss the many patients in common, which made congruent patient planning rather difficult. I reminded them that this consultation was being procured and paid for by their agency's administration, which indicated a certain good disposition or at least a good organizational moment. I invited them to suggest how they would propose to structure those inter-agency meetings on a regular basis in ways that would not disturb the routine of the current programmes. We also discussed who would have the decision power in each agency to formalize such meetings, and the complaint evolved into a plan of action to propose the meetings as a regular part of clinical practice.

Returning to the conversation about Bruno's predicament, another "damned-if-you-do, damned-if-you-don't" situation became apparent, this time not between the expectations of the staff of two agencies but within the residential facility: this patient's socially appropriate, "good" behaviour triggered plans towards what the staff defined as a *reward*, namely, the graduation; however, the predicament was that this was probably perceived by the patient as akin to an expulsion from his home and de facto family. Correspondingly, the response of the staff to Bruno's "bad" (or "mad") behaviour—namely, his demotion and the consequent delay of any talk of discharge—was defined by the staff as a negative reinforcement, while there were good reasons to assume that the patient experienced it with relief. However, the reactive behaviours of the staff to Bruno's relapses—disappointment, anger, decrease of interest in him, and reduction of his participation in activities and responsibilities that would define him as a member of the "family"—deprived him of the much-needed social/emotional nourishment from his primary group and entailed a social pressure that motivated him to behave once again in responsible, "healthy" ways to re-initiate the cycle.

Through this evolving conversation we were developing a new consensual description of this patient's predicament. The residence was, for all purposes, Bruno's home. The residence's staff and to a great extent that of the day hospital constituted for him his most meaningful personal social network. And, because of unclarified contradictory expectations between the staff of both institutions and between them and Bruno himself, he was enveloped in two sets of incompatible messages/behaviours, with an unavoidable paralysing, if not crazy-making, effect, in the best style of the "double-bind" trap.*

Of the two sets of incompatible messages enveloping Bruno, the first stemmed from the conflicting assumptions between the teams, one of them expecting evolution and change and behaving according to this expectation, the other expecting steady maintenance and behaving according to that assumption. (This is reminiscent of Weakland's 1960 discussion on the double-bind and the three-party interaction.)

The other set was lodged in the incompatibility between the assumptions of the overnight therapeutic community and those that may have been guiding Bruno: what the residence personnel considered a reward—the "graduation" of the patient to a less restrictive residence for chronic psychiatric patients—meant for the patient the loss of a great part of his rather feeble meaningful surrogate family and close social network.

_____

*The double-bind is a rather universal pathogenic situation, as discussed in Sluzki and Veron (1967), following the landmark theory proposed in Bateson, Jackson, Haley, and Weakland (1956). The ingredients of the double-bind experience include the presence of two (or more) contradictory injunctions placed at different logical levels (e.g. one explicit and one implicit; or one at the level of a class and another at the level of a member of that class), occurring in a meaningful context and within a relationship of dependency, in which it is impossible either to leave the field or to clarify the contradiction—situations in which such attempts result in punishment or the contradictions are never perceived as such by their originator, and, alas, the experiences are repeated. There is a clear one-on-one match between this set of ingredients and those of Bruno's predicament.

I commended all the participants (myself included) for having generated collectively such a sophisticated field hypothesis and suggested a method to test it—namely, that they invite Bruno to a formal meeting and, in a rather ceremonial way, pose to him that, upon much deliberation, they have reached the conclusion that they have been in error when suggesting to him his possible move to another house; instead, they now thought that it would make more sense that he consider living in the current house indefinitely. If Bruno would agree with this change of plans, they should tell him, he would have to assume a series of responsibilities, to indicate his status as permanent member of the community. I underlined to the team that this proposal was not to be considered a "paradoxical intervention", aimed at obtaining a contrary effect, but an actual redress of the previous ambiguous situation.

I explored which responsibility could be appropriately assigned to Bruno so as to increase his chances of success. They concluded that as he had always shown interest and ability in being in charge of the house's pantry, he could therefore be in charge of food supplies, maintaining an inventory of goods and making the weekly shopping lists. The fact that this flew in the face of the previous experiences of inappropriate actions by Bruno precisely in that very area did not escape anybody and was the source of many jokes and of some serious discussion about the risks of this idea, but everyone ended up by agreeing that it was worth a try. The consultation ended in a cordial and rather jovial tone.

Bruno was never again the focus of our consultations in subsequent meetings. A follow-up discussion on the subject one and six months later showed that Bruno was still living in the residence, that his unpleasant behaviours were sporadic and minimal, that he was a responsible pantry-keeper, and that his diabetes was under control. I reminded the house staff to make occasional comments to the patient that would reaffirm (to him as well as the staff!) the notion of the stability of his citizenship as member of that community.

The staff also informed me a month later that a new process had been formally established in the agency—namely, twice-monthly meetings between the personnel of both sectors in order to circulate information and elaborate conjoint plans about their many patients in common. Obvious as may be *ex post facto* the advantage of scheduling meetings on a regular basis between members of sectors that share patients and of unifying records between agencies with an overlapping population of patients, this new activity was described by the consultees as a revolutionary change in the culture of their institution. Even further, it took place in what was perceived by them to be an amazingly easy fashion: they made the suggestion to the upper echelons, who found the request very reasonable, and it was instituted. Also, and as a grass-roots change of policy, the staff of both sectors decided to make themselves available on each other's on-call list to cover a turn when somebody in one of the sectors was sick, on leave, or what-ever, instead of resorting to a larger on-call list of per-diem person-nel. This was not only economically advantageous for those who wanted additional work, but explicitly done in order to increase their familiarity with the other sector's routines and challenges. Last but not the least, the staff also informed me with pride that the directors of both sectors and the director of the umbrella agency had agreed to the establishment of a unified record system for all patients that would collate information from both sectors, in-cluding goals and objectives (formulated in terms of assets and strengths, as we were doing consistently during the consultations) and including detailed family and network resource variables (also in line with an emphasis followed during those meetings).

The latter represented the presence of a perhaps more subtle change that became apparent in the participants: a comfortable and meaningful change in their language and logic signalled the incorporation of a systemic slant in dealing with patients. Ques-tions along the line of "why now?", "in which way are we participating in generating or maintaining the problem?", "how can we formulate the problem in a more constructive way?", and "who else is part of the daily network of this patient?" began to permeate their practice, with a concurrent noticeable reduction in the utilization of psychiatric categories and labels when referring to patients.

Not surprisingly, the overall director of this consortium of agencies joined us as a visitor in one of the subsequent monthly consultations "just for the pleasure". In fact, she participated very lucidly and constructively in the case discussions, and I praised her both for the quality of the staff and for the solid evolution that the consortium was showing under her aegis. During the year that followed, she joined the consultation group fairly frequently—which remained focused on the residency but included on a stable basis members of the day hospital.

Discussion

What different levels of transformations could be specified throughout these series of consultations and their institutional effects?

At the most story-specific level, the team shifted their original narrative about Bruno. That story placed all the participants in a bad light, unable (the staff) or unwilling (Bruno) to achieve the staff's original goal. This failure entailed that there was somebody there upon whom blame had to be placed (the staff, the staff of the other agency, the patient, or the administration). That story was transformed throughout the consultation into one where, within his own limitations, Bruno was in fact trying to be consistent both with his own needs and with the community's expectations, and his oscillating responses were a reasonable expression of alternative compliance with those contradictory expectations. As the social ecology of Bruno acquired centre stage, he—and, hopefully, the rest of the patients or former patients they served—ceased being conceived of by the staff as individuals-in-isolation. The new story contained new problems and hence new solutions, and it placed them all—patient and staff alike—in a reasonably competent position. One of the correlates of all this was a transformation in the staff's rhetoric from one that was contingent upon diagnostic labels to one based on interpersonal processes, conjoint responsibility, and attainable goals—hence shifting the responsibility of failure and success regarding the patient's disorder to the collective calibration of objectives: success or failure becomes everybody's responsibility. Another correlate of this shift has been, indeed, a change in the staff's own behaviour, as they generated a solution that was empowering for all in lieu of a description that entailed incompetence or failure.

At a broader level, the team experienced itself as able to think: the consultation entailed conceptualizations and favoured the enactment of behaviours that go beyond their description of themselves as "just front-line doers", as following other people's designs. As a result of this shift in professional identity, they began to take the responsibility of promoting a change in procedures that furthered their professionalism—namely, the inter-agency case conferences, organized under the aegis, and acting as reminder, of what they called their new way of thinking about and acting with their patients. In turn, this resulted in what may be considered an anchor of this epistemology—namely, the unified record-keeping—which reflected and required psychosocial, integrated, systemic thinking as it contained many variables explicitly eliciting the new language and practices. In all this, the patients benefited from participating in a therapeutic environment that was more empowering, respectful, participative, and non-oppressive.

This consultation, hence, had as one of its effects the empowerment of the counsultees. It should be noted that this was facilitated by a reflective stance on the part of the consultant that favoured the generation of potential solutions to difficulties by the consultees themselves, rather than by the consultant. This is in fact not a new creed. System therapists have in recent times enacted their dominant epistemological shift towards social constructionism by means of behaving during the consultations according to a set of principles:

- *transparency*: that is, avoiding aloof/disengaged stances and the use of privileged information and, in general, knowledge as power—an evolutionary offspring of the original interactional–strategic notion of "one-down" (Watzlawick, Weakland, & Fisch, 1974; cf. also Furman, 1990);

- *curiosity*: that is, maintaining the assumption that descriptions are hypotheses, without any one being intrinsically correct (Cecchin, 1987)—in turn an evolution of the concept of "neutrality" (Selvini Palazzoli, Boscolo, Cecchin, & Prata, 1980a), akin to that of "multi-partiality" (Boszormeny-Nagy & Spark, 1973) or "poly-ocularity" (de Shazer, 1985);

- *positive connotation*, or assumption of good intent: an active effort on the part of the interviewer to place all participants in locus within stories that are favourable to them without being unfavourable to others—a powerful stance that has been facilitated by the powerful tool of "circular questions" developed by the Milan team (Selvini Palazzoli et al., 1980a; Penn, 1982, 1985; Tomm, 1985, 1987, 1988) and a series of other tools—such as reframing and relabelling—that have evolved in the field of family therapy to facilitate the co-construction of new, qualitatively transformed stories by all the participants (Sluzki, 1992).

The overall style emerging from these principles has been identified above as *reflective conversations*.

It may be proposed that the true change in the organization described in the prologue took place not when we started the new programme but when the language and the experience of those processes became part of the participants' assumptions about themselves and about the goals and practices of the organization. The same may hold true in the case of the clinical consultation: the organizational change began to materialize when the participants' newly acquired language/epistemology (and the embedded ethics that included empowerment and a new definition of self as co-participation in institutional processes) became enacted in practices and record-keeping procedures that reconstituted that epistemology and—even more important—kept alive the reflective conversation among staff members and with their patients.

CHAPTER THREE

Connecting personal experience to the primary task: a model for consulting to organizations

David Campbell

A s an organizational consultant, I always take time to introduce myself and my biases to the people I am working with, and I am going to do the same here. Although I was born and bred in America and trained there, I have been working as a clinical psychologist in the British National Health Service for twenty-four years. As a systemic practitioner for most of that time, I began applying my systemic ideas to consultation in small units within the health service, social services, or education, such as multidisciplinary teams, area teams, or school staff groups. I also work as a freelance consultant, which has taken me further afield to do work with private sector organizations. This chapter is based on work in various settings, but I have tried to reduce my experiences down to those ideas and techniques that have proven most effective over the years.

Professionally, I have been influenced by my training as a psychologist and psychotherapist to value people's emotional lives in whatever context I find them, including organizations. Exposure over the years to group relations events has left me humbled but also fascinated by the power of a group to create a "life of its own", to maintain its beliefs and culture in the face of external pressures to change (see Bion, 1961; Menzies Lyth, 1988; Miller, 1989). The third major influence has been my commitment to systemic ideas and their application to organizational life (see Campbell, 1995; Campbell, Coldicott, & Kinsella, 1994; McCaughan & Palmer, 1994; Selvini Palazzoli, 1986; Senge, 1990; Wynne et al., 1986).

In my work, I find I repeatedly fall back on core values that underpin my approach to organizations and influence the way I ask questions, tease out crucial dilemmas, and sometimes make interventions into the process of an organization's development. In my work, I do not claim to be neutral. I want to give equal validity to all the views I can gather, but in doing consultation I am clearly trying to create certain contexts for discussion and thinking which are shaped by my own values. Since values accrue during a lifetime, it is difficult to trace specific sources; however, these following works have more recently influenced my own values as a therapist and consultant: Anderson, Goolishian, and Windermand (1986), Boscolo, Cecchin, Hoffman, and Penn (1987), McNamee and Gergen (1992), Foucault (1980), and White (1995). My core values about change in organizations are conveyed in my consultation work in the following ways:

- presenting the view that we are simultaneously "at the mercy" of the organization, but also autonomous and able to initiate changes;

- allowing people to experience their connectedness in the organization;

- providing the opportunity to step back and become an observer of oneself;

- creating a climate in which existing belief systems can be examined and challenged;

- supporting examples of change, risk-taking, and new connections whenever they occur.

I try to take an organization back and forth between the experience of reflecting on the meaning of the behaviour and creating new strategies and structures based on the understanding of meaning. First, it is important to understand beliefs that people want to hold on to, including, for example, my own ideas about systemic thinking; it is then important to turn them upside down, examine the opposites, consider that which has not been said, and bring forth alternative accounts (see White, 1995).

I believe that theorizing is important as a means of creating a language to explain our experiences to other people. But I am also sceptical, because I think that we all underestimate the degree to which our theoretical explanations merely justify our actions that confirm our values. Therefore, I am not a theoretical purist, but I am interested to know what it is that people in organizations find helpful; this has more to do with watching and listening carefully than it does with conceptualizing. I may use many different conceptualizations depending on whether they "grab" people and whether they affect their possibilities for finding new ways to move forward together. I do not think that one consultant is going to "understand" what is happening in a complex system like an organization, but I find that identifying themes and making partial observations of the underlying meaning system can act like beacons of light that allow individuals to go further and see aspects of their own experience differently—and that has the possibility of creating ripples, through interaction amongst people who work together, that can lead to change in organizations.

So, what is an organization? My model, very briefly, begins with a clustering of people in society who come together to produce something or provide a service for other people. They either serve to a certain standard in the public sector or they produce to make a profit in the private sector. Out of the necessity to fulfil a primary task (see Miller, 1976; Miller & Rice, 1967), this group must work together, communicate a range of ideas, bring in supplies and technologies, and maintain its premises and its position in society. The complexity of coordinating these processes to carry out a task over time requires a structure, which I will now call an "organization".

Over time, patterns of working behaviour become established so that workers can observe that "this is the way we do things here"; the organization is no longer an abstract set of structures, but in peoples' minds becomes a living organism that has a culture and that powerfully affects—and is affected by—individuals' values, beliefs, and behaviour. It is at this interface between the organizational structures and individuals' beliefs and behaviour that I choose to act as a consultant. In other words, I can be effective as a consultant if I can help individuals to create and support the structures that allow the organization to continue to carry out its primary task within its constantly changing environment.

Getting to work

In this chapter I describe my model of consultation to organizations. It goes without saying that the culture of each organization is unique; however, I have found over the years that some consultation processes seem to be helpful for most organizations. In order to bring them alive here, I have chosen a case study in which many of these processes were used; some, of course, are emphasized more than others because of the nature and timing of the presenting problem. I am therefore asking the reader to keep in mind that I will be making general points about my approach to consultation as well as specific points about the particular case study.

The most frequent request for help which I get is usually something like this: "We would like some help to resolve internal conflicts so that we can get on and plan where we are going as an organization." I would then begin to negotiate how I might work with the organization—for example, whether to meet an executive or steering group to plan the work. I have learned from bitter experience that starting off on the wrong foot can lead to ineffectual work—taking the time to understand and make hypotheses right from the initial phone call always reaps dividends later on. I would negotiate between the organization's view of what they want, how much time they have, and the money available, and my own views. Ultimately, I must feel that I have the commitment from the staff to work with me in a manner that I feel allows us all to work productively together.

Once the "contract" has been agreed, I plan a loose structure for the consultation work; that is, I am aware of wanting to take an organization through a process of discussion, understanding, and creating new structures, but I will never know how this process will develop until I begin to work and can understand some of the problems that the organization is facing. I am also constrained by the time available to do the work. There is a big difference in what can be accomplished during a one-day staff "away-day" as opposed to six days of consultation over a six-month period. Nevertheless, I do try to take most organizations through a process that contains the following steps (though not necessarily in this order):

1. Creating a climate for working together.
2. Understanding the effect of group dynamics on the organization.
3. Seeing the organization in the wider system.
4. Clarifying internal resources:
   —personal
   —professional.
5. Developing the mission statement.
6. Implementing the mission statement with a strategic plan:
   —matching internal and external resources.
7. Building structures to support the strategies in relation to:
   —communication
   —groupings and meetings
   —lines of accountability
   —feedback loops.
8. Management and leadership.
9. Stepping back to understand the new group process.

In this chapter, I will be illustrating my ideas by referring to ongoing consultation work I have been doing with Refuge, an agency of about fifteen staff providing therapeutic and counselling services to political refugees and victims of torture, as well as consultation to other relevant workers. In this case study, it was appropriate to change the sequence of the above steps in the consultation. Also, while the entire staff came to the two-day consultation, this is not always the case. But my comments in this chapter apply to small organizations, with four or five up to fifty or so personnel, all of whom can fit in one room and take part in a collective consultation. I would always expect to spend some time working with the whole group, and some with sub-groups.

Several years ago the director asked me for an individual consultation (what I would call a role consultation) about his untenable position as leader of this agency. He felt that he could not get the staff to support the changes that were necessary to move the agency forward, and the staff felt that they could not cooperate with the management style that he was using. An impasse had clearly been reached, and much of the consultation centred around whether he should try new ways of tackling this dilemma, or whether he and the staff had gone as far as they could together and he should therefore leave. At the end of the consultation, an agreement was made to work with him and the staff group in several months' time. In the meantime, the director made the decision to leave, but the staff group wanted me to keep my agreement to work with them because they did not know whether the organization would survive; they also wanted to understand more of what had happened between them and the departed leader.

Creating a climate for working together

I begin by asking myself and the group how we can create a climate for working together. In order to expose themselves to change, the group will need to feel safe with each other and safe with me. For example, I often invite them to discuss experiences that they have had with other outside consultants, and their experiences of trying to change things in the organization. Working together in a group with an outside consultant can feel like a great personal risk—and so it should be if any significant change is going to take place. However, organizations can also create overly safe, protective environments for individuals, sometimes at the expense of sweeping difficulties under the carpet, or allowing rancour and bickering to conceal personal insecurities about the workplace.

My first task is to create a safe environment. In many organizations, a lack of safety results from the feeling that there are dreaded issues lurking beneath the surface which will all be "unleashed" by the consultation. I must address this. I try to convey that some of the dreaded issues will need to be discussed before progress can be made, but I will take responsibility for ensuring that the issues are addressed without getting out of hand. I also make it clear that the consultation work I undertake is different from group relations work; that is, that whereas the aim of traditional group relations work is to bring about understanding through interpretation of the group dynamics, this is usually only one part of what I would do during a consultation. The aim of the consultation is to create a better working environment and clarity about where the organization is going in the future. Many things need to be explored, and the relationships within the group will only be one of them. Exploring any dreaded issues is a means to the end, not an end in itself.

My first question is usually: "What does it really feel like to work here?"

I usually ask people to discuss this with one or two others with whom they have fairly neutral relationships. Sometimes I let them discuss the question "What does it feel like to work here?" for a few minutes; then I ask them to discuss, "What does it *really* feel like to work here?", to move the discussion along. Then I gather the responses and unpack them until I and the others have some understanding about what is actually happening that makes people feel the way they do—for example, "What specific things do you observe that lead you to feel so terrible?"

People give many reasons for feeling uncomfortable in the workplace, but my impression is that most of these experiences boil down to feelings of being treated unfairly. Gender differences, racial differences, professional differences, favouritism, pay and conditions, personal alliances, organizational influence—all of these have been presented to me at one time or another as the major obstacle to an organization being able to work together. My experience leads me to the assumption that if any organization is serious about working together, it must be fair—and be seen to be fair—to all employees.

Once I have identified a pattern of underlying problems, I then make another basic assumption, which is that the organization is like a human relations laboratory whose task is to mirror conflicts in the external or internal environment so that they can be worked through and resolved. In other words, the organization creates and maintains conflicts in order to have an opportunity to solve them. I prefer to use this formulation rather than a formulation that leads the organization to think of themselves as harbouring pathology. I find that if people think of their organizations as active, problem-solving laboratories, and even if the problems they are trying to solve are shown to be painful, anti-task ones, they feel more positive about the strengths and capacities for change within their organization.

At this stage, I think that my task as a consultant is to enable the organization to get to "this place" where dilemmas can be felt by all those in the organization. Over the years, I have used a number of metaphors, such as a "precipice", a "cutting edge", "between the devil and the deep blue sea", or a "twilight zone"; it is, however, an uncomfortable place, one where people feel a sharp recognition that if they remain inactive they will continue to have problems, but neither can they move forward without experiencing loss and sacrifice.

Once we have all arrived at "this place", my second task is to help the group stay with the dilemmas until there has been sufficient airing of contradictory feelings and opinions. I think that it is important to convey to an organization that solutions lie at the end of a process. If a brilliant idea emerges very quickly in the discussion, or if one person should appear to sum up the feelings of the entire staff group, I try to elicit other ideas, and unspoken feelings, to create a fuller picture of all the experiences in the organization. I also make it clear that reaching a premature closure may relieve the tension, but it is unlikely to underpin organizational change because the tensions and differences amongst the staff have not been sufficiently woven into any final decision.

This is difficult work and should sound familiar to those experienced in group relations work. I have personally been greatly influenced by my group relations experiences (although they were early in my career), as well as by the more recent writings of Gergen & Gergen (1986), and White (1995) and the social constructionist movement (see Burr, 1995) on the subject of bringing a client's subjugated story to the surface.

Understanding group process

In doing consultation work, the first question I ask myself is: why do organizations get stuck in the first place, and why should they ask for help? Whereas I agree with Bion that organizations get into trouble because group process gets in the way of carrying out the "primary task", I prefer a simpler working definition: that organizations are always straddling the double-edged task of being a group and being an organization—one is for belonging whilst the other is for producing.

When I arrived at Refuge for the consultation the director had left the organization, and I was met by a senior member of the staff. The process of seeing the director depart had been traumatic for everyone. There were splits between those who supported the director and those who did not; anger about the way the departure was handled; and hurt, guilty feelings that the staff had participated in a process that was hurtful to many people. It was as though a bitter, destructive process had developed that had then got out of control against their wishes.

I began by discussing a plan for the two days that we had together. I was clear that we needed to address the feelings that people were holding inside themselves as well as the future of the organization and the leadership vacuum, which suddenly seemed like a lot to do in two days. We had an open discussion with the entire staff group for several hours. The issue that emerged as most divisive and distressing was a recent change in salary levels such that the different disciplines, who previously had been paid at the same rate, were now, with the support of their unions, going to be paid on differential scales. I was listening carefully for the group dynamics themes that perpetuated the atmosphere of tension for all of them. For example, they were working with people who had been abused by society; they were confronting "ultimate evil", as one of them put it. And this seemed to lead them to believe that they had to create an experience of "goodness" to combat the evil. Everybody in the organization should be equal. They demonstrated a loyalty to the ideal of fairness, a desire to create a good, safe, and enclosed world in the organization, but some staff felt that their different skills and levels of training were not recognized within the agency, although they were recognized in the outside world.

I dealt with this by acknowledging their personal feelings about the content of this issue, but also offering another idea, which was that this could also be seen as a group process. I suggested that if one task of the organization was to resolve conflicts between good and evil, it would be likely that this dynamic would be played out within staff relationships. Splits between good staff, those who wanted equal salaries, and bad staff, who wanted differentiation, would be one way for the organization to confront and resolve the issue of good versus evil. I challenged the view that their distress was caused by personal battles by suggesting that it was the result of the good-versus-evil struggle being played out, but not yet resolved, within the organization.

Although this brief description is very condensed, I think that this approach helped the staff step back from the process that gripped them. They could see their colleagues less as enemies and more as actors in a group relations drama. It was a larger process than they could control, and it actually had some meaning in relation to what they were aiming to achieve with their refugee clients.

This was a difficult discussion for many of us, but at the end there was sufficient agreement amongst the staff that we should now move on, as we had planned to look at the future of the organization. I was aware that some staff were still upset by the discussion of recent events, and I hoped that their feelings would be addressed in other discussions during the consultation.

Developing the mission statement

An Italian psychiatrist, Luigi Boscolo, once said that his father told him that in life there were two kinds of jobs: "those in which you keep your head down, and those in which you keep you head up" (personal communication). I have always enjoyed this metaphor because it captures an important organizational process. Organizations can easily keep their collective heads down in order to get on with the job. When this happens, everyone sees their work and their relationships in a more narrow context. When changes then impinge (from inside or outside), the organization lacks the breadth of vision to see things differently and find solutions.

Therefore, I usually spend time with an organization charting its position in the outside world. I draw large diagrams that place the organization in the centre surrounded by all of the individuals or groups that have a strong, vested interest in the future of the organization. The first step in this process is to identify those groups that I prefer to call "stakeholder" groups, based on the work of Guba and Lincoln (1989). The second step is to identify what these groups are looking for from the organization, and the third step is to explore ways in which these multiple requests can be forged into plans and strategies for the future.

There are many terms in the literature to describe the process of clarifying the aims and strategies for an organization's future. Until something better comes along, I use the term "mission statement". I have found that it is the process of creating a mission statement, rather than the statement itself, which unifies and focuses an organization on its central task; I have also found that the sequence one follows in this process makes a difference to how a staff group commit themselves to the mission statement.

Clarifying internal resources

With the staff group at Refuge, I began by asking them to move into the sub-group where they felt they could most easily discuss their own professional development. In this case, they initially broke into discipline groupings: psychotherapists, social workers, psychologists, physiotherapists, administration, and translators. Within those groups I asked them to talk in pairs about their own futures. How did they want their career to develop over the next few years? What specific activities or projects did they want to develop within Refuge? What would they need from and what could they contribute to Refuge? I chose this way to begin because they all seemed discouraged by what had recently happened, and I thought that they needed first to be reconnected with their own sense of a future.

I made it clear that I wanted each of them to share only what they wanted to share with the whole staff group when we reconvened, and in doing so clear differences emerged. Some staff wanted to develop their counselling and therapy work, both psychotherapy and physiotherapy, with individual clients based in the agency; others wanted to move more into the community, working with extended families and consulting to other professionals working with refugees. After some discussion of their experience of these splits and possible meanings in terms of group dynamic process, I told the group that I wanted them to keep these internal resources in mind as we now turned to look at the position of Refuge in the wider community.

Seeing the organization in the wider system

I first went to the flip chart and wrote the name "Refuge" in the centre of the paper. Then I asked them to tell me the names of other groups who were interested (or who had a stake, i.e. a stakeholder) in the future of Refuge. I asked them to think of groups such as clients, referrers, other agencies, or government departments who would have some vested interest in the decisions that Refuge makes about the future direction of its service. When these groups were put on the page surrounding Refuge, the next step was to identify what each of them wanted from Refuge in the future. For example, they identified that clients were asking for a service that did more work with their families in their own communities; other refugee organizations wanted a clearer profile of Refuge in relation to the other agencies, and they wanted more collaboration on joint courses and use of translators; the government departments expected Refuge to become less dependent on the government and to seek out alternative financial support.

I often use the following exercise to facilitate this process: I ask staff members to form themselves into role-play groups representing the most relevant stakeholder groups in their community. Then after 15 minutes they come back and present the stakeholders' views to the whole staff group.

Once the different interests or expectations of stakeholder groups are available for everyone to see, the next step is to discuss the competing expectations and then work towards a consensus about the priorities for the organization and the preferred strategy for addressing the expectations of the outside world.

I asked them to move into four small mixed-discipline groups, whose task was to propose the elements that should be contained in the final mission statement and incorporate these different approaches. They came back as a whole group to give initial feedback, and I wrote their interim ideas on a flip chart for all to see. Then I asked them to go to their small groups once again and to reduce these ideas to one final sentence that constituted a mission statement. This was to serve two purposes:

1. The statement specified aims of the organization which all the staff could sign on to and work towards for the next year.
2. The statement was a clear communication that would help the outside world understand what Refuge was trying to do.

Finally, as a large group, we amalgamated the four proposed mission statements into one, combining ideas and sharpening the language. The final combined mission statement read as follows:

"Refuge would aspire to be an interdisciplinary treatment and consultation centre for refugees, asylum-seekers, their families, and those who work with them"

Although the statement itself may seem anodyne, in the process of creating it many differences were aired and new working practices were discussed. When we finished this work and were coming to a coffee break, I said that I wanted all the staff to take the felt-tip marker and sign their name under the statement to show that that each was prepared to work towards those goals. When we returned from coffee to begin a new piece of work, I noticed that one person had not signed the statement. I made a light-hearted comment and decided not to press the issue. It was only later that I realized the significance of this abstention.

Implementing the mission statement with a strategic plan

Once the aims or mission statement have been clarified and the individual resources elicited, the next step is to devise a strategic plan that matches the internal resources with the external demands and addresses the question: "How will we use our resources to achieve our aims?" I prefer to call this a matching strategy, to remind everyone—including myself—that the aim is to link the external with the internal. This helps avoid the tendency to become unrealistic by emphasizing either the external demands at the expense of what the staff are truly willing or able to do, or being over-enthusiastic about the staff's personal goals when there is simply insufficient demand for that particular activity. The process is one of moving back and forth between the internal and external, checking the viability of one in the context of the other, and repeatedly asking such questions as: " What client group will want to use or pay for that service?" "Which of you amongst the staff want to re-organize your work to respond to this external need?" "How will you get job satisfaction if you decide to shift to a new direction?" I have found it helpful to keep Hampden-Turner's diagram in mind, adapted to this process (in Campbell et al., 1994), as shown in Figure 3.1.

Figure 3.1 illustrates, on the left, that internal resources only take their shape, or gain their meaning, in the context of external demands; and, on the right, that external demands can only be defined in the context of internal resources. As in the earlier stage of "creating a climate for working together" during which I work

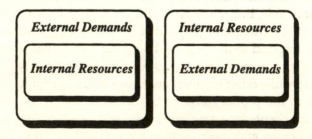

FIGURE 3.1

with dilemmas, my role here is to move back and forth between the internal and the external to ensure that one is defined by the other. I have to hold the tension between them and try to avoid premature decisions being made without sufficient discussion.

The Refuge group decided to implement their mission statement by supporting five strategic proposals. Each proposal was identified, and a "lead person" was given responsibility for ensuring that it was carried out:

1. Two social workers agreed to meet social welfare offices in the community to discuss ways in which Refuge could work with them.

2. A monthly meeting would be organized for translators.

3. Relevant staff members would meet in small groups to plan the development of family and group work services within Refuge.

4. One staff member took responsibility for raising the issue of interdisciplinary work at relevant meetings.

Building structures to support the strategy

Changes do not just happen in organizations, but they are initiated by individuals and then supported by (1) formal policies such as operating procedures, job descriptions, and contracts and (2) structures such as lines of accountability, channels of communication, work groups, and ad hoc meetings—all depending on the task and size of the organization.

Most of the organizations I meet will say that they need to "improve their communication". The need is ever-present, and it is always laudable, but consultants will get bogged down in the mire if they set out with the vague goal of "improving communication". I usually respond to this request by saying, "For what purpose do people want to communicate—to whom and about what?" Communication, like other organizational processes, is best understood in terms of the primary task of the organization. If the task is to work with clients by using one's own and one's colleague's personal responses and feelings, then a more intimate, informal type of communication, and an organization that promotes trust, will be most helpful. Other organizations with other tasks may need to communicate about academic ideas, about the interface between design and manufacturing, or about the relationship between sales staff and the customers. Therefore, the structures of an organization—in this case, communication—must be designed in the context of the primary task, the mission statement, and the implementing strategies of the organization. Structure must follow strategy—not the other way round.

Management and leadership

In the case of Refuge, we could not go any further in our consultation until we had answered the question of who was going to be responsible for implementing these changes. We had to confront the leadership crisis. I chose to deal with this in three ways:

1. I wanted to stimulate an agency-wide discussion about leadership: What did leadership mean to all of them? How did they all contribute to it? How could they support or undermine leadership? My aim in doing this was to promote a sense of corporate ownership of the leadership process, so that it was not seen as an "us vs. them" phenomenon. I knew that the staff had been hurt and demoralized by the departure of their leader and as a result they might be wary and stand-offish with a new leader; alternatively, they might expect the new person to be a saviour who would redress the problems of the past. But either way, it seemed to me that the danger was that they would be putting their hopes and worries into another person instead of owning them for themselves, and under those circumstances it would make leading an impossible task.

2. I wanted to look carefully at their strategic plans to discuss what a leader would need to do to develop the plan, and what qualities would be required of the leader and the staff. To develop this theme, I discussed with the group the systemic relationship between "leadership" and "followership".

3. I wanted to work with the staff on the issues about choosing their next leader.

The American playwright Arthur Miller was recently asked why there did not seem to be so many great writers in the world today, and he replied: "Probably because there aren't so many great readers." I find it helpful in organizations to discuss the ways that leadership is influenced by followership, and vice versa. I hope through this that staff members see their own, and the collective, responsibility for the leadership in their own organization. I also present a concept that I have adapted from the writings of Peter Drucker (1990) which he calls "information responsibility", which I have recast in systemic language as "feedback responsibility". This clarifies that feedback, which is truly the lifeblood of a systemic organization, does not just happen; individuals must take active responsibility to identify what is important feedback and to whom it should be passed. The failure of the organization to understand the changing expectations and needs of the staff is a responsibility shared by all.

In designing an organizational consultation, one must periodically change the mode to keep the participants fresh and interested, and on this basis I ended this discussion with a brief exercise for all the staff. I asked them to write statements for themselves, about the following: "What I personally will do to make leadership more attractive to someone . . ." and "If I were going to be a leader, this is what would need to be different for it to be attractive to me . . ." (the latter sprang from the possibility, discussed earlier, that the new leadership would emerge from within the current staff). Their comments were then passed to me, read out anonymously, and discussed.

The group felt that the risks of having another leader appointed from outside far outweighed the risk that appointing an internal leader could create divisions and conflicts within the staff group. At least an internal person would need less time to adjust to the culture and personalities at Refuge, and this thought seemed to offer some security to the staff group after what they had been through. We also discussed the possibility of a "leadership team" of two or three rather than a single leader, and the conclusion was that the group, which valued consensus decision-making where possible, would prefer a leadership team because all decisions would be discussed among the team, which would model the consensus process for the organization as a whole.

It was clear that there would not be time during this consultation for the new leaders to step forward and assume responsibilities, so I wanted to be sure with the little time I had left that there was sufficient agreement about the next step to be taken after my departure, and this led us to discuss the process by which new leaders would actually be selected. It was agreed that at a staff meeting in about one month's time, those interested would put their names forward as prospective leaders, and this would be discussed by the staff group. Then, if there was sufficient support, these persons would present themselves to the Board, who would make the final decision and agree all the official terms and conditions of employment. The staff group preferred this option, to avoid being lead by someone they did not approve of, which prompted me to raise the dilemma that they would have to surrender some of their control and security if they were going to allow a leadership team to develop its own ideas and authority. It was as though the organization needed strong leadership at a time when the staff also wanted to control the process to prevent the organization re-living some of the previous difficulties.

The two-day consultation finally came to an end, and the Refuge staff were left to their own devices. At the subsequent staff meeting, three staff members put themselves forward to become the leader group, and the Board supported the principle of an internal leadership team. After several months, a rift developed between the leaders over the unresolved issue concerning one discipline's right to have different pay and conditions from other staff members doing similar work. Although the principle had been accepted, there were many angry feelings which did not abate, and eventually the leader representing this discipline decided to apply for another job and leave Refuge. The two remaining leaders stayed in their roles, and the pay and conditions issue has become more acceptable, presumably because it was no longer embodied in the daily activity of one of the leaders, and the staff at Refuge feel that they have moved on to a less tumultuous and more productive period.

Stepping back to understand the new group process

The final step in the consultation process is one of placing all the staff in an observer's position so they can reflect on what they have learned through the process (see Campbell, 1995). I assume that if the consultation has been effective, the participants are coming away with a new understanding of why the organization "feels" the way it does, what they each contribute to this process, and what kind of structures they need in order to support development in the future. I try to consolidate this new thinking by giving people the time to discuss, either as a large group or in small groups, their experiences. I emphasize that they have created these new understandings themselves and that the responsibility for the organization's future belongs to all of them collectively.

If it seems necessary to clarify or consolidate points made during the consultation, I might remind people of some of the key issues that were raised, such as, in the case of Refuge, the necessity of identifying the badness and danger "out there" and the subsequent struggle to create a moral, non-abusive organization that could treat everyone as equals, while at the same time recognizing the differences between the professionals and their ties to the outside world.

Conclusion

There are good reasons why there are so many dismissive jokes about consultants. "A consultant is someone who borrows your watch in order to tell you the time." I think that many clients are disappointed in the results of consultation because of unrealistic expectations, but I want to caution any reader embarking on consultation work not to collude with the hope that you will be able to perform miracles. Oh, if it were only possible! My own experience leads me to the humble conclusion that there is a limited amount a consultant can do to effect changes in organizations with long histories and to create sufficient momentum to carry any changes into the future. I think that it is important to be clear about what consultation can do and that the real work must be done by the organization after the consultant is gone. It behoves us all to encourage the establishment of organizational structures, such as meetings, to allow the consultation work to carry on after the consultant is gone. Follow-up visits are another important means by which one can monitor the change process begun during the consultation. In these ways, I think it is also possible to help clients become observers of their own processes of change.

CHAPTER FOUR

The feelings of the consultant as indicators of problems and solutions

Gianfranco Cecchin
with Alan Cooklin

Editor's note: *The questionnaire sent to authors (see the Introduction) had a complex result. It could have provided very stringent constraints on thinking had one followed it slavishly; or it could, on the other hand, have channelled thinking in creative new ways. There is probably an analogy here that is applicable to organizations: structure and order may lead to creativity if they are defined benignly, and if they really have the support of those on whom they are imposed. If one considers the questionnaire as a prescription in response to which the authors are expected to act with compliance, then one could only conclude in this volume that either the level of compliance was low, or the constraints imposed were inappropriate. If, on the other hand, one considers the questionnaire as a probe that has the capacity to elicit specific information, but could also itself be a form of information to which the authors may respond, then it could be said to have elicited some useful information about how creative individuals respond to "institutions" (in this case, the "institution" of this volume). Thus, the way that Gianfranco Cecchin has responded has made it essential that he*

*and I enter into a written dialogue. The readers must judge
whether or not, as I suggest, this is congruent with his thinking
about, and style of, consultations. However, the way in which
this chapter is presented is a combination of two forms: the
outline essay that Cecchin wrote, and the discussion we had of
his thinking behind what he did.*

A s you can see the situation is quite enmeshed and I am
trying to find a way out of it.

ALAN COOKLIN: But Gianfranco, I haven't seen anything yet. What
is it that is enmeshed?

GIANFRANCO CECCHIN: Well, it is not what you have seen, but what
you will soon see. Perhaps I need first to explain how I understand the term "enmeshment". I define this as "obligated by
loyalty". As you will see, my participation in the consultation I
describe was obligated or trapped by my own loyalty to the
group, and by the group's loyalty to me.

AC: Do you mean the whole group was loyal to you?

GC: No, if the group as a whole had been loyal or disloyal, I
could have easily handled it. The problem was that a part of the
group was loyal to me and I needed to be loyal to their attempts
to form a group. That is, they were a group trying to follow a
belief system that they knew that I supported—namely, the
systemic approach. They were trying to implement this. I was
trapped in trying to support something that they knew that I
believed in.

AC: Do you mean that that's a definition of loyalty?

GC: Yes, being stuck is being trapped by people being loyal to
something you believe in, and as a result you cannot be irreverent to your own loyalty.

So, as you can see I am loosely following your suggestions
given to all the authors about how to organize our thoughts. First I
want to make my position clear. I am a family therapist, doing
family therapy, family therapy supervision, and teaching family

therapy in different institutions. On occasion, I become a supervisor of organizations.

In this chapter, I describe a situation in which these two positions became overlapping. In 1994 I was invited to supervise a group (one of whom had been a former student at our Family Therapy Centre) in their activity as family therapists in a public institution. They specifically wanted me to go to their own institution, rather than coming to my office as happens with most other groups.

AC: Did you have some thoughts about why they wanted you to go there at that stage, or at that point were you just innocently thinking you were going to them for supervision? Did you have some thoughts about what they were after?

GC: Yes—I assumed they wanted my support in the face of their colleagues' resistance to their attempts to introduce systemic practice in their institution/organization, and therefore I went as an ally. If they had come to the Milan Centre, their colleagues would have treated them with some contempt as going to some kind of "guru" outside the public system, and following some private fantasy or agenda of their own.

You have to understand that these people were in training, and they worked in a public institution and were feeling some honour at creating a group to do family therapy within a systemic framework. From my own point of view, it was important for me to support them and also for me to recognize them. However, what they were doing was not really supported by their institution. Many people did not really support what they were doing, but were kind of ambivalent. They thought that they should in some way be supporting the *idea* of working with the family and therefore could not exactly say no, but they did not really support the implications of the change in practice that this would represent.

There is also a political component to this which is very important. With the closing of the mental hospitals in Italy and the development of the community programmes, in the face of the power of many traditional approaches to mental health care, the systemic approach has gained in prestige and power. As a result, in this institution the staff were always looking over their shoulder, worried about their future. They would not dare reject something that they thought might become powerful in the future, in case they might themselves become redundant and lose their jobs.

When I arrived at the institution I found my former student, three others who had in the past trained with us, and four more people whom I had not met, who came from a variety of different professional backgrounds. One of the latter group was male.

> AC: Why did you think that it was particularly significant at that stage that one of them was male? Were all the others women? If so, what did you think was their relationship to you?

> GC: Yes, all the others were women. In Italy there often is a hidden competition between men and women, which is partly a result of the way in which in women the whole role of feminism, while present, is in fact hidden. For me, the fact that there was only one man present suggested that (as men represent the more dominant discourse in Italy) the idea of the group was not really supported by the institution. The psychoanalytic tradition tends to be much more associated with "maleness" in Italy, whereas because systemic thinking relates to relationships, this is often more associated with being more "female". This constellation, therefore, made me suspicious about the role that I was being asked to play in the organization. However, I did not voice this thought. I thought of it, but my immediate reaction inside myself was that if I voiced any such idea they would all have denied it immediately—both the man and the women.

One of the group was a psychiatrist, two were social workers, and the rest were psychologists.

The work began in a way that was quite familiar to me with many of the groups I consult to. We considered some of their cases, and I interviewed a family, with the group observing behind a one-way mirror. I gave some comments and suggestions and then left.

There were two more meetings like that, and things seemed to be going along well enough. On the third day, I began to realize that something was not working. I began to feel bored with the group. I realized that only two or three of them were active in the conversation—the one who had invited me, plus two of the former students. The others remained passive and appeared unimpressed or even quite negative towards my approach, including how I made hypotheses and thought about and responded to issues. They looked disappointed and frustrated, and I assumed they felt "unable" to fire me. I had the same problem with them.

AC: Do you mean by "fire" here as in the American sense, i.e. to "sack" them from their jobs, or do you mean to "fire" them with enthusiasm?

GC: Oh, I mean it in the American sense, to fire them—or to sack them, as you English say.

AC: But then why couldn't they get rid of you, and why couldn't you get rid of them? Was it just out of loyalty or politeness, or did you feel in some kind of bind?

GC: Well, it was out of loyalty not out of politeness, but, as we discussed before, it was a kind of loyalty that creates a bind. Even if I did not think I could do anything, I couldn't abandon them. When you can't rebel against your own loyalty, then you become the victim of bind.

After I realized what was happening to me, I asked them not to bring any clinical cases to the next meeting because I wanted to talk about our relationship.

AC: So, did you tell them that that was why?

GC: Oh, yes. I said to them that I did not think that we could produce any useful clinical experience together if we could not understand the relational context in which we were working.

I had accepted an invitation as a "Clinical Consultant", and I had then taken the initiative to change my role to something that increasingly became that of an organizational consultant. However, what is unclear at this stage is whether *I* really changed my role, or whether I just began to fit in with the unexpressed demand (through the medium of asking for a clinical consultation) that I "sought out the organization". Given that those who did not know me were treating me with relative contempt, whilst I suspected that my ex-students might have been treating me with if not a degree of reverence, then at least with the hope that I would be some kind of saviour, it seems not unlikely that they were nursing such a hope. Thus, in the next meeting I began by asking a number of questions:

- Why are the eight of you together?
- Who had the initiative to organize the group?
- Who was it that *wanted* to do family therapy? Who was the prime mover for this change in the organization's practice?
- How do you get permission to spend a day a week together, taking time out of your usual jobs?
- Who is officially in charge of the group, and who is responsible for the results?
- How do you get your clients referred?
- Are the clients obligated to come, or do they have some choice?
- How did the secretarial staff respond to these initiatives?

AC: What are the initiatives that you are responding to here? Is it the initiative for them to be employed in the first place, or the initiative for change in their job? For some reason, you are very unclear about this.

GC: Well, I think I am unclear because of the particular role that secretaries play in institutions in relation to the bureaucracy of hierarchy. Somebody in the hierarchy had told the secretaries to do some work for this group. This person can in some way tell them that they should "do a bit of work for the group", but there can be an implicit secondary message not to take this work too seriously or give it any priority. This was my question. The importance of this is that the secretaries really represent the hierarchy of the organization because they are directly employed by the organization. In Italy, this is different from the professional staff, whose career is not totally dependent on the institution, because they can oscillate between pieces of private and public work, to some extent at will.

AC: It seems to me that these questions you have listed are not ones that you would automatically ask before you go into any kind of consultation supervision. That is, your style is very much to respond to the process of the moment, to see what happens, and then to begin to make hypotheses and to organize your role. If you remember, when we did the joint workshop together in Sorrento that was one of the most interesting differences in our approach. In a funny way, that seems to be analogous to me to the way in which you responded to being asked to write the chapter. You said yes, but only as we got into the process did the process of the struggle to define it begin to unfold between us.

GC: Well, I must admit I wasn't completely aware of all of this before I started, but then you are right—it is my style not to particularly worry about that, but to enter the system, take a risk, and see what happens. Sometimes I pay for that, but that's how I operate. As you know, this is a bit analogous to the way I do family therapy.

So, I asked them to compose an organizational chart—that is, simply a chart showing the lines of accountability within the hierarchy. The form of what they constructed was a pyramid, on top of which was a director of the Mental and Social Service Department of the USL [Local Health Unit], which is the local health provider, funded by the state for a population of about 200,000. There are two more directors on the same level for medical and surgical services. The Director of Mental and Social Services had four departments within his control: social services, child care and development, family care and consultation, and long-term care. Each department had a director under whom were a number of unspecified "responsibles", who were responsible for a range of different functions within the service and for different catchment areas. Each "responsible" was in charge of three to four professional staff who did the "real" work. This was as much information as I could elicit from the group. The eight members of the group all came from different departments, only one of whom was "responsible" for an office, whilst the others were at a lower level.

AC: So what was your thinking at this time, given that you carried on working with them? Were you surprised at how relatively junior they were, and, if so, what was it that somehow got you to accept this invitation in the first place?

GC: Well, they were young, but not so junior. I have already explained to you about the loyalty I felt to ex-students who were trying to really implement our thinking in the public sector. Also I felt that being junior, or not so junior, was not so important in this situation. For me, the important factor was the structure of the organizational chart, the way that the people were organized within the institution.

Our former student had convinced her director that the service required a systemically orientated family therapy team. She had been working in the Child Development Department, in which supervision had been provided by a psychoanalyst for several years, and she had wanted to introduce a different way of thinking. She had managed to convene the group (with whom I was meeting) and had asked the social worker—the most senior member of the group—to be responsible for the group. What was curious, however, was that this social worker was the one who had arranged for the original supervision with a psychoanalyst. Two of the other participants in the group had been specifically asked by their "responsible" in the Family Consultation Department to participate as a form of training.

AC: So, what did you make of this? I would really like to know what you were thinking at this point.

GC: I need to remind you that Italy is essentially a very fundamentalist country. Things are either this or that, and you are associated with either the psychoanalytic tradition or the systemic tradition. It's very difficult to imagine the two being complementary to each other. Intellectually, people may be able to talk to each other or talk about both kinds of thinking, but passions run high in institutions that have become dedicated to one or the other tradition.

AC: What did you make of the fact that this "responsible" who had invited you in was the same person who invited in the psychoanalyst?

GC: Well, my idea was that her interest was political rather than based on intellectual curiosity, or any real understanding of systemic practice. I think she feared that being totally dedicated to psychoanalysis might have weakened her position, perhaps left out some important factors that might have given her power as she progressed through her own career. That is, I think she was afraid that if she totally sold herself to psychoanalysis she might become marginalized; as a result, she wanted to ride two horses.

AC: What made these "responsibles" think that this training would actually be useful? Had they in some way been influenced by the one who had been your student, or were they just short of any form of training?

GC: Well, I think that they were genuinely curious about the systemic approach, and actually suspected that there was something valuable and perhaps powerful that they could benefit from. However, they couldn't quite commit themselves to it, in case they could be attacked by their colleagues. Therefore, their solution was to send some of their underlings for training in the hope that they could learn through these underlings what might be valuable, but without they themselves being exposed. Also, the "responsibles" shouldn't actually show their enthusiasm— that would make them too exposed to attack and competition from their colleagues, so they had to do this in a covert manner, and sending their underlings was the ideal way to achieve this. The only drawback was that the underlings had to be modelled on their bosses, because to be loyal to their bosses they had to show the same kind of contempt that was implied by their bosses' actual lack of commitment. So the way in which these people behaved in the group was both to be curious and to show contempt—an uncomfortable position, but very effective in preventing themselves from learning anything useful. I do suspect (though I say this with full humility) that a naive consultant could have been quite destroyed by this manoeuvre— facing a mixture of curiosity and contempt at the same time is most soul-destroying for somebody trying to work with a group.

Thus at least half the group were there because they had been compelled to attend. Only the organizer of the group and the two other junior members (who had trained with us) seemed to have some genuine interest in what was going on. Of the directors, only one (that is, the one who was responsible for the "responsible" who had set up the group) seemed to have any interest in making the group work, and she was a personal friend of the organizer. Some members of the group, however, questioned this director's motivation in supporting the formation of this task group.

AC: Why did they question the director's motivation? What do you think they assumed was behind her motivation in setting up the group?

GC: Well, the first thing was that although she organized the group she did not show up. She did not attend herself. She *said* "I would like to attend", but she was always busy and never arrived. So they suggested that maybe she was simply supporting the group for her career, or just out of loyalty to her friend who was the "responsible", or that she had some other reason that was not being made explicit. Whatever it was, they perceived her as having an impediment to making any kind of real commitment to this group or to what changes in the institution that this group represented.

AC: So what are the changes that this group's success would have meant for this institution? What were the real implications of being committed to what this group represented?

GC: Your question fits in with the solution that I tried out, as you will see in a minute. The fundamental problem was that the success of a group promoting the systemic approach would lead to a change in the philosophy of the whole organization. The effect of this would be the same as that of any major change in an organization: namely, that the whole hierarchy becomes upset and turned upside down, because what used to be valued becomes less valued and what becomes newly valued takes precedence. As a result, those who had been following psychoanalysis, or other particular approaches such as biological psychiatry, would become lower in the actual hierarchy and would lose status.

Some of the other directors had also sent members of their staff to participate.

AC: It does seem to me, given that there were only four people who had not been members of one of your training groups, that the figures do not quite add up. There cannot have been several people sent by one director and others by the other directors because it would come to more than four extra. Can you explain this?

GC: Well, there were four regulars from the "positive" director's group and others sent from the other directors' groups who sometimes came regularly and sometimes came and went. It was unclear whether these people had come to join the group or to try to control the group, or had come in order to then boycott the group, or just as spies.

Anyway, these staff clearly felt that they had been pressurized to attend under the guise of choosing "freely" to become part of the group. Some were actually bitter and asked if they had been "singled out", "rather than my colleague who had more time".

With these factors having been elicited, I began to ask myself the following questions:

1.   What are the assumptions that keep this project together? How come they received referrals? Why is (apparently) nobody trying to kill the project yet?

2.   Why has the group accepted having a consultant like myself enter their system?

3.   Should I try to help them organize an efficient family therapy consultation system, or a consultation service whose purpose is satisfying to the bureaucratic hierarchy but may have little relevance to their clients?

4.   Or could I achieve both the aims in Question 3 at the same time?

Comment

Most theories of organization assume that efficiency of results is related to clarity of the hierarchical structure of the organization. The system here, on the other hand, only seemed to exist by maintaining a lack of clarity, and I began to think that it might cease to exist if the structures were in fact clarified. I began to think that if I tried to clarify the usual organizational issues such as who was in charge, who makes decisions, or who is really responsible for what goes on, then I would be ejected (fired) as a consultant. I was not against being fired, but I did not want to do this until I had made some kind of significant statement. In that case, being fired might have been the best way to intervene. The experience of defeating a consultant can often have a salutary effect. The reason I wanted to stay in, as I have said before, was because of my loyalty to my group. The reason I did not want to clarify things too quickly was because I had in mind an analogy with what happened on the Italian Stock Market when stockholders tried to analyse closely the accounts for a major company. Their attempts to clarify what was going on actually meant that their stock was "killed", and they lost much of their money. I did not want to be in this position in this organization. Also, I felt that so far I was too irrelevant to take such a posture as yet. Another thing, apart from my loyalty, that kept me in the consultation was a fascination or curiosity about what made an Italian public organization tick.

My solution

As I said, I could have just left, but to be true to my own tradition I needed to do something that gave a positive message to the organization about the way that it actually is, in just the same way that I would to a family.

> AC: It sounds like you are saying that as a matter of your own honour you really had to do this thing, otherwise you couldn't honourably leave?
>
> GC: Yes, you are quite right, it means I have to leave with honour. To leave with honour means that I have preserved my own style.

I therefore said to the group that I thought that the ambiguity as to their task was whether they were expected to succeed or not, whether there was really a role for the systemic approach within the institution, and all this had its strong advantages. Although to some extent this ambiguity slowed down their development of effective practice, on the other hand it reassured the senior people in the organization that they would not be causing too much trouble or generating too much change, it prevented conflict between the different directors of the different parts of the organization, and overall it carried out a supportive function for the organization. Therefore, I recommended that they needed to organize the group so that this ambiguity remained, because ambiguity would be part of the preservation of the system as they and their colleagues knew it. So maybe they needed to suspend their attempts to become effective as clinicians and devote themselves, or at least define themselves, as a research group. I suggested that what they needed to do was that when they observed families and observed the family approach, they should each take very detailed notes and write reports of their observations as a form of research. They equally, or perhaps even especially, should note those things that did *not* work. They should write all of this up, and they should circulate copies of this to all the directors. They should post them to each director personally. This is because, in Italy, the bureaucracy highly values the printed word. Some of them protested: "but these directors won't bother to read this". I answered "That does not matter—what is important is that they can receive it and own it", and as a result they can be quite sure that nothing is happening behind their backs. My thinking was that by doing that we satisfied (a) those who were curious, in that they had an opportunity to explore and do research; (b) those who were spies, in that they did not need to carry out their job because we were doing it for them; (c) those who had many doubts, as they could check out their doubts by writing everything down; and (d) those who wanted to boycott the group, as they could delegate their job to those who received the printed word because these people in more senior positions would themselves be able to find out all the things that did not work. This intervention seemed to me to be one that allowed all the needs to be satisfied, whilst allowing the group to go on functioning. The need to be a spy, the need to do research, the need to boycott the group, the need to be just curious, all could be satisfied whilst also allowing the group to get on and do some work. Also, the organizers could feel that they were doing justice to their jobs by receiving and, if they wished, writing important papers.

The feedback

The result was that the referrals to this group suddenly began to increase. The membership of the group became more stable, at about eight people, and the group began actually to talk about families and to think about how they could help families for a time. The issues about the organization began to take second place.

Comment

I had also encouraged them to let their colleagues know that this was not necessarily a permanent group. This would be a "research" group that might have a limited life of, say, three years to try something out. This limiting of the idea of the group in terms of its time-frame dramatically limited the degree to which it was perceived as a threat by others in the organization.

> AC: But how much do you think that both the presentation of the problem and your kind of response was organized by strong cultural elements in Italy?

> GC: In Italy, everybody is often looking for some fundamental solution—permanent jobs, truth—from whatever organization, whether political or religious. At the same time, when people are within these kinds of institutions of "truth" they become restless and dissatisfied.

So what has been presented in this chapter is both an organizational change and the impact of the society or sociological influences on the organization, and vice versa.

My belief is that it is also true of any business organization that it is to a large extent a reflection of the culture in which it is developing and active. My impression is that American consultants, for example, consulting with Italian businesses often find themselves feeling quite ineffectual in achieving change because the rules that they are used to simply do not operate. Alternatively, perhaps they are stuck with the idea that there must be some kind of business organization that works in any country and any culture. From the way in which I have presented this case report you may see that my idiosyncratic approach is commensurate with my way of thinking about The Family and perhaps a function of something that fits the Italian culture.

CHAPTER FIVE

Black people working in "white institutions": lessons from personal experience

Suman Fernando

In popular language, "race" is synonymous with colour, and "we speak casually of Africans (or African–Caribbeans) as one race, Asians as another, Europeans or whites as a third" (Malik, 1996). These everyday perceptions, rather than any scientific or biological evidence, form the basis for the term "black people" as used in this chapter. Another way of describing the use of this term (in this chapter) is by reference to its "political sense"—that is, as indicating people who trace their ancestry to populations that were and/or are subjugated and exploited and so forth by people who are known as "white people". Thus in Britain, Africans, African–Caribbeans, Arabs, Bangladeshis, Greek and Turkish Cypriots, Indians, Iranians, Palestinians, and Sri Lankans may be seen as black people. However, issues around race and racism are much more complicated than this brief reference to "black people" indicates and are discussed later in the chapter.

Black professionals are becoming increasingly evident in British institutions that deal with health and social services—in other words, these institutions are overtly multiracial. However, few black professionals achieve positions of authority within these institutions, and those who do often find themselves involved in a continuous struggle within them to prevent becoming marginalized. Many British institutions now have "Equal Opportunities Policies" (EOPs), which are supposed to prevent discrimination on grounds of race, as defined in the Race Relations Act (Home Office and Central Office of Information, 1977). However, the experience of many black people working within institutions, including those that deal with health and social services, is that racism is as strong as ever, even if overt, easily identifiable discrimination is difficult to find—although, of course, this is manifested from time to time. Because of this, and for various historic reasons, British institutions dealing with health and social services are generally envisaged (at least among most black people) as "white institutions"—that is, as a part of what they perceive as an oppressive racist society in which we all live.

Institutions are composed of individuals, and, as in a family, each person involved in a particular institution has his or her own degree of dependency on others within it as well as on the institution itself—both for financial and/or emotional reasons or for reasons of status or occupational need. But "dependency" in such a situation is different to "dependency" (on one another) in a family—even a large family. In an institution—at least in most British institutions—individuals within it are not generally linked by ties of "kith and kin" or ancestry as such, although tradition may play a part in its ethos, its "culture". Again, membership of an institution is neither involuntary nor lifelong, unlike the membership of a family which is generally on a like-it-or-not basis *for life*. One can always resign from an institution, but not from a family.

Individuals within an institution influence the policies and ways of working of the institution in various ways and to varying degrees, depending on the positions they occupy, the power they wield, and their own particular agendas. Naturally, the power they wield would depend on knowledge and understanding of the particular field in which the institution functions as well as (and perhaps more importantly) on personal factors such as the ability and willingness of the individual to wield effective power, his or her self-confidence, perseverance, sense of "mission"—and indeed having a "mission" at all—and so on. At one extreme, an individual may be a passive player (almost a "sleeping partner") working according to the rules—both explicit and implicit—without asking any questions, careful not to rock the boat. At the other extreme an individual member, perhaps working in conjunction with others, may influence his or her institution to such an extent that the institutional rules appear to reflect the person's views completely. Finally, although most institutions are hierarchical with an identified "head" (who has significant scope for wielding power), members of the institution lower down in the hierarchy may influence the workings of the institution as much as, or more than, the designated institutional "head" does.

Each person ("player") within an institution comes to his or her institution from a particular background and, whether aware of it or not, with sets of ideologies on various matters, including race. In a setting where either the institution is overtly multi-racial or the purpose of the institution is concerned with issues of race, sooner or later the politics of race become a significant process within that institution.

"Institutional racism" may be described as "systemic inequality which results from institutional processes which are racially discriminatory" (Ben-Tovim, Gabriel, Law, & Stredder, 1986); its difference from personal (racial) prejudice, briefly referred to later in this chapter, has been discussed at length elsewhere (Fernando, 1991). The extent to which black professionals working in "white institutions" are aware of institutional racism varies. Some think that they are immune from racism (within their institutions), usually because they feel that they are treated colour-blind as "honorary whites". However, it is the experience of others (perhaps the majority) that racism strikes in the professional field too—and sometimes in the most unexpected ways—so much so that black professionals who wish to confront racism in institutions that deal with social services and health often wonder whether they could ever get very far doing so *from within*. For example, it is not uncommon for a black person who raises issues about racism to be depicted as someone with a "chip on his/her shoulder" or "a bee in his/her bonnet". Again, most institutions expect loyalty from their members, and a black person who feels accepted by the institution as an "honorary white" may find it difficult to argue against the majority who voice liberal sentiments without understanding the strength of institutional racism.

This chapter describes some personal experiences of the author in his association with a prestigious institution—the Mental Health Act Commission (MHAC). The chapter illustrates some of the difficulties that black people have in confronting racism within institutions but, at the same time, shows how black people within the "system" (however racist it might be) *can* effect changes—however limited. Although describing true experiences, it is not intended to blame any particular persons individually for the racism of the institution concerned, nor suggest that the MHAC, as an institution, is any more racist than most other public bodies in the health field.

The MHAC has a remit to protect the interest of people compulsorily detained under the Mental Health Act (Mental Health Act Commission, 1985). Its members, usually called "Commissioners", are appointed by the Secretary of State for Health and include both black and white people. Since black people are disproportionately over-represented among detained patients (Department of Health/Home Office, 1994)—a fact well known for several years (Fernando, 1988, 1991)—the Commission was inevitably involved from its inauguration (in 1983) with issues of race. I was a member of the Commission from 1 October 1986 until 31 October 1995. As one of ninety-two ordinary members, I started off with little influence. But, as time went on, I became influential through membership of working parties and, later, of the national standing committees of the Commission and, finally, the policy-making Central Policy Committee. Two series of events (experiences) in which I was involved are described and appropriate lessons are then drawn.

Race and Racism

The ideologies about race prevalent in West European society can be explored by considering its historical context. The classifications of races, devised in Europe in the eighteenth and nineteenth centuries and largely based on skin colour, were constructed by biologists, physicians, and anthropologists, later influenced by Darwinian ideas of evolution. They occurred in a context where the words "black" and "white" had been associated in the English language with heavily charged notions of good and bad and went hand in glove with prejudice from the very beginning. Then came slavery and colonialism, which fed into racial prejudice and vice versa, consolidating the dogma of racism.

The concept of "race", meaning some biologically determined entity recognizable by external appearance (or, rarely, by nominal religious affiliation or language), has in scientific circles been dismissed as a basis for dividing up the human race (Jones, 1981). In the book *Not in Our Genes*, Rose, Lewontin, & Kamin (1984) state: "Human racial differentiation is indeed only skin deep. Any use of racial categories must take its justification from some other source than biology." However, the tendency to think of people in terms of their "race", referred to by Barzun (1965) as "race thinking", persists; it is prevalent in many societies, underlying ideologies such as anti-Semitism, orientalism (Said, 1978), and, of course, skin-colour racism which is the ideology generally referred to as "racism". All too often, people are perceived, classified, discriminated against or favoured, and even destroyed on the basis of what is seen as their "race". In short, race, as we generally conceptualize it, is a biological myth but a social and political reality and, as such, a very powerful determinant of individual and group behaviour and of sociocultural systems and institutions.

Race prejudice is basically a psychological state, a feeling or attitude of mind, felt and/or expressed as "an antipathy based upon a faulty and inflexible generalisation" (Allport, 1954); at a deeper level it may be likened to a superstition (Fryer, 1984). Racism, however, is a doctrine or ideology—or dogma. As Wellman (1977) argues in *Portraits of White Racism*, once racial prejudice is embedded within the structures of society, individual prejudice is no longer the problem—"prejudiced people are not the only racists". When implemented and practised through the institutions of society, racism is called "institutional racism".

Experience 1

When I was appointed to the MHAC in 1986, I realized straight away that I was one of the very few black members of that body, and it soon became evident that I was one of very few commissioners to be sufficiently independent of the institution (in, for instance, not needing to be a member for financial reasons) to raise issues of race and culture in the mental health field openly and with some persistence. Within a short period of time, I formed the view that the MHAC was open to change towards becoming an institution that addresses issues of racism. I did so for the following reasons: (1) although the Commission had a relatively small number of members who wished to face up to injustices of the psychiatric system, many were prepared to see themselves as promoting good practice within the established psychiatric system; (2) the majority of commissioners were liberal-minded and were afraid of being considered racist; and (3) the Commission's structure was such that active campaigning within the Commission would pay dividends if pursued tactfully.

The Commission was (at the time of my appointment) divided into three geographically based regions. In the region I worked in, a "liberal" white member had already formed a working party to consider "Black and Ethnic Minority Issues". I joined this group but, in spite of pressure to do so, did not take its chair, for two reasons. First, the chairperson at the time, being well established within the Commission, had the contacts through which influence could be brought to bear, and (most importantly, as I then saw it) had the ear of the chairman of the Commission; and, second, I did not wish to get labelled as "pushy" so early in my career as a Commissioner. This working party acted as a pressure group or lobby within the MHAC. As a result, the first public conference of MHAC was around ethnic issues in mental health. Subsequent biennial reports (Mental Health Act Commission, 1987, 1989) highlighted issues of race and culture. Having convinced the then chairman (a barrister, white man, and hereditary peer) of the need for much higher numbers of commissioners from black and minority ethnic groups, we noted that the Department of Health specified the need for more persons from these communities in its circular letter to professional bodies asking for nominations. By 1988 at least 10% of commissioners were identifiable as being from "ethnic minorities", although many were lukewarm about becoming involved in issues of race.

In 1989, a new chairman was appointed to the Commission—a white Jewish barrister with a reputation for radical politics and forthright approach. The regional structure was replaced with a central office, and national standing committees (NSCs) were instituted, some replacing working parties/committees already in existence. However, the Central Policy Committee (CPC) of the Commission, consisting of commissioners directly appointed by the Secretary of State, continued. The Working Party on Black and Ethnic Minorities was replaced by the NSC on Race and Culture. The stage seemed to be set for further progress towards an antiracist and culturally sensitive Commission. I agreed to take on the chair of the NSC on Race and Culture, and several new members joined this group, all identifying fairly strongly as being from black and ethnic minorities. My chairmanship was confirmed by the members of the NSC. We considered thinking of the NSC as a "black" group (using black in a political sense) but decided against this as we felt that a "black section" would be counter-productive. Instead, we made efforts to recruit white members to the NSC, with some success. We started discussing specific policies, such as asking for all complaints to the Commission with a racial or cultural component to be referred to our group, planning training for commissioners, and so forth.

In October 1989, all commissioners had a memorandum from the Commission chairman stating that all NSCs would in future be chaired by commissioners appointed by him, and a few days later the names of the appointed chairpersons were listed. Whenever they were available, named nominees were commissioners who were already sitting as chairpersons of the respective groups, the exception being that I was not nominated in the case of the NSC on Race and Culture. I questioned this action. In a telephone call to me, the (white, Jewish) Commission chairman told me that he did not think that a black person should chair this committee, giving as his main reason: "If a black person chairs this committee, the issues will get marginalized ... the best way of carrying forward the issues is by having a white chairman." When I related this conversation to other members of the Commission, several white members considered that the reasons given were sound, although others recognized a flaw in the argument. All the black members I spoke to recognized immediately the reasons given as camouflage for a racist action, but mostly they were against my making a fuss, in case we lost the gains we had made—for example, in having an

NSC on Race and Culture. I was in a dilemma as to what action to take. With strong support from the secretariat, I wrote to the secretary of the Commission, to get the matter discussed at the CPC—and the item was included on the agenda. However, the papers that I sent were not circulated to members of the CPC. I then realized that I had to carry out background work if the CPC was to exert its authority in my favour. I lobbied several individual members of the (all-white) CPC and also spoke privately to individuals at the Department of Health. My case was taken up by a Jewish woman member of CPC, and I circulated letters to each member of the CPC, giving my case. Also, I obtained legal advice on the applicability of the Race Relations Act in appointments and made this fact known within the Commission.

I learned later that, at the meeting of the CPC where my letters were discussed, the chairman agreed that my presentation had been accurate. He had pleaded that (a) he himself experienced anti-Semitism and so cannot possibly be racist, and (b) he firmly believed that issues of race cannot be taken forward unless people from the dominant racial group speak up, quoting his own experience when he faced anti-Semitism at school, and therefore that a white chairperson was needed to speak on race matters. However, at the insistence of the CPC, he changed his earlier action by confirming me as chairperson of the NSC on Race and Culture, and he apologised to me in writing.

At this point, I decided that the reversal of action carried out in private was not satisfactory since our plans (at the NSC) for progress on ethnic issues were unlikely to materialize in a situation where the committee I headed would be marginalized in practice. I decided to expose the whole affair at a general meeting of the Commission (from which information was often "leaked" to the press) in order to obtain a stronger commitment to ethnic issues within the Commission. When I sounded out the support that I might expect get for this from the (predominantly white) membership of the Commission and from contacts at the Department of Health, I did not get the impression of widespread support, and, indeed, I was strongly advised to "sort it out" privately. The main motivation of many people, both black and white, within the Commission seemed to be a desire not to rock the boat, because they had reached some accommodation with the chairman of the Commission. Essentially, they feared the repercussions of losing his patronage. Meanwhile, I had several telephone calls from people whose membership of the Commission had not been renewed (having presumably lost his patronage) advising me to "go public". I then realized that I should not become a pawn in other people's games but think things out for myself, based on my own agenda.

The end result of this episode was a compromise. In negotiating with me through an intermediary, the chairman of the Commission agreed to my proposition that the Commission as a body should have a "Race Policy" that would place on record the basis for the prevention of both direct and indirect discrimination on racial grounds. In turn, I agreed not to take the dispute into the public arena and to present the conflict to the general meeting of the Commission as a misunderstanding. The "Race Policy" was accepted at a full meeting of the Commission, ratified by the CPC on 1 February 1990, and published in the Commission's Biennial Report (Mental Health Act Commission, 1991). The NSC on Race and Culture remained active for some considerable time (see below), organized training, and monitored the implementation of the Race Policy by, for example, getting black membership of the CPC.

LESSONS ABOUT RACISM

1. Racist action can be camouflaged by overt liberal sentiments, often without the person responsible realizing it. In this case, a (liberal) intention of a wish to highlight racism concealed what amounted to actual racist practice.

2. People who have experienced racism may feel that *they* cannot be racist, whatever they may do. This is not true: victims of racism may, and often do, act in a racist fashion.

3. Those who may gain from racism and those who may suffer from it may both collude with racism for what they may perceive as pragmatic reasons—a type of rationalization that may be open to manipulation by systemic forces in a context where patronage works through "divide-and-rule" approaches.

4. If a person deals with racism in a particular way, she or he

may think that *that* is the way to deal with racism in all situations. Since the manifestations of racism changes, strategies to deal with it must change too. When racism is subtle, it requires subtle thinking for its analysis and perhaps subtle strategies of resistance.

LESSONS ABOUT SYSTEMS

1. A person caught up as a victim of racism within a powerful system may well have a dilemma about how to confront it. It is always necessary to confront racism; direct confrontation may be satisfying, but careful thought is needed on the most productive approach. Here, a consideration of context becomes crucial—the exploitative tendency of the media, the power structure within which action may be taken, and the weaknesses of individuals when it comes to the "crunch" must all be taken on board. The outcome is seldom fully satisfying or conclusive. It may merely open up a new stage in developing anti-racist practice within the institution.

2. When resolving an issue of racism, a personal resolution (with an apology, for instance) may appear to be adequate. However, unless some systemic change can be initiated, the personal racism is very likely to be repeated. Anti-racist policies incorporated into the workings of the system are one way of making a lasting change. But such a policy must include within it some means of monitoring the implementation of the policy.

Experience 2

A new chairperson of the MHAC was appointed in 1994—the first woman to hold that position (although called "chairman") and a non-barrister. She did not come with any particular reputation on "radicalism" but expressed interest in promoting the increase of black and ethnic minority membership and confronting issues of race in the psychiatric system A restructuring of the MHAC had been agreed before her arrival on the scene, including within it a new recruitment process whereby the MHAC itself would advertise and recruit commissioners although the final decision for appointment rested with the Secretary of State for Health. The new (restructured) Commission was scheduled to take effect from 1 November 1995.

As a part of the process of restructuring, NSCs were abolished and the CPC replaced by a Board of Management, apparently without a remit for making policies. A small group (essentially a twosome), called the "change team", was appointed by the Chief Executive to carry through the reorganization—and this included rewriting all the policies of the Commission. The "change team" appointed a group to rewrite the "Race Policy" in order to widen its scope by addressing the work of the Commission with outside bodies and recruitment to the Commission of new members. As the chair of the outgoing NSC on Race and Culture, I was appointed by the "change team" to chair a "Project Group" to consider issues around race and culture, including amending the existing "Race Policy" to take account of recruitment and training.

This "Race and Culture Project Team" produced an agreed re-drafted and re-named "Policy on Race and Culture". This was considered by the CPC at its meeting on 24 May 1995 and agreed with some amendments. This amended version was included in the training pack for new commissioners and referred to during the training as representing the agreed policy of the Commission. While the activities of the "change team" were progressing, the Commission office had been in the process of preparing the Sixth Biennial Report of the Commission for the period 1993–1995. In mid-October, all commissioners were sent a draft of this biennial report and asked to comment and/or point out mistakes, as necessary. On perusal of this draft, I noticed that some crucial wording in the "Race and Culture Policy" (to be included as an appendix within the report) was incorrect. This concerned Paragraph 2.3 of the policy, which had been agreed to read: "[That the Commission would] work towards establishing an ethnic mix of its membership and staff that reflects the ethnic composition of detained patients visited by the Commission." In the version within the draft Biennial Report, the words "detained patients visited by the Commission" had been replaced with the words "British Society".

Assuming this change in substance of the policy to have been an error, I wrote to the office asking for the matter to be corrected. I received no assurance that this would be done, so on 22 October 1995 I wrote to the Chairman of the Commission asking that she should make sure that the wrong wording of the policy (as printed in the draft of the Biennial Report) should be rectified so that it adhered to the wording agreed by CPC. The response I had from the Chief Executive about a week later made it clear that the changes had been made deliberately (and were not errors, as I had assumed) because (as he wrote) "the objectives as expressed in the draft Biennial Report were preferable". Meanwhile, the CPC had been disbanded as a part of the reorganization! After consulting with other ex-members of ex-CPC, I wrote to the Chief Executive asking for a reversal of the changes in wording made by the office (presumably by the chairman of the Commission). I had no response, and on 31 October 1995 my term of office as a member of the Commission came to an end. In her letter to me thanking me for serving on the Commission, the chairman stated that "your invaluable work has left us with a firm foundation on which to build", but he did not mention the change that had been made in the wording of the Race and Culture Policy. The Sixth Biennial Report of the Commission (Mental Health Act Commission, 1995) included the Race and Culture Policy with the wording as altered and not as agreed by the CPC, representing the Commission, and without any statement explaining this change of wording after its approval as MHAC policy.

LESSONS ABOUT RACISM

1. People who are unsure about their own feelings on racism may foster open debate of racial issues and seem to support anti-racist action, but take action behind the scenes that does the opposite. In the last analysis, actions speak louder than words; so whilst one may welcome good words, one has to wait to see action before closing the book.

2. Racism permeates systems so strongly that one needs to be on guard all the time; gains made over years of hard work may be undone in a very short time.

LESSONS ABOUT SYSTEMS

1. Policies are only effective if there are structures to ensure that they are implemented. In the case of the MHAC, the structure until early 1994 included a National Standing Committee on Race and Culture with a remit to monitor the Race Policy. This worked so well that some progress was achieved in ensuring the need for training in race and culture and having black people appointed to the CPC. However, once this NSC was disbanded, no structure was put in place to ensure that the new Race and Culture Policy (even with the wording amended in the office) would be implemented.

2. People in authority may well have good intentions, but they are inevitably influenced by systemic forces that oppose change. "Good intentions" is a valuable asset, but adherence to policies openly discussed must be the basis for successful institutional change.

Conclusion

Since black people are over-represented among people detained compulsorily under the Mental Health Act, it is reasonable to expect the MHAC to (1) place considerable emphasis on informing itself (through training of its members, etc.) about issues of race and culture in connection with compulsory detention and mental health; (2) focus on these issues in the course of its visits to institutions and bodies involved in detaining people under the Mental Health Act; (3) aim to include within its membership a large number of black people; and (4) report on issues of race and culture in its Biennial Reports to Parliament.

My experience is that, by working within the system, I (together with other black members) was able to promote progress within the MHAC on all the items listed, to varying degrees. The most successful area was in ensuring the consistent reporting of racial issues in successive Biennial Reports, especially the ones issued in 1991 and 1993 (Mental Health Act Commission, 1991,

1993), reflecting to some extent the extent to which these issues were addressed by commissioners in their day-to-day work. However, my experience taught me that it was not just a matter of persuading commissioners and getting policies accepted through the normal processes: the work involved constant attention to details of activities within the MHAC, in order to prevent slipping back after progress, and persistent vigilance to prevent, and if possible expose, actions taken behind the scenes. In other words, it was not a matter of pushing open doors that gave way, but of constant pushing against doors that were being pushed shut—and were firmly shut given any drop in vigilance. In the case of the MHAC as an institution, the way in which changes were made involved persistent attention to whatever was going on, using circumstances as they arose but aware of the personalities involved in the institution. To the question "was it worth while?", I would give the answer "yes, the achievement was very little, but more than I could have achieved from outside the system".

So, in analysing the personal experiences of a particular black professional in a particular white institution, the general conclusion is that, in spite of embedded institutional racism, black people who wish to fight racism must become involved in British institutions, pushing their way forward if necessary, but once they are involved, they must (in order of priority):

1. be constantly vigilant and not mistake words for action;
2. push the frontiers of anti-racism as far as possible, making alliances with anyone who wishes to cooperate;
3. be prepared to confront racism thoughtfully and realistically.

Personal epilogue

A black person in Britain who strives to fight racism will seldom, if ever, become top dog in an influential "white institution", but achieving a senior position in such an institution is not unlikely. That is what I achieved as a senior influential person in an organization of some importance in the field of mental health. At first, I was viewed with some suspicion by most of the colleagues on the Mental Health Act Commission. But gradually I achieved a position of some trust and influence, having proved myself as reasonably reliable and consistent—a "proof" of worthiness that most white colleagues did not have to show in order to achieve equivalent or even higher positions. Looking back on my experience in this particular institution, I would name the following strategies that worked *for me* in bringing about change:

- Forming alliances with carefully selected individuals, especially white people.

- Developing a strong pressure group that was clearly identified as "pro-black", but including within it a minority of white people.

- Selecting a few areas to focus on, and persevering until change was effected in these areas.

- Threatening to "go public" when confronted by overt racist practice, but being willing to compromise in order to achieve tangible gains.

Strategies that did not work *for me* are as follows:

- Developing a direct link with the head of the institution, even though the person concerned had a reputation of liberal-mindedness.

- Seeking to display loyalty to the institution by abiding with a majority view, *when such a view was racist* or may have colluded with racism.

- Taking a submissive stance in order to maintain the "honorary-white" status.

CHAPTER SIX

Organizational change in the Probation Service

Lennox Thomas

I was invited to do some long-term consultancy work with probation managers in "Midshire" around the area of organizational change in the light of recent government proposals, the management of equal opportunities issues, and the specific changes in the role of the senior probation officer. Like many of the other 56 probation areas in England and Wales, Midshire was in the position of developing new policies for the management of the organization and the practice of probation officers. Both central government and local staff were considering changes in probation. The independence of developing policy and practice at its own pace in the 1970s was replaced by a series of policies emanating from government in the 1980s. These policies were arriving in waves at local probation services, who sought changes in the organization of hierarchical structures, financial management, values, training, and day-to-day practice of working with offenders. Never before had the Probation Service been faced with such challenges, and some of the probation areas have parried the blows, others adopted a fearful resignation. The effect of such rapid and at times radical policy changes and proposals has ultimately served to strengthen the professional organizations. The

National Association of Probation Officers, representing a broad practitioner view, and the Association of Chief Officers of Probation, representing managerial views, evaluated and responded to the effects of these policy changes.

For the purposes of confidentiality the name "Midshire" is fictional. Other details about the organization has been changed in order to prevent identification. The method of the consultancy is similar to that of work done by the author with other organizations.

Prompts for change

The changes at the beginning of the 1980s in the form of the Criminal Justice Act 1982 were in part a result of a new government's wish to reduce crime. The bill preceding the act contained many new measures such as curfews and negative requirements as component parts of probation orders. Probation organizations rejected these measures and considered them both unworkable and undesirable. In rejecting these, probation officers used arguments based on both social work values as well as on the practical application of the measures. It appeared that the social work values that underpinned the work of the Probation Service had created a source of unease in civil servants charged by government with the task of making these changes. Most of the policy papers from the Home Office have since drawn attention to the redundancy of some of these values in a modern probation service. Even the language of social work, the description of concepts and behaviour, had come under attack. This was evident in a paper by David E. R. Faulkner of the Home Office, delivered at the Clarke Hall Conference in Cambridge in July 1989.

The Probation Service is acknowledged to be a service having its roots in social work, having a social work base. It has rightly moved on from the days when it saw itself as a social work agency: It is much more than that today. But it is not always clear what a "social work base" does and does not mean.

After quoting Professor Bottoms's five key social work values (Bottoms & McWilliams, 1979), Faulkner went on to say that these values were not unique to the Probation Service, and indeed police officers and even civil servants could subscribe to them as well. In his bid to dismantle the social work component of the Probation Service and reshape it into a community correctional facility, he had, perhaps deliberately, missed the point that values are grounded in practice, and he represented a particular way of doing probation work which is different to the work of police officers and civil servants.

In April 1988, John Patten's speech to probation committees, *Home Office Policy for Criminal Justice*, he discussed punitive changes in probation, stating that this would require a shift in attitudes and types of work but not in the fundamental values of the service. He added that if sentencers were to make more use of probation, the services must develop sentencing measures that demanded more from offenders, unlike the conventional treatment model. The Probation Service—and in particular its three principles of advising, assisting, and befriending—had been under strong criticism from central government, whose wish it was to change this long-held basis for its existence. Whilst the early documents made subtle comment about change, later Home Office documents—the 1988 Green Paper in particular (Home Office, 1988)—were unequivocal.

The 1989 National Probation Audit Report, *Home Office: Control and Management of Probation Services in England and Wales*, and the 1989 Audit Commission report, *The Probation Service, Promoting Value for Money*, both restated the role and power of the Home Office to put forward the broad direction of probation policy. In the 1970s, control from central government was deployed to probation areas. The reason for this stated in the National Audit Office report was to allow local probation committees to stimulate development and exercise their own responsibilities. The shift of power back to central Home Office control was a result of the Home Office wanting to see improvements in local management and performance. The findings of their audit were that management had not kept pace with developments.

After the Criminal Justice Act 1982, the Home Office issued a paper, "The Statement of National Objectives and Priorities in 1984". This introduced a top-down model for developing priorities and policies for local probation areas. The probation services in

England and Wales had to produce objectives so that performance could be monitored against them. The areas were encouraged to set out their local conditions and factors that affected the nature of their work. This was an early move from the Home Office, largely influenced by its Probation Inspectorate, with its aim to achieve stronger management of the local services. This policy was welcomed by many managers in the service who acknowledged that the Probation Service was in need of direction. The Statement of National Objectives and Priorities (SNOP) involved every level of management. Prior to this, systems for managing a service of its size and position in the Criminal Justice System were not effective. Teams had the task of producing clear and systematic objectives which were later amalgamated and set in order of priority by chief officers. These Statements of Local Objectives (SLOPs) were returned to the Home Office. Local objective setting proved to be a useful exercise in co-ordinating services locally as well as identifying the extent to which probation officers were out of step with the purpose and direction of the services that employed them.

After receiving the local statements from the services, the Home Office identified the need for management training in the Probation Service. During this process, civil work with divorcing parents and their children and prison after-care duties were ranked as low priorities. This perhaps coincided with the subsequent view of the Home Office that civil work should be dealt with in separate units away from the main body of work with criminal courts and sentencers. After-care, as distinct from parole, was not given high priority, and indeed this was not changed in later policy papers from the central government. The emphasis of the Green Paper (Home Office, 1988) was on the development of tougher probation and new non-custodial measures for Crown and magistrates courts. The profession considered the reduction of after-care work with prisoners a short-sighted move.

In addition to changes required by government, local, and national agencies concerned with penal policies, The National Association for the Care and Resettlement of Offenders (NACRO) and the Runnymeade Trust expressed concern about sentencing practices in relation to women offenders and black offenders. Research papers from these bodies indicated a disproportionate increase in imprisonment of both groups. Policy groups were concerned about equality and sentencing practices, and probation services were rightly prepared to consider their part in this, particularly the preparation of reports to criminal courts.

The organization's history and culture

Midshire Probation Service is a small area serving both urban and rural populations. The organization has a very clear, formal managerial structure. Probation officers are employed by probation committees who appoint senior probation personnel to carry out day-to-day managerial tasks. The committees are usually made up of a variety of people from the community, particular those closely associated with the Criminal Justice System—for example, magistrates, judges, forensic psychiatrists, and so forth. Technically, it is the committee that has the main contact with the Home Office, which funds the Probation Service for 80% of its running, the other 20% being given by the local authority.

Midshire Probation Service employs a chief probation officer, a deputy chief probation officer, 6 assistant chief probation officers, 20 senior probation officers, and 196 probation officers and assistant probation officers. On the administrative managerial side, the staff consists of a chief administrative officer, 3 senior administrative officers, 14 administrative officers, and 52 secretaries and clerks. Other staff are employed for day-centre work and for the bail hostels. Bail hostels provide a place for defendants to live until returning to court. They were introduced to reduce the number of people in prisons awaiting trial and to provide some measure of surveillance on the movements of those who might otherwise have been remanded in custody.

The organization's objective is to provide a statutory service in conjunction with the other three arms of the Criminal Justice System: that is, courts, police, and the prison service. Probation officers supervise offenders in the community and provide a prison-visiting and after-care service to people who are incarcerated and those who are subsequently released on license. They prepare pre-sentence reports in order to assist courts in the sentencing process, and they generally offer advice, assistance, and befriending to offenders in order to help the individuals and families break criminal patterns. The methods they employ are varied—individual, couples, family, and group casework—and they also provide practical and welfare advice and contribute to policy development on poverty, crime, and homelessness. Midshire seems to have a very smooth administrative structure and very clear lines of accountability and supervision. Woven into the structure of supervising offenders is a very complex organizational structure; a comparatively recent comprehensive handbook details ways to deal with the particular problems that such a large organization throws up. Midshire had also made its own recent forays into working with equal opportunities. This had created a great deal of dissatisfaction and concern among the workforce. Both staff and middle management expressed concern about what might be expected of them.

The chief officer's group described the workforce as predominately white and middle class, although some increase in the very small proportions of black staff and of staff from working-class backgrounds had been noted. The cultural norms from the 1960s and 1970s which had been non-conformist and anti-psychiatry had become more anti-establishment in the 1980s. The feeling was that new entrants to the Probation Service were either more sensible or much more concerned about keeping their jobs. Those employing staff in the 1980s saw a group of people who were much more concerned about espousing the values of difference and tolerance, which had been the centre of discomfort amongst the staff around the issues of equal opportunities. The more experienced staff saw this as a threat to their own way of thinking and as, possibly, fashionable sloganeering. Newer staff, particularly those who valued difference, found that change was slow and that management was not particularly interested in seeing changes brought about. There certainly was a dilemma for older, more experienced staff who had got used to the notion that black people were clients and who found it hard to think of black people as colleagues with an equal right to be in the building as themselves. An example of this was an incident that arose when an experienced white probation officer confronted a young black man in the corridor. He was trying to get into his office. She asked him what on earth he thought he was doing. He told her that he was a new probation officer who had been introduced to her some days earlier. She apologised and said that "one always needs to be careful when you see young black men with keys". Whilst this had caused the young man some distress, he felt too new and unsupported to make a complaint about this or to talk about his feelings.

The overall task of the organization is that of the management of offenders in the community. The Probation Service was founded as a result of the efforts of nineteenth-century penal reformers who wanted, on the one hand, to increase sentencing options open to courts to reduce the harsh measures of transportation or imprisonment of poor or misguided young people, and, on the other, recognition of the need for social reform (Holmes, 1900). The idea of giving someone a second chance before imprisonment, as the final measure, caught on and has always been under the watchful control of magistrates and other influential people in the community. The history of Midshire Probation Service is indeed the history of most of the probation services in the United Kingdom and abroad. Commonly, since the 1930s and 40s staff entered the service as a second career, or as a first profession for social science graduates. It was essentially a middle-class profession with a well-supported and well-regarded professional association developed from very early in the life of the Probation Service.

The human structures developed in response to or connection with the primary tasks in that offenders were seen as a people apart, quite different from officers. This was an attitude that pervaded many decades of the Probation Service. Woven into the professional duties were attitudes of paternalism and ideas of transforming offenders into moral human beings. There was indeed a great deal of missionary zeal underpinning the professional task. The early Probation Service was in fact called the "Court Missionary Service". Older probation officers would see their identity as being different from that of social workers. In the 1960s, the probation services changed their job titles from their ungendered form of "assistant principal" and "principal". The underlying motives behind this revision was unclear. However, the stated aim was that of bringing probation in line with the police and other services. This change to "chief", "deputy chief", and "assistant chief" moved trained social caseworkers further away from the titles used in other areas of the personal social services. Their identities are a very closely balanced act: on the one hand to gain confidence and credence in relation to magistrates and judges, whilst on the other to have street credibility for the clients they work with. There are taboos about crossing both boundaries, particularly about getting too close to "client-land" or "going native". This caution for distance is part of power holding and the maintenance of difference. Whilst it is important to get close enough to influence, getting too close often serves to render the office useless. This situation gives rise to many "games" that are played with defendants facing the criminal courts. Such a "game" played by probation officers might be seen as similar to the ways in which lawyers attempt to "get people off", which has led to the possible implications that defence lawyers and probation officers are both "on the side of the angels". That picture of officers dedicated to their work and always acting in the best interests of their client is not the universal picture. The staff at Midshire were only too aware of themselves as the soft underbelly of a sometimes harsh and unfair Criminal Justice System.

Staff were similarly managed in a paternalistic way. As a personal social service, the policies that should serve to ease the flow of decisions often came late and were often drafted by committee. Probation officers often complained that there were too few policies, and then when policies were put in place they complained that they felt hindered by these policies and tied up in red tape. Newer entrants to the service found the idea of working to policies much easier to cope with and often put pressure on managers to develop such policies. In recent years, staff have complained that there did not seem to be a sense of common task or purpose, and that it did not seem that all staff members were after the same ends. Staff sometimes found themselves polarized as either loony, unrealistic liberals or conservative and punitive dinosaurs. The introduction of new ideas and new policies, particularly equal opportunities policies, created much conflict in many offices. Staff took up entrenched positions; battle-lines were drawn, and the senior probation officers, often with their own individual agendas, found themselves completely immobilized by the strength of feelings in their staff teams. The introduction of equality policies in some teams appeared to set people taking up positions (some genuine, others not) for or against a particular issue. Some people argued that the mere existence of probation officers was *prima facie* evidence that they were concerned about inequality, and that looking to one particular group or another was therefore unequal. Others argued about the disproportionate numbers of black people who were imprisoned, yet others at the disproportionate numbers of women in custody. Many took this as an implied criticism of their role hitherto, and they expressed a deep sense of personal outrage as a result. For some, it posed a very challenging learning task, whilst for others the same ideas posed severe threats to their own personal identity. It would be fair to say that some teams in Midshire took the task of change seriously, questioned their practices, and sought to make changes in the way they went about their duties, and particularly the way that they used their power. The influential power that probation officers have in the preparation of their reports, and the recommendations that they make to Courts, became a focus of work for some. Few would see the issues of structural change in the Probation Service as easy, and even fewer would deny the existence of personal challenges and personal threats to their thinking and beliefs. Many felt that the introduction of equality-monitoring systems marked an end to the personal autonomy that probation officers have traditionally guarded. Management clearly needed to introduce a consultative system for dealing with the dilemma of change. The way that the organization had developed afforded a great deal of autonomy to probation officers, but made for difficulties allowing the structure to change. There were strong feeling that the management were leaving the probation officers, the main grade, to get on with it by themselves. Staff talked with conviction that this was indeed the writing on the wall. Some saw the changes as a great left-wing conspiracy, others as an instrument of the right.

Like many other services, the development of the Midshire Probation Service was incremental. From its origins of two or three probation officers attached to a particular magistrates court in the 1920s, the organization developed rapidly in the post–Second World War period. From being a group of "equals", senior probation officers were appointed to administer and coordinate small teams. Since the early 1960s, sentencing policies have changed, introducing fresh options to the courts, both those supervised by probation as well as others without supervision requirements (e.g.

conditional discharge and suspended sentences). The role of the
Probation Service has expanded into taking over the care functions
as well as supervising licensees on parole (Edmunds & Thomas,
1978). In the 1970s, hostels, day training centres, and community
service were all new measures that required different organization,
and concomitantly the structure of the organization adjusted.
There were changes in Midshire, which, like other probation areas,
served urban populations and reorganized to offer this new range
of options to both clients and courts. Alongside these changes,
the tradition of autonomy in practice, so dear to the Probation
Service, often remained unchanged. The notion of independence
also seemed part of a mythology and perhaps reflected a form of
blinkered thinking in those who had failed to recognize or to face
the structural changes in the organization. As a result, a gulf grew
between how things are done and how they are traditionally
believed to have been done. Because the managerial structure was
not cohesive, personnel could continue in the belief that they
were autonomous in the way that they carried out their work. In
Midshire this notion that rules did not have to be taken seriously
when working with offenders (who were constantly breaking
rules themselves and were, as a result, at the risk of incarceration)
seemed unwise. The maxim developed that one could break any
rule other than "sleeping with the client or fiddling the petty cash".
There was a sense of security in having a job for life and of not
being bothered much by managers. What had been the culture of
the white, liberal, middle-class backbone in Midshire, which itself
developed out of the Christian culture of Victorian prison reform,
had in the 1960s then become something more—a more politicized
way of thinking. The individualistic, objective tradition of writing
reports and supervising offenders led in part to probation officers
not paying sufficient attention to the development of psychological
techniques for helping their clients change. The social context
of, for example, poverty, abuse, or discrimination was given little
attention as part of the professional task. On the other hand, probation officers saw themselves as helping to prevent and reduce
crime. The ethos of advising, assisting, and befriending sometimes
seemed difficult to square up with more direct confrontational
imperatives for change in criminal behaviour. The easygoing
assumption that offenders changed and developed through the

medium of the casework relationship alone was losing its credibility.

General resistance to being managed by seniors sometimes led to the blurring of the managerial role, which is for many a role of supervising, managing and providing some pastoral care to staff. However, many preferred to see the senior as no more than a supportive peer. The assistant chief probation officer, the next grade up, was often viewed as a visiting grandparent. The deputy and the chief grades were seen as the ultimate powers or those with ceremonial roles, often therefore reviled as being "long gone from practice" and "out of touch". The administrative assistants and secretaries in Midshire were, by contrast, efficient and often held to the task of keeping the organization running smoothly.

Whilst in many ways Midshire had developed as a response to changes in legislation and Home Office directives, these changes often took place in isolation from staff, who complained about not being informed or sufficiently consulted. Senior managers in Midshire sat and pondered on change for some time before staff were informed of the proposals, whilst the implementation through the different grades continued to be delayed.

How the organization might improve is functioning

If I were asked about another structure that could serve the needs of the probation staff and their clients in Midshire, I would encourage the probation officers to have more specialist interests in their work: for example, sex offenders, welfare rights, or substance misuse. In order to do this, senior probation officers need greater security in their role. It would seem useful to provide senior probation officers with more consultancy, particularly on those difficult-to-manage issues that face them, such as persistent criminality, psychological problems in clients, and interventions for behavioural change. I would suggest that the senior role is less administrative and more of a supervisory function. The senior administrative staff would therefore take up the administrative and managerial aspect in the office and work in conjunction with the senior probation officer. It would require a considerable shift in the way that personnel are devolved in the Probation Service, where the probation discipline appears to hold all the power and the non–probation managers and administrators are therefore seen as merely "supportive". The assistant chief probation officer (ACPO) would have a greater role than both the senior administrator and the senior probation officer and would have an inspectorial function. This would not only be in relation to how the local organization was run, but also in terms of the policies and practice of the probation discipline staff.

In Midshire, it seemed that staff needed to be encouraged to use greater teamwork in carrying out certain functions in the organization. This would allow for diversity in terms of work skills as well as a sharing of ideas on day-to-day practice. The Senior Probation Officer grade would be key to introducing new policies and new ideas to teams of main-grade officers and other administrators in the office. It seemed that in Midshire the thinking and commitment of senior probation officers, who are much closer to the everyday tasks, were not used. The old-fashioned idea of chief, deputy chief, and ACPO as being part of the "top table" of decision making was something that needed to be changed. A new emphasis on sharing and collaboration would help to shift staff away from thinking of themselves as autonomous professionals towards thinking about themselves as part of a group of people employed in a shared corporate task. It was the view of the consultants that in order for change to take place, first-line managers needed to be valued more.

Midshire developed partly because of the piecemeal way that the Probation Service grew in the post-war era. Officers who joined the Probation Service in earlier decades had been professionals in other areas of work and came to probation as a second career. The choice of this career was often as a reaction against previous jobs where they felt that they were working in over-controlled environments or in uncaring hierarchies, and therefore did not receive adequate job satisfaction. A career in probation had a semblance of giving staff a great deal more individuality and more self-worth. The work seemed highly valued, and the personality of officers seemed not only to matter but to be crucial to the job of working with offenders. The one-to-one casework—the main thrust of the work—had seemed particularly attractive to many of the people who came to it. This, the central task, coupled with the changes in the Criminal Justice System in the 1960s, 1970s, and 1980s, seemed to have caught the organization's structure "on the hop". The fact that the Probation Service was largely a single-discipline organization contributed to a stagnation of thinking. There are analogies here with the police service, who also found it difficult to hand over tasks to civilian staff members during the changes in the 1970s and 1980s. Many of the changes in Midshire were in fact initiated by professional managers and administrators who had been employed at the head office. The staff in research and information seemed more abreast with the new policies being introduced and more optimistic about change. Midshire needed a task evaluation of its key staff grades. Several staff members there were unhappy with the organization's functioning and structures.

The task of introducing ideas of change to Midshire senior managers was not easy. Consultancy often did not seem to be that of inviting change, but of helping the personnel to feel good about the decisions that they had already made about change. For the organization to achieve a different structure, a much broader view had to be taken of the probation task, and each tier of the organization needed clearer objectives. The personnel would have to think about themselves more as "professionals" than as "befrienders". Managers would have to put more emphasis on evaluating the work of the service, and the organizational philosophy of assisting, befriending, and being with defendants had to be squared with the behavioural change that courts and the public expected. Probation officers and senior probation officers would have to consider taking advice from experts on psychological and behavioural change. Also, more clarity was needed about the context of poverty and disadvantage and the part that these played in offending behaviour, without these being an apology for criminality. Managers would have to take much more seriously the desire and capacity for motivated staff to genuinely facilitate change in their client group. Probation officers would have to think about themselves as having a more positive role. The identity of officers as society's agents of control does not necessarily lead to changes in the behaviour of defendants that the public and judiciary expect. There was a need for cultural change as well as change in the organization that supported the work.

Engaging with the organization

Some colleagues and I were approached by Midshire Probation Service, requesting consultancy and training for some of their staff. All consultants were known for providing services to organizations in both the public and private sectors. They had backgrounds in health, education, psychotherapy, family therapy, social work, probation, and management. The group was brought together in the mid-1980s as a result of being participants in race and gender equalities training, being part of group relations programmes, men's and women's self-help development groups, or black self-help development groups. They shared beliefs that organizational structures required change if those groups who were socially marginalized or oppressed were not to be further marginalized or oppressed in their place of work, that systems like people could change, and that crazy or dysfunctional aspects of organizations could be subjected to modification and change in behaviour. This, we believed, could come about as a result of systematic organizational analysis and by the introduction of perspectives of equalities (e.g. class, gender, race, etc.) to provide a particular scrutiny of the organization. An equalities lens would ensure that these ideas could permeate values and practice and could also stand up to objective measurement when the consultancy is evaluated. Esme Roberts (1991) argues that social work organizations are set within the context of wider society and are therefore subject to a range of social, legal, cultural, and attitudinal influences of that society. Whilst Roberts recognizes the possibility of conflicting values, modifying these externally and internally should not be avoided. This is based on the view of social work as an agency of social change, yet the political climate in the late 1980s and early 1990s was manifestly that of reversing the influence and scope of social welfare organizations. Midshire, whilst responding to central government's call for change in the organization, also expressed a wish to see fair treatment for those from disadvantaged groups. The group of consultants operated as a collective, doing mutual development work together using outside consultants for themselves. As part of the group's commitment to social justice and social change, each quarter a charity was selected to whom 5% of the earned fees were donated. Having attended training as participants, we felt that as a group of black and white men and women working together, we had something new to offer. We agreed from the outset that we could afford to be selective about the organizations we chose to work with. We believed that the professional fee could not be the only reward for such harrowing and sometimes thankless work. The belief and the mission of the consultants group and how they measured success was itself a reward.

The initial contact from the commissioning agencies and our letter setting out our terms for working with them often led to organizations choosing not to go ahead with consultancy or training. Some enquiries were about training only. It was our policy always to consult, and not to go ahead with a simple request for training without knowing more about the organization's hierarchy, what the training was for, and how it was tied in with policies. Our experience was that training served a variety of functions for organizations, and we thought it wise to be both clear about this and have it acknowledged. For those agencies without policies concerning equality, we encouraged them to begin the process, not without our assistance, but primarily to be clear about the uses and efficacy of training in a vacuum in the absence of policies written in collaboration with the workforce.

In the case of Midshire, policies existed but were unused and therefore were untested and unfamiliar to staff and hence inadequate in many areas. The policies did not seem to have been built for use but perhaps to indicate that something was being done. The chief probation officer of Midshire, having initially found the scrutiny of consultants difficult, later became a trusted ally in the process of the consultancy. Unfortunately, the same could not have been said about his deputy and assistant chief officers. We had the impression that we were being obstructed or at any rate not cooperated with. The hunch that they had a different agenda was later confirmed. The first contact was made by Medicare's training officer to discuss training for probation officers. We were told that the chief was "very busy" and would not take kindly to being asked to meet with us. I explained to the training officer that the organization needed to "own" the consultancy and that life would be much easier for her department if the mandate for training came from the head of the organization. A meeting was then agreed with senior management, who decided to update and improve their equal opportunities policies and statement. It was also agreed that they would circulate the updated policies to their staff with a note about the forthcoming training strategy and the ongoing consultancy, this only after numerous telephone conversations with the training officer. We were curious to know why Midshire, which seemed a quiet backwater probation area, was apparently keen to look at equalities practice and organizational change. They had no management staff from black or minority ethnic groups, and no women staff above the senior grade. The training officer was probably in the highest-profile job held by women in Midshire. There had been some pressure from staff, and the Home Office had recently issued reports on race and gender inequalities in sentencing and staffing. These initiatives were hot on the heel of documents and research papers from a variety of voluntary agencies concerned with penal affairs. The National Association for the Care and Resettlement of Offenders (NACRO), the Runnymeade Trust, and the Rainer Foundation had expressed concern about issues of equality for some time. Midshire was clearly behind with these issues compared with metropolitan areas, but was not too different from other county areas. Midshire's principal town differed from those in its bordering counties in having substantial populations of migrants from Eastern Europe, Asia, and the Caribbean who settled there after the 1939–45 war.

We soon learnt that whilst some staff were keen to see these developments, just as many others were apprehensive, whilst some talked of being insulted at the suggestion that they required training. The implication was that to take part in equalities training meant that their practice was discriminatory, and that they were unable to provide a fair service to users. Senior probation officers, as first line managers, were very involved in these discussions with teams. Some staff were just curious, whilst others were genuinely interested in training. The consultants decided that all three of us needed to meet with the senior staff group. The consultants defined training as a discrete piece of work commissioned by an organization, the need for which is decided by the latter. Consultancy, on the other hand, was defined as engaging with an organization over a range of issues perhaps not yet clearly defined by them but probably involving advice, examination of systems, and discussion over some time. The outcome of this might be change in the structure, delivery of services, research, or training for personnel. Other styles of consultancy work (Obholzer & Roberts, 1994) might involve psychoanalytic perspectives brought to bear on the processes of collaborative behaviours and relationships in work groups. We chose a more active model of helping the organization to countenance change in relation to policies and to develop systems to manage its effect.

The consultancy informed the training, and together they formed the two main components of the overall strategy. It was important that training in itself was not seen as the only remedy that the organization needed, since there was also a requirement for structural change (Ferns & Madden, 1995). Those with the power to make this happen were the members of the chief officer group. It was important for us that members of the consultancy with debriefing functions helped to steer the trainers and consultants in the right direction so that a comfortable and effective working distance could be maintained. The fact that two of us had professions very similar to that of the senior managers made it both easy to understand their dilemmas and yet opened up the possibility that we might be sucked into what was going on in the organization and its hierarchical structure. The opinion of the one member who had not been in a similar role was therefore crucial. Training was arranged for senior managers, and it was decided that at least one of the consultants to the organizations should be selected as one of the two trainers. The other two consultants remained as debriefers to the whole training and consultancy strategy. The consultancy collective viewed this process as most important, so that the work with this organization was discussed monthly. For us, this reflection was most useful. It helped us see both obstacles and resistance to change, as well as how we might help the client group achieve this. In discussing our "rules of engagement, the rationale for starting to train the managers first was eventually accepted by them as a useful model.

In their written statement to the staff about consultancy and training, the senior management group said that, it was a priority that all professional staff were to attend for the initial training and that administrative and support staff would be trained in the second round. Some participants to the training defined the consultants and trainers as the cause of their discontent. A few were sufficiently candid to state at the outset that all they were prepared to do was "attend". Others festered with discontent, whilst many welcomed the training openly, proclaiming that it was long overdue. The consultancy had ensured that staff had received copies of policies and the guidelines on equalities, which had in some way given permission for these issues to be talked about in team meetings and for the implications for practice to be faced. Training of the senior management group seemed to reveal some of the dilemmas that the whole organization was up against. Some expressed bitterness with change, claiming that they had suffered from change in the organization over the past twenty or so years. Others said that they felt under attack by the "left", who they considered had played a central role in these ideas of sensitivity to black people, people with disabilities, and women. Although some staff complained that people only paid lip service to these ideas, at the same time they appeared to seek a new language "so that we can talk as though we know and understand these things".

There were some personal pleas like "do not upset my staff", or "beware—all this is like a red rag to a bull", and so on. Some senior staff had given real thought to these issues, and their reflections demonstrated this. Other concerns were that the trainers and consultants were giving permission to difficult people like radical black staff and women in the unions to make unnecessary demands on the organization.

Outcome

Our engagement in work with Midshire lasted two years. The training evaluation forms and discussion of the process with the managers suggested that the whole enterprise was considered successful. The greatest impact was on main-grade probation officers, who felt that they had a greater investment in the organization as well as having a duty to the users of the service. This group went on to introduce new initiatives for women offenders and were trying to do the same for young black offenders. The issues about disabilities were exercised in the senior management group, who had to consider promotion for someone with a disability in the administrative section. A few staff who expressed very strong racist feelings were difficult for the management to confront. This was particularly so in the case of one member of staff in middle management. However, Midshire did eventually effect organizational change. They developed new policies and new ideas for practice. They saw women, black people, and people with disabilities progressing into management and, in the case of women, into senior management. Midshire became a leader in equalities issues. There were, however, some failings: The consultants mistook enthusiasm of a few as a total commitment by all, which proved to be false. The discomfort of ACPOs in the consultancy and training programme remained a problem. The deputy and the chief were heads of the organization and had no single areas of responsibility. Each assistant chief had a geographical patch, as well as heading up operational aspects of the probation and after-care task such as civil work and hostels. It became clear that they saw themselves (or were seen as) "barons" responsible for their own individual areas. This generated competition and distrust. The atmosphere of competitiveness was combined with determination to be seen as in control. A remaining impression is that their performance ranged from "pleasing the boss" on the one hand, to "playing the maverick" on the other. On reflection, the consultants' unawareness of this factor left the ACPOs as the group who benefited least.

We only learnt subsequently that the chief probation officer was considering early retirement, which was an open secret among his senior management group. It had been his wish to begin organizational change, and it seems that this was his "last difficult task", perhaps as an act of generosity to his successor. Receiving this information late in the consultancy explained much of the competitiveness of the ACPOs. I wondered whether they saw the consultancy process as a covert protracted encounter group or perhaps an assessment technique that would decide their suitability to apply for the coveted job at a future date. Whether or not this single factor played an important part and organized their behaviour is a matter of speculation, but it was clearly a factor. Another area of difficulty was the small group of staff who presented the organization with long-standing problems. Two were encountered during the training as being particularly racist and resistant to any change. Another was a person whose performance in the job was consistently poor. Although these people had long-term reputations as being problems for Midshire long before their particular assistant chief was appointed, the macho principle of having sorted things out prevented the ACPOs from giving open acknowledgements of these difficulties. We were concerned about the degree of personal accountability that the ACPOs were carrying, and we wondered whether they feared being seen in a negative light as not having succeeded where so many others had failed. We believed that their job role called for review. These pressures seemed to be an impediment to honesty and openness and also prevented them from developing shared stragedies for staff management. Alternatively, this personal accountability might have been a way of protecting the chief and his deputy from criticism or rebuke. Whilst this would have been an honourable intent, we felt that running for the chief probation officer's post was the dominant goal. If, indeed, protecting him was the stated wish, then having his job was the payback.

Returning to Midshire for a review six months after the consultation period had ended, we found that many changes had taken place and that others were being planned. Senior probation officers were in the process of devolving some of their managerial duties to administrative officers, many of whom had been experienced senior secretaries in Midshire. The management of the day-to-day finance and ledgers, the logging of sick notices, and other office managerial duties were handed over or shared. The administrative officers' pay scale was enhanced to take into account their increased responsibilities, some of which they were already performing as a supportive function for hard-worked senior probation officers. This change seemed to have been quite satisfactory because the talents of a group of mainly female workers was used.

As part of the Home Office directive that probation areas should develop partnerships with local voluntary organizations,

Senior Probation Officers became involved with local organizations that provided services for offenders and other groups. Some of these organizations served ethnic minority populations, and the collaboration even at the planning stage proved useful to probation officers and their work. This informal local consultation assisted in the proposal to set up a young black offenders' group in one area that had a substantial population of African-Caribbeans. Many of the senior probation officers were part of policy implementation groups and felt more involved in the management process of the whole organization, not just their teams.

There were some senior probation officers who did not enjoy the increased scope of their work, and some complained that their work took them out of the office rather more than they liked. Some probation officers complained about not having sufficient access to the seniors, and some of the seniors worried that they would be seen as too identified with head office management.

The new developments for the senior probation officer grade were reported positively. The officers considered that they had the backing of the senior management group and were optimistic about the future and about the further policy changes from new legislation which had to be implemented. One senior probation officer said that she has always worried about being caught between her loyalty to her team and her loyalty to senior management. She said that she might not be as popular now, helping her team to face many difficult issues, but her role as a manager was less muddled, her tasks better defined, and her mandate clearer.

The consultancy was very interesting and taught us a great deal. We were able to identify some of our own failings and vulnerabilities as a consultant group and particularly to recognize the effect on us of working in a very stratified "macho" type of organization. We were able to recognize how the values and ways that the client organization operated was beginning to affect us in some way. The degree of understanding and accommodation that is necessary as consultants working with client organizations began to permeate some of our own meetings and in turn challenged some of the principles held as a collective organization. In short, we began to emulate some aspects of the behaviours that were present at Midshire. Seeming to be in charge and in control at all times, becoming reluctant to recognize personal failure and share these difficulties, and being concerned to "watch out for our backs" were difficulties that threatened our consultants' group during the time of our work with Midshire. We then sought facilitation to help us develop ideas around what we recognized were difficulties in the group.

ACKNOWLEDGEMENT

This paper could not have been completed without the help of Irene Winifred Edmunds [1924–1996], probation officer, campaigner, and educator.

CHAPTER SEVEN

Collaborative inquiry: a postmodern approach to organizational consultation

Harlene Anderson & J. Paul Burney

Our collaborative approach to consultation is collegial and egalitarian. It is the framework for a partnership in which consultant and client combine expertise to explore their dilemmas and challenges and develop new possibilities for resolving them. Whether we work with individuals or a group, members of a family or an organization, our collaborative approach remains the same (Anderson, 1990, 1997; Anderson & Goolishian, 1988; Anderson & Swim, 1995; Goolishian & Anderson, 1987). In organizational consultation, the method is a way of integrating people and business strategies in building pathways to change and success. In this chapter, we describe and illustrate this postmodern approach to thinking about, and working with, human systems and the problems they present.

In its simplest form, postmodernism refers to an ideological critique that departs radically from modernist traditions in its questioning of the mono-voice modernist discourse as the overarching foundation of literary, political, and social thinking. Although there is no one postmodernism, in general it challenges the singular modernist notions of knowledge as objective and fixed, the knower and knowledge as independent of each other, language as representing truth and reality, and human nature as universal (Derrida, 1978; Foucault, 1972, 1980; Lyotard, 1984; Ricoeur, 1983; Rorty, 1979). Consequently, the postmodern perspective challenges the technical and instrumental nature of consultation and the notion of the consultant as the expert on organizational culture. It favours, rather, ideas of the construction of knowledge as social, knowledge as fluid, the knower and knowledge as interdependent and thus knowledge as relational, and the multiplicity of *truths*. Said differently, knowledge—and language as a vehicle for creating knowledge—are the products of social discourse.

We view human systems as language- and meaning-generating systems, in which people create understanding and knowledge with each other through communicative action (Anderson & Goolishian, 1988; Goolishian & Anderson, 1988). Communicative action involves dialogue within a system for which the particular communication has relevance. An organization is one kind of language- and meaning-generating system that has a relevance specific to itself. For organizations seeking consultation, our relevant role is to join them as they seek a solution to a problem.

From a postmodern perspective, then, organizational consultation is a linguistic event that involves and takes place in a particular kind of conversational process, a dialogue. Dialogue, the essence of the process, entails shared inquiry—a mutual search and co-exploration between client and consultant, as well as among the client system members—into their narratives about the organization and its members (Anderson, 1995). The shared inquiry is fluid, and it encourages new ideas and viewpoints to be advanced in the conversation. Client and consultant, and client system members, become conversational partners in the telling, inquiring, interpreting, and shaping of the narratives.

We contrast dialogical and monological conversations. By monological we mean those conversations in which people are talking to each other rather than with each other, in which one idea or a group of ideas dominate the space, and in which no newness occurs (Anderson & Goolishian, 1988). Dialogical conversation involves both internal and external dialogues as people talk with themselves and with each other. The internal dialogue consists of a person's internal unformed, and forming, thoughts and ideas. In this process, possibilities come from within and are generated in, and through, the inherent and creative aspects of language, dialogue, and narrative. Transformation occurs within such a collaborative process as the participants generate and explore multiple descriptions, stories, and perspectives; that is, through dialogue, through the evolution of shifting, clarifying, and expanding meanings and understandings, and as a natural consequence of it, new narratives and new possibilities emerge. We think of this newness as self-agency: the ability to act, or to feel that we are capable of acting, to handle our dilemmas in a competent and autonomous manner.

As consultants, our aim, expertise, and responsibility is to create a dialogical space, a metaphorical space providing sufficient freedom for individuals to explore ideas and to facilitate a dialogical process. How does the consultant achieve this aim? We assume what we refer to as a philosophical stance—a way of being in relationship with, thinking about, acting with, and responding to people (Anderson, 1995). It is a way of being that serves as the backdrop for the conversation. The stance is characterized by an attitude of openness to, respect for, curiosity about, and connection with the *other*. It entails flexibility and willingness to follow the client's ranking of what is most important to him or her. Although, as consultants, we may initially have a structure or outline for the consultation—a stepping-stone towards the process—we do not operate from a set agenda of our own or with preconceived ideas concerning the direction that the conversation should take, or what its outcome would be. Any idea about the format or direction of the consultation is tentative, and we are poised to change it at any time. The task is to create and continue the dialogue and discover with the client what is significant.

The most critical aspect of this stance is *not-knowing* (Anderson & Goolishian, 1988). *Not-knowing* refers to the assumption that we do not know what is best for others or how they ought to be conducting their business. We do not suggest that we are *tabulae rasa*, but rather that what we do know—or what we think we know—is only one perspective that is always open to challenge. Nor do we imply that if someone were to ask us a question we would not respond. The difference is in the manner in which, and the intent with which, we would respond. The consultant's *not-*

knowing invites members of the client group to be the teachers, the experts on the circumstances of the consultation, and it naturally acts to involve them in a shared inquiry with us and with each other. Shared inquiry only happens, however, when the consultant's curiosity maintains coherence with clients and is not too far removed from their experience (Anderson, 1994; Anderson & Goolishian, 1992). Questions asked from a stance of *not-knowing*, for instance, should not cause the client to be distracted from his or her train of thought.

As consultants we are more curious and interested in each person's ideas about his or her organization and the manner in which it operates than in proposing our own ideas. This is not to say that we will not offer reflections on ideas and thoughts when asked by the client for feedback or opinions. Our ideas and thoughts, however, are set forth in a manner that allows the client to consider them and to correct us if they are not consistent with the client's point of view. We offer our contributions tentatively, with genuine interest and a desire to hear more of the client's narrative concerning the organization's dilemmas and challenges, including the client's expectations of the consultation.

This conversational style and attitude entails a natural curiosity about the client's dilemmas and a desire to acquire understanding. We listen actively to the narrative being presented to ensure that we have not misunderstood, and we continuously check out what we think we have heard. By asking conversational questions in a manner that encourages the client to say more about the subject being discussed, and by verifying, rather than assuming, that what we think we have heard is what the client wanted us to hear, we explore the client's part in the conversation. *Conversational* questions are questions that are informed both by what has been said as well as by what has not yet been said. The intent is not to receive an answer, steer in a direction, or create a narrative that we deem more useful or correct than the one we are hearing. The intent is to learn, explore, and clarify the client's narrative in a manner that enhances the dialogue. At the same time, we know that the context of the consultation, the manner in which it is conducted, the client's intent, and the experiences and prejudices we bring to the consultation are all variables that influence our curiosity and the style, choice, and type of our questions.

When a consultant assumes this stance, consultation is changed from an archaeological, hierarchical, and interventionist relationship between an *expert* and *non-expert* to a collaborative, egalitarian, and mutual endeavour by people with different types of expertise. Client members who view themselves as important parts of the dynamic process of change become actively and enthusiastically engaged. Consultants become facilitators of the dialogue regarding the concerns of the client instead of experts expected to provide solutions. As we become conversational partners with our client, the dialogue brings forth new ways of thinking and acting regarding dilemmas, problem-solving, communications, relationships, and ourselves as individuals.

In this kind of process the consultant is also at risk of changing. In our experience, the approach is a philosophical one: the consultant's beliefs and biases are not only part of the consultant's professional work, they become a way of being in our professional and personal lives. Our approach frees us to work in a variety of organizational settings, with individuals and groups, without regard to gender, culture, or type of dilemma. Interestingly, we have found that, in a sense, our stance models new and alternative ways for client system members to be with each other, even though modelling is not our intention.

In this chapter we present a narrative of our consultation with Friendly Travel, a corporate client, as illustration of the collaborative inquiry process. We hope to show how the consultation set a collaborative tone, and how it provided the opportunity for multiple, criss-crossing dialogues, by which the client system's members collaboratively defined their dilemmas and created possibilities for addressing them. We hope also to show the evolution of newness through collaboration and shared inquiry, and how it was peculiar to the conversational process.

Organizational setting and history of the consultation

We were invited to provide a seven-and-a-half-hour consultation to a small organization in the travel–tourism industry, to address issues of communication and interpersonal staff relationships, and to help create a more cohesive, effective team. The client organization, Friendly Travel, is a full-service resource provider to individuals, businesses, and organizations in a small recreational, agricultural community in Texas and has as its market a larger, countywide suburban residential and technological business community. The company has an owner and 17 employees, all of them women. The agency has one main office and two satellites.

A member of the consulting team is an acquaintance of the owner, who, in previous conversations, discussed some of the internal and external dilemmas she was experiencing in her organization. The internal changes the client wanted to make concerned staff interpersonal relationships and enhanced service to her customers. She expressed ideas about building the foundations for a better team and developing connectedness within her organization. In her words,

> "The dominant culture of the airline industry has had a major impact on us. The negativity directed at us, as travel agents, from the airlines, and the continuous change in the industry, has caused us to be reactive instead of proactive. We need to find a way to circumvent it."

Not only did this represent a major dilemma for her company, but its current structure and employee relationships, she believed, did not allow the agency to address such issues successfully.

The owner expressed interest in a day-long consultation that might be somewhat different from one conducted by a consultant retained by the organization in the past. She said that she hoped that plans could be formulated that would be helpful to her and her employees individually and to the organization as a whole. She warned, however, that the employees would be reluctant because of the negative experience with the previous consultant and resistant about attending on their day off.

The owner has a high profile in her community; she volunteers a large portion of her time to civic organizations such as the County Fair Association, Performing Arts Society, Chamber of Commerce, and the American Cancer Society, and she serves on the board of directors of the local community college. Part of her motivation is that she is known as a talented, energetic, and well-respected business person in the community, someone who can get things done. Another consideration is that community involvement is personally rewarding and makes good business sense. The organization is uniquely positioned in a continually changing industry that requires rapid response and leaves little time for proactive measures.

The structure of the consultation

Our consultation began with an interview with the owner and discussion of her objectives. The consultants then discussed the structure of the consultation day and confirmed it with the owner. It was to consist of introductions, opening comments, an experiential activity, partner interviews, small and large group discussions, and reflective conversations. Ninety days later, a follow-up interview by one of the consultants with the owner led to plans for a second consultation.

Conversation with the owner: shared inquiry begins

A consulting team member met with the owner before the group consultation to determine how the consultants might help her and what she hoped to accomplish. By introducing the client to the collaborative inquiry process, their initial meeting began the consultation. The consultant set the stage for collaboration by inviting the owner, as the expert, to participate in a conversation about her organization and its dilemmas (Anderson, 1994). The consultant's inquiries concerned the focus of her business, her main objectives and special challenges, as well as what she considered to be her organization's strengths and weaknesses.

In the initial conversation, we learned that her primary goal was to build a better team that gets along and works together more efficiently. She characterized her organization's current dilemma as disorganization. She felt that her organization's greatest weakness was lack of teamwork. This affected the organization internally through employee relationships and organizational structure, as well as externally by making it less responsive to the requirements of clients and the travel–tourism industry. A more efficient team would help the owner accomplish three main objectives: to increase overall business, streamline internal operations, and expand meeting and convention business. The organization's strengths were, she said, "our knowledge and personal attention to our customers' concerns and our longevity in the business". The employees were knowledgeable, and they devoted a great deal of personal attention to each customer's needs. Their services had, in fact, become so individually tailored that they thought of the organization's customers as "my clients". The owner's attempts at changing this attitude had been unsuccessful because of the staff's concerns that change in their customer service would affect the quality of their product. Thus, an asset—concentration on individuality—had become a liability.

The consultation day

INTRODUCTIONS

An important consideration for consultants is the manner in which to begin the consultation day so that the staff will understand that the day's interchange depends on their input. We wanted to begin by continuing both to position ourselves collaboratively and to generate ideas publicly with the staff as we did with the owner. We therefore gave some thought beforehand as how to introduce ourselves to the group and present what we knew, at that time, about their organization and its problems. That is, in our experiences, our relationship with the consultees (in this situation, the staff) begins before we even meet them. They develop ideas about us, make assumptions about our agenda, and have expectations of us. We want to position ourselves to talk and act in ways that may dispel any preconceived assumptions that attribute private agenda to us or that place us in authoritative roles. In other words, we want to behave unexpectedly with their expectations. We want to create a different reputation to the one they have constructed.

We introduced ourselves briefly, discussed our experience, and expressed our enthusiasm for the opportunity of working with the group. We shared what we had learned from the conversation with the owner about the internal problems of teamwork and communication and the external problems with the travel–tourism industry, as we understood them. We also expressed our wish that the group would use the consultation day in a manner that would be most helpful and productive for them. We presented the non-expert concept: as consultants, we were not experts who knew the solutions to their dilemmas but were present as collaborative partners in a process of mutual discovery—a process we do *with* them rather than *to* them (Anderson, 1990, 1994; Anderson & Goolishian, 1992). Ideally, the process would generate new thoughts and useful ideas for their organization.

Then we asked the owner to share her version of the history that preceded the consultation day, her agenda, and her hopes. She briefly summarized the first official consultation conversation and discussed Friendly Travel's previous consulting experience, acknowledging publicly her view that it had not been helpful or productive. The previous consultant had lectured them about what was wrong and what needed to be done, rather than addressing their specific concerns. The owner also acknowledged the resentment experienced by many of the staff about scheduling the consultation on a non-working day, since many staff members were vocal when they arrived about "being here on my day off because the owner signs my pay cheque". She expressed her expectation to the staff that this consultation would be different. She presented her ideas, as told to the consultant, about their shared organizational dilemmas. We invited the staff members to introduce themselves and to discuss why they were here and what they hoped to gain from the experience.

Several elements were important in setting the stage for the collaborative inquiry process. First, the consultants' introduction was non-hierarchical in manner, and it included their understanding of the organization's dilemmas and expectations for their consultation, based on the conversation with the owner. The consultants' role was one of inquiry about the situation, rather than expertise. As facilitators, we hoped to initiate a process of discovery, exploring innovative ideas that might prove beneficial to the organization, rather than providing solutions to the organization's problems. Second, the owner, in her brief introduction, discussed the reasons for the consultation and her belief that it would be different from a previous, unsuccessful one and that the consultants' collaborative style would benefit the organization. Third, the owner presented to the group her perceptions of the organization's concerns, emphasizing that these may or may not match those of the other group members. Fourth, the invitation to staff members to introduce themselves and to state why they were present and what they hoped to gain from the consultation helped to initiate the collaborative inquiry process. In our opening greeting we had acknowledged that some were there under duress, and we expressed our awareness of the inconvenience and their annoyance. Some in introducing themselves reiterated their displeasure, but all expressed a desired goal for the consultation, ranging from interpersonal aspects to technical and pragmatic ones.

Our aim in using the collaborative inquiry philosophy is to create a dialogical space and stimulate conversation focused on hypotheses set forth by the client (Anderson, 1995). That is, we are interested in the individual group member's hypotheses about her or his organization, rather than in hypotheses of our own. In our experience, the collaborative manner in which participants are encouraged to express their ideas and opinions differs from the organization's usual hierarchical operational style. Clients report that this process allows them to feel more free to express themselves and to be creative, thus leading to possibilities where there seemed to be none before and to more productive outcomes.

EXPERIENTIAL ACTIVITY: GROUP JUGGLE

We chose an experiential activity that we hoped would be inviting and would aid the client in developing a different style of team communication. Designed to be enjoyable while also allowing the group to become more relaxed mentally and physically, the activity—Group Juggle—increased the possibilities for interaction within the group. Experiential activity and physical movement can be effective stimuli in engaging participants and providing an opportunity to be open, active, and creative. Activity is also a basis for discussing important aspects of communication, such as focus, concentration, and the ability to listen effectively. Experiential activities effectively set the collaborative tone: members of the group participate on an equal basis, instead of the clients participating as a group and consultants observing as outsiders (Fluegelman, 1981).

The group was asked to stand in a circle as one of the consultants placed ten balls in the centre of the floor. Asked to throw the balls to one another, they began by throwing balls indiscriminately while dropping most of them. They described their first reactions to the activity as total chaos. The consultant then addressed one of the participants and, gently, threw the ball to her. After she had caught the ball, she was asked to name another group member and throw the ball in the same manner. The sequence continued until everyone in the circle had caught and tossed many balls.

The consultant asked, "How many balls do you think you can toss around the circle without dropping any?" A discussion ensued about setting a realistic number, and the group attempted, rather unsuccessfully, to juggle three balls. As the discussion continued, the group suggested changes that could be made to improve their performance. In their next attempt, the group successfully juggled three balls around the circle and gave themselves a round of applause.

Asked about this change in performance, the participants said that communicating what they needed from each other and group concentration had made the attempt successful. The consultant challenged the group to use their new knowledge and repeat the game with a new goal concerning the number of balls. They agreed on ten balls. When the activity ended, there were thirteen objects in the middle of the circle, including a rubber chicken, a bat, and an alligator. This time the group achieved their goal very effectively. The activity was fast-paced, and the introduction of the last three objects caused a lot of spontaneous laughter and confusion.

Each participant then had the opportunity to reflect on her or his impressions of the experience. The introduction of new elements in the activity, and the effect on group effort, led to a discussion concerning the organization's styles of communication, which they felt may take place in unanticipated ways. One member commented that no one had been able individually to juggle three balls, but together they had juggled thirteen objects. Ongoing, effective communication had allowed the group to accomplish more than any one individual could do, and it had allowed the introduction of new and unexpected elements. Experiential exercises, as *physical metaphors*, illustrated concepts of effective communications and teamwork for the group.

THE PARTNER INTERVIEW

The group members were asked to form teams of two and to interview their partners. They were asked for their initial responses to four questions:

1. "Why are you here?"
2. "What do you hope to leave with?"
3. "What do you see as your organization's primary dilemma?"
4. "What do you see as your organization's primary strength?"

Two other questions were optional:

5. "What do you think people need to know about you?"
6. "What misunderstandings do you think people have about you?"

Each team member introduced her or his partner to the group and reported the responses. Each respondent was encouraged to listen and reflect on the manner in which the partner presented her or his answers and to hear how the partner interpreted and expressed her or his answers. Throughout the day, the consultants recorded each team's responses on a 24 x 36 pad displayed for the other group members. Recording discussions for the group to see highlighted the fact that the consultants listened carefully to the group members' comments. The group members had the opportunity to see as well as hear the responses, which were referred to during subsequent discussions and provided the group with permanent notes about the consultation.

An important part of the collaborative inquiry philosophy is that, throughout the consultation, information is publicly shared. The partner interviews allow team members to develop and share ideas about the organization and their expectations concerning the consultation. Many group members had concerns about being criticized or fixed (meaning, nothing would change) and that only the owner's ideas would be presented.

This type of activity has several other advantages. The participants are eased into working together in a new fashion by starting, in pairs, with a small activity rather than a large group-oriented one. However, they become comfortable in presenting ideas to the group by introducing their partners and his or her ideas, rather than first discussing their own.

SMALL GROUP INQUIRY

We began the Small Group Inquiry by dividing the clients into three groups and asking each group to spend thirty minutes discussing six questions:

1. What is the organization's number-one dilemma?
2. How does it work against the effectiveness of the organization?
3. What factors contribute to this dilemma?
4. How have you tried to resolve this dilemma?
5. What needs to be done to resolve this dilemma?
6. How would the organization be more effective if this dilemma were resolved?

The consultants asked the participants to think of the questions as a springboard from which to generate and develop ideas, as well as an opportunity to brainstorm about possibilities. The owner was asked to move among the groups as a silent observer, for two reasons: to give the participants the opportunity to talk without her involvement, and to allow her to listen to the discussions first-hand, because it is difficult to recreate the richness of a conversation.

Small group members enthusiastically shared their answers to the questions with the whole group. Group I stated that their primary dilemmas were communication and a lack of leadership. Group II said that their problems were a lack of communication throughout the organization, the unavailability of management, and a lack of personal responsibility. Group III listed their dilemmas as the attitudes of their clients, co-workers, themselves, their employer, and their families and the consequence to the organization's effectiveness. Group III also stated that effectiveness was diminished by leaving problems unaddressed and unresolved, which leads to conflicts, frustration, and confusion resulting in errors, anger, and negative attitudes.

The groups described a number of factors that, they believed, contributed to the dilemmas: a lack of respect for each other, inconsistency in leadership, failure to follow through on tasks, fear of reprisal, negativity, and rudeness. They also expressed concerns that management did not spend enough time on-site with them and that personnel training was inadequate. Staff meetings were the usual mode of resolving dilemmas, but there was no follow-through on proposed solutions, which, ultimately, led to an avoidance of the issues. They concluded that what was needed was consistent leadership, training, realistic policies, rules, structure, and more positive interaction. They stated that positive change and reinforcement needed to start at the management level and filter down. If they were able to resolve their dilemmas, they said, the organization would become more productive and efficient, which would lead to better understanding and a more pleasant, helpful work environment. Developing confidence and unity in the office would result in improved customer service, they said.

The short, impressionistic answers given to the questions by the small groups introduced multiple perspectives on topics of importance to the organization. The Small Group Inquiry provides the opportunity for multiple voices as well as the individual's voice to be heard, and it encourages participants to engage in their own conversations concerning the organization. This process initiates conversations for the larger group process, and it dramatizes the importance of group members' presentation of their ideas and solutions while the owner and the consultants listen (Anderson & Goolishian, 1992).

LARGE GROUP REFLECTION

Ideas about the dilemmas, initially generated by the Small Group Inquiry, were expanded during the Large Group Reflection. The discussion created the opportunity for generative conversations. The participants were invited to think about the various ideas and suggestions offered by the small groups and to find common threads and similarities, as well as distinctions, among the groups. A great deal of comment concerned communication—primarily, the lack of open communication within the organization. The small groups also stated that there were too many chiefs; they felt understaffed and stressed; there was pettiness and jealousy, along with negative attitudes and a few combative personalities.

While engaged in the collaborative inquiry process, our experience has been that individuals described as resistant or combative in their personal relationships often change, very quickly, to a response characterized by openness, and that they communicate without fear of reprisal. The open and non-hierarchical manner in which the consultants began the workshop, and their continuing collaborative stance, was a critical factor in creating a safe environment in which people talk and relate with each other openly and in a manner that is more synchronic and less discordant. In our experience, at this level of open communicating and relating people invariably readily engage in the process with enthusiasm. Even those members who in the beginning expressed strong resentment about the consultation were eagerly adding in their thoughts, opinions, and questions. As the group's agenda evolved, perceptions of problems and interpersonal relations began to change, with participants reporting feeling respected, being heard, and taken seriously.

The Large Group Reflections generated many ideas concerning dilemmas: lack of effective communication, lack of responsibility, lack of adequate continuous training, turf (or territorial) issues, and management issues. Group members identified the lack of effective communication within their organization, with their clients, and with the industry as their primary concern.

The group members expressed a need for consistent information open to everyone. Poor communication, in their words, creates a hesitancy to ask or answer questions. In one employee's words, "I have a fear of asking questions because of reprisal". The group members characterized this dilemma as the cause of pressure and stress contributing to decisions being made in crisis.

Problems in coordinating the agency's activities from three separate locations were identified as another factor in the overall lack of communication. Several office locations received company mail, memoranda, and tickets on a timely basis, while others did not. They described the agency's inter-office communications system as if everything fell into a black hole; information was not received in a systematic or timely manner. The lack of effective communication resulted in no follow-through on tasks, a lack of respect for each other, and expectations being unfulfilled.

ORGANIZATIONAL DILEMMAS

Several group members talked about the influence on the staff of the owner's involvement in charitable and civic organizations. Some ideas expressed in group discussions were that "she [the owner] works better under pressure, but some of us do not, and that when she is pressured, it affects all of us". The added pressure of upcoming community events was also expressed as a dread of the Cattle Barons' Ball or the Chamber of Commerce events.

A hectic atmosphere prevailed in the offices, and "just do it" was the staff's attitude and approach to tasks. They characterized the organization as one that had grown in response to the community's demands for service, not necessarily as the result of an opportunity to develop a long-term strategic plan.

The staff struggled with aspects of team cooperation while dealing with the practical dilemmas of systems hardware, communication, and the internal operations of the organization. The staff characterized the feeding-frenzy environment as contributing to a contagious attitude of individuals treating others with little regard or respect for boundaries. The staff had trouble with issues of relationship integrity, while communication was indirect, instead of direct, open, and inclusive. Adding to the contagious attitude were pressures from the travel–tourism industry and the organization's clients.

The staff members' conversations identified concerns and insecurities about turf (or territory), about fear of losing their clients to the organization, and they raised such questions as: "Whose clients are they?" "Does the client belong to us [the employees] or are they Friendly Travel's clients?"

Another area identified as problematic was a lack of responsibility in implementing procedures concerning client relations. Who had the authority to implement procedures was unclear to the staff. They also discussed a lack of compassion and acceptance among staff members regarding different personalities and work styles.

Among management issues, the group identified inadequate policies, procedures, and job descriptions, all of which, they believed, resulted in multiple and overlapping responsibilities and thus confusion. The staff characterized the management team as being unavailable and the chain of command and responsibility as being blurred. They raised questions about the management team's inability to take time to listen patiently to their concerns and suggestions.

To allow her more time to pursue other interests, the owner had appointed a manager for each office to supervise daily operations. The entire group agreed that an individual staff member's relationship with the owner was of great importance. Concern about the underlying sense of competition was expressed by the comment, "Everyone wants to be the owner's pal".

They described inadequate training as hindering new employees from being easily incorporated into the organization's work force. The absence of continuous training for the staff made it difficult to stay current on changing policies within the organization and with the dynamics of the travel–tourism industry. Despite unanimous agreement on this issue, this problem had gone unresolved for more than two years.

The Large Group Reflections and *cross-talking* about ideas initiated the process of conceptualizing possible solutions to the group's dilemmas. In a collaborative consultation, solutions develop and evolve continually. The solutions the group determined to be most effective for their organization were the end-result of the process, and they are presented later.

CONSULTANTS' DISCUSSION

The collaborative inquiry process, introduced during the early stages of the consultation, tends to create a conversational attitude, so that informal discussions continue during breaks, at lunch, and over coffee throughout the day. Group members reflect on various ideas that surface during informal conversations, and they often bring their insight to the larger group discussions.

During the lunch break, with the group members listening, the consultants reflected on the morning's activities and brainstormed about the afternoon's (Andersen, 1991; Andersen, 1995; Anderson & Goolishian, 1991). By talking openly, we allow clients access to our thoughts, shared ideas, and discussions, reinforcing the collaborative aspect of the team's reflections. There were no secrets about our impressions of the organization and the staff's concerns.

The afternoon began with an *As If* group activity, whose content had evolved from the lunch-break conversation.

THE AS IF GROUP ACTIVITY

The *As If* group activity and discussion stimulates an awareness of thought processes and invites the participants to voice their ideas (Anderson, 1990; Anderson & Goolishian, 1990; Anderson & Rambo, 1988; St. George, 1996). The *As If* group's multiplicity of perspectives mirrors that of an individual who, at any given time, may think about many, often contradictory, ideas. The individual, while engaged in the act of listening, is concurrently engaged in an inner dialogue.

The group activity provides participants with an opportunity to (1) develop awareness of how each participant in the organization experiences and thinks about various dilemmas; (2) experience the diversity of individual perceptions and points of view; (3) discuss ideas in a public forum instead of an exclusive or private setting; (4) experience shifts or changes in perspectives; and (5) experience the style and types of questions or comments that invite conversation, while becoming aware of the types of statements that cut it off (Anderson, 1990; Anderson & Goolishian, 1990; Anderson & Rambo, 1988; St. George, 1996).

Determining which dilemmas would be presented, the group decided that the owner would present a dilemma to the *As If* groups from her view of the situation. The participants, organized into three groups again, were asked to listen *as if* they were members of one of the following groups: the travel–tourism industry, the organization's clients, or the organization's staff. They were asked to listen while placing *on hold* any emerging ideas, questions, or comments.

The *As If* groups were asked to talk about the presented dilemma, pose questions, and offer suggestions or advice they thought might speed its resolution. The owner moved among the groups and listened. Each group then shared a synopsis of the group members' discussion of the dilemma from the various *As If* perspectives of industry, clients, or staff. The owner and the other two groups listened without questions or comments. After each group concluded its report, the other participants reflected on what they had heard. Thus, the *As If* groups were a catalyst for the large group process; they generated a wealth of information and led to a spirited discussion of solutions, including establishment of short-term goals and the proposal of a new business structure for the organization, all developed solely from the participants' ideas.

PROPOSED SOLUTIONS

The *As If* exercise solidified a shift in focus from problems to possibilities. In the general discussion that followed, the participants generated various ideas about their goals and possible strategies for initiating change in their organization. They developed specific ideas about job descriptions, training manuals, policies and procedures, communication, and changes in the organizational structure. They characterized their solutions as new beginnings for their organization. Several participants were astounded by the "openness and freedom of expressing our ideas" and said that "she [the owner] listened to us". They expressed a desire to create an ongoing dialogue with their co-workers and the boss.

They determined that an organizational structure was needed that specified individual responsibilities and levels of decision-making authority. They proposed a new structure in which the owner would have the final say, while other responsibilities would be delegated to three managers who would report directly to her. The managers would be responsible for accounting, personnel, and training. The new structure would also create two divisions in the agency: one for leisure travel and related activities, the other for corporate and convention business.

Plans were discussed to develop job descriptions and training manuals, as well as organizational policies and procedures, telephone technique improvement, and more effective communication with each other and their clients. The group members expressed the unified opinion that the organization needed a technologically updated communication system, and that personal interactions needed more attention. All believed that the proposed improvements and shared recommendations would increase the organization's productivity and profitability. As one person expressed it: "Friendly Travel would become 'Friendlier Travel'."

REFLECTIVE CONVERSATION WITH THE OWNER

Afterwards, one of the consultants engaged the owner in a reflective conversation about her thoughts, the information generated by the group, and her experience of the consultation as a whole. The reflective conversation was not intended to be an evaluation of the consultation day, but it is an aspect of the collaborative inquiry process of sharing thoughts in a public, inclusive fashion (Andersen, 1991, 1995).

In this case, the interview was spontaneous rather than planned. While one of the consultants talked to the owner, the group members were asked to listen without comment. Often this process creates new awareness for the interviewee, the group members, and the consultants. The owner responded during the interview that she "was amazed by the great ideas, the group's enthusiasm, and how helpful and freeing the experience has been".

The consultation day was concluded as each participant voiced her ideas about the owner's reflections and the day in general. The owner and consultants offered closing comments as well. Several participants mentioned their initial resistance to the consultation: "I did not want to come today, but am glad I did because it was totally different from my expectations" and "Even though I had to come on my day off, it was worth the effort". The participants described the day as passing quickly, and that the experiential exercise had created the opportunity to view dilemmas in the office in a different way. Several comments concerned the experiential activity and that "It has been a while since we've laughed and had fun together". The participants had enjoyed the enthusiasm and moving around rather than sitting and being lectured. They expressed amazement at the wealth of information produced in a short time and mentioned the open and non-judgemental way the consultants had related to the group.

Several participants discussed new impressions of their co-workers. The consultation had allowed them to relate to one another in a new way, outside the office, and this, they felt, would carry over when they returned to work. They also discussed the ways the group members had communicated with one another. The owner expressed her appreciation to the consultants for their time and efforts in making the day a unique and helpful experience and thanked the group for doing a great job.

The consultants commented on the amount of information the group had discovered in collaborative conversations and a continuing fascination with the process. They remarked on the group's spirit of enthusiasm and on the positive attitudes that had developed over the course of the day, despite some of the participants' reluctance. The consultants concluded the consultation by thanking the owner and the staff for sharing their collaborative experience.

Ninety-day follow-up with the owner

About ninety days after the consultation, the owner of Friendly Travel and one of the consultants met for a follow-up conversation. This kind of meeting is an important continuation of the collaborative inquiry process, and an opportunity for both client and consultants to review and reflect on the consultation.

The owner commented that the style of the questions and the manner in which they were asked by the consultants had helped the group to achieve a high level of openness. In fact, she said, "The group has never opened up like this before, and they really loved the role-playing".

Since the day of the workshop, she has noticed a difference in the roles that staff members play in the organization. She described the employees as being less secretive and she said that problems are now discussed with no stigma attached to the person who brings the problem to the other's attention. Her sense was that "We are working 'smarter', showing more consideration for one another, and seem to be on an emotional upswing". She also indicated that the staff seemed to appreciate her being more open and approachable, spending more time with them, and showing less partiality or favouritism. With the exception of one person, the employees have been more open in talking with her.

The owner outlined how she has changed her role in the organization since the consultation. She has become more active in the business and has reorganized her management staff while delegating more authority.

She has implemented a training programme and begun to address the technical communication problem. Two employees, both with broad expertise in specific areas of the agency's business, have been chosen as designated troubleshooters. The owner retains the final decision-making responsibility for all of the company's activities.

Staff initiatives

The monthly staff and management meetings are more open and productive, the owner reported. The staff requested that meetings be scheduled after office hours rather than using time devoted to their clients. The owner said that she believes that this represents a real change in her organization. The staff also proposed eliminating guest speakers from the meetings, to devote more time to discussing organizational matters. The staff has expressed a new reliance on the support, input, and feedback from their fellow staff members in problem-solving and new perspectives on old problems. Before the consultation, she said, if someone was snowed under at the end of the day, at five o'clock, the others would just leave instead of asking whether that person needed help. Now the staff members are more considerate towards one another.

The owner was impressed that all of the staff seem genuinely interested in keeping the wolf from the door, and the agency is now generating more business, for which staff members receive an override commission. She said that she has revealed to her staff, for the first time, the total dollar amounts represented by the override commissions, so that the managers will understand more about the organization's financial situation. The owner now provides, monthly, each staff member's ranking in the company's total sales, income, and commissions. She expressed an interest in scheduling another collaborative day in six months "as a checking in on my staff's true feelings".

Summary

Based on the collaborative inquiry approach to working with organizations, the consultants chose to operate from a non-expert, non-hierarchical position, applying their expertise to the art of creating a dialogical space. They facilitated conversations concerning the client's thoughts and ideas about various dilemmas that her organization was experiencing. Such conversations often lead to solutions created by the participants, and they usually produce meaningful and durable results. The experiential activity encouraged both physical and mental movement, which, in conjunction with collaborative conversations, became a catalyst for new awareness and insight.

Setting a collaborative tone, which is an important part of the collaborative inquiry's style, begins with the initial interview of the organization's representative. The collaborative tone here was reinforced by the manner in which the consultants introduced ideas, as they understood them, concerning the organization's dilemmas, and it facilitated continuing conversations as the consultation progressed. Ideas and thoughts were pursued from the organization's perspective.

The experiential activities, the Small Group Inquiry, and the Large Group Discussions were arranged so that the participants were gradually introduced to a non-threatening way of generating and sharing ideas. Such an atmosphere created an open and safe space in which dialogue could occur, and it encouraged the participants to express their thoughts, ideas, and suggestions without fear of ridicule or reprisal. An important part of the process was recording the group's ideas and suggestions, so that the information was continually available to everyone. The *As If* activity was especially important in that it provided the opportunity to listen, think, and express views from different perspectives.

The collaborative inquiry process often creates conversation that continues after the initial consultation. Such conversations occur among employees informally throughout the day, over coffee or lunch, and they continue formally during staff and management meetings. Once introduced to a new way of communicating, organizations often discover that conversation becomes a springboard for advancing innovative ideas and creating solutions. As organizational members become more responsible for implementation, and rely less on external consultants as catalysts, the organization becomes empowered to act as its own agent of change.

CHAPTER EIGHT

"Inside" consultation through self-differentiation: stimulating organizational development in the IDF's care of intractable, war-related, traumatic disorders

Yoel Elizur

The focus of this chapter is on the epistemological shift that occurs when a member of a human-service organization who has been educated in its professional culture, and who works within its normal paradigmatic practices (Kuhn, 1970), becomes a systems consultant to the organization. It is proposed that the new organizational positioning is insufficient by itself, and that in order to negotiate this transition successfully and to be able to impact the institutional culture and structure, the new consultant needs to achieve a wider meta-perspective with respect to the institution's guiding theory and organizational structure. In family systems terminology, the ability to move from a member to a supervisor/leader role and to modify some basic aspects of the system's structure and function (second-order change) depends on

---

The opinions that are expressed in this article are the personal opinions of the author and do not represent nor oblige the IDF. Military censorship forbids revealing the size of army units. Therefore, the terms junior and senior officers are not used in a strict sense but only when it is necessary to differentiate between levels of military hierarchy.

the establishment of differentiation *vis-à-vis* the organization. When consultants maintain a differentiated "I" position, they have latitude to consider the implicit and explicit roles assigned to them, to reflect from an outside position on the system's organization and guiding theory, and to do the three things that systems therapists and consultants do: (1) enhance uncertainty, (2) introduce novelty, and (3) encourage diversity (DiNicola, 1994). When this personal/professional process is not worked through, there is a risk of over-accommodation on the part of the consultant. Consequently, dysfunctional institutional processes are protected, and the consultant's work does not challenge the staff to grow and does not lead to organizational development.

The risk of over-accommodation that is faced by "inside" consultants is located at one end of a continuum along which we find "imperialistic" consultation at the other end. Imperialistic consultation is a common risk for "outside" consultants who do not join and accommodate to the local therapeutic culture with sufficient sensitivity and respect (Jenkins, 1991). Outside consultation is the more usual situation, and the characteristics of its consultant–institutional interface have been extensively explored (see Elizur & Minuchin, 1989; Imber-Black, 1988; Wynne et al., 1986). Consultants in these types of situations are advised to be open to learn from local experience and to use flexibility in adapting their model of work to the institutional context. Clearly, these suggestions respond to the difficulties of outside consultation but do not answer the needs of inside consultants. For those who have developed their approach within the local institutional culture, the more difficult and challenging task is to move in the opposite direction, clarifying diffuse boundaries and reassessing traditional beliefs in light of new knowledge.

The starting point for reflecting on inside consultation will be the process of change at the level of the person of the consultant. How can a member of an organization differentiate himself or herself in order to gain the outside position and point of view that is necessary for becoming a consultant? Obviously, this is a mutual process since the system also has to accept and relate to the consultant as an expert who emerged from its own ranks, someone who, on the one hand, can be trusted to safeguard the organization's crucial interests and, on the other, can become a professional leader. Without some openness to change on the part of the system, the consultant's role will be limited to maintaining the status quo. At the same time, the flexibility of the system is only a potential whose actualization depends on the consultant's initiative and leadership. It is suggested that the inside consultant's ability to assume a leading position is established by going through a developmental passage, which can be likened to the process of "separation–individuation". In this process, consultants develop a more detached and objective outlook with respect to the system and increase their manoeuvrability to act as agents of change. Though no consultant can be an "objective" observer who is completely separated from the observed (Keeney, 1983), the inside consultants' recalibration of boundaries is a *sine qua non* for their ability to provide the organization with fresh stimulation. As a result of this process, a more complex suprasystem becomes established, in which consultants and organizations are able to carry on their transactions as two differentiated subsystems. When this process is negotiated successfully, the two subsystems collaborate and empower each other (Elizur, 1996).

Some aspects of the process described theoretically above will be demonstrated by the author's experience in the Rear Care Installation that was established by the Israeli Defence Forces (IDF) in order to provide intensive care to soldiers who suffer from intractable combat-stress reaction. The first part presents the cultural and organizational background necessary for understanding the context of this work. It begins with a description of the toll of war paid by Israeli society, putting the emphasis on mental health casualties, and continues with the front-line and rear-line organization of care. The second part is a personal account of the author's experience and development that coincided with the movement from one role to another: joining as a regular staff member, becoming a family supervisor three years later, and becoming the installation's chief supervisor during the last year. This account leads into the third and major part of the chapter which is focused on the deconstruction of professional/cultural "truths" and the development of a broadened perspective concerning the treatment of combat stress. This most basic act of differentiation became possible following a review of the installation's cultural and historical context and, in particular, the unveiling of three different facets of denial: denial of the prevalence and severity of acute combat-stress disorders, denial of the long-term and spreading impact of post-traumatic stress disorder (PTSD) on both veterans and their families, and denial of the limited effectiveness of treatment. The point that is underscored by this description of the author's preparation for his new role is that an inside consultant needs to undergo a process of self-differentiation in order to attain a degree of leadership that is necessary for restructuring the system of which he is a part.

Cultural and organizational background: the toll of war

From the age of 18 to 50, all able Jewish and Druze men in Israel are required to serve in the army. We begin with a three-year regular service and thereafter are called for an annual reserve duty of on average one month. Altogether, five-and-a-half years of our mature lives are devoted to the safeguarding of Israel's security, a period that is incomparably longer and riskier than the demands made of their citizens by all other democratic countries. But this is only a part of the story, for our sons and daughters, fathers and grandchildren, siblings and members of our extended families, friends and colleagues are all serving or are going to serve in the army. Their lives are at risk, and, inevitably, most Israelis have personal connections with families whose members were either killed, maimed, or injured in military duty.

Among the casualties that have been diagnosed during or immediately after the war, 23% were identified as combat-stress reaction cases (Solomon, 1993). Combat-stress reaction is an acute disorder more widely known under terms such as "battle shock", "shell shock, "war neurosis", and "combat exhaustion". It occurs among soldiers who have been exposed to traumatic stressors, and it has a labile and polymorphic nature that can change in appearance from one war to another. The six major manifestations of combat-stress reaction are: (1) a paralysing anxiety state, (2) depression, which is usually manifested by guilt, unremitting fatigue, and withdrawal, (3) acute psychosomatic symptoms, (4) psychic numbing, (5) disorientation that creates a dangerous break from reality, and (6) profound feelings of loneliness and vulnerability (Solomon, Mikulincer, & Benbenishty, 1989). The severity of this condition is such that there is a breakdown of functioning and, consequently, the removal of the soldier from battle. Since combat-stress reaction is not diagnosed unless the soldier becomes clearly dysfunctional during the war, there are many veterans who are later found to have suffered from undiagnosed acute stress disorder. One large group of soldiers cover up their condition, do not seek help, and manage to stay in their units with the support of their "military family", even though their functioning is often impaired. Another group is composed of soldiers with only a few or no unusual symptomatic reactions at all during combat, but who develop a delayed stress reaction at a later stage. Hence, unlike the physically injured, whose number can be determined by the end of the war, the number of psychiatric casualties that are identified by the mental health establishment continues to rise after the termination of war. Research estimates indicate that over the years the prevalence of affected veterans more than doubles (Solomon, 1993). Many of them will suffer from the pervasive disturbance of PTSD, which will also affect many other veterans who did not experience combat reaction.

The organization of combat-stress reaction care

FRONT-LINE CARE: STRUCTURE AND FUNCTION

Front-line treatment is organized in a two-echelon system: (1) forward treatment of up to 48 hours is done in small medical units that operate right behind the fighting forces and work within the battlefield area, close to the place and time of the combat reaction; (2) intensive treatment of up to seven days is provided by a larger installation that is located in the rear area of the fighting command zone. These installations are located in military camps, and the environment, which is both supportive and military, creates a strong suggestive atmosphere that is crucial for the success of front-line care (Levy & Neumann, 1984). The treatment is based on Salmon's three principles of proximity, immediacy, and expectancy (Salmon, 1919). The soldiers, who are physically and mentally exhausted, are supported and at the same time pushed to recover from their "temporal disability" and resume their functioning. A treatment milieu is thus created that maintains a clear and constant focus on the following goals: (1) to return functional soldiers to their original military roles within their military units, (2) to prevent discharge of less functional soldiers by reassigning them to less demanding military roles, and (3) to help the least functional soldiers improve their functioning and reality orientation, and thereby prevent psychiatric disability and hospitalization. Altogether, it is a highly efficient treatment-delivery system. A controlled outcome study that took advantage of the natural quasi-experimental design that was created during the war in Lebanon confirmed that front-line implementation of Salmon's principles increased the soldiers' chances of returning to their units and contributed to their subsequent civilian adjustment (Solomon & Benbenishty, 1986). These results provide crucial support for the staff who often feel torn in a duality that is difficult to reconcile: as therapists they want to alleviate individual suffering and to protect their patients from unpredictable levels of stress and danger, while as officers they are expected to use their authority and help provide the army with able men. The evidence that soldiers who did manage to reorganize and to confront their fears are better off after the war, and continue their lives without the stigma that is associated with psychiatric breakdown, helps to deal with the apparent conflict between individual mental health and military considerations.

REAR-LINE CARE: STRUCTURE AND FUNCTION

The soldiers' response at each echelon determines whether they will be returned to army functioning or moved into the next line of treatment. Consequently, the most severe cases will ultimately be referred to the Rear Care Installation. This is the army's central and largest mental health installation, and it provides realign care to referrals from all parts of the county. It is the last level of residential care within the military framework. The wish to provide the best possible care to those who were most severely traumatized led to the creation of an intensive four-week pro- gramme administered by the most experienced clinicians on reserve duty. The treatment environment has been constructed with the following goals in mind:

1. to work through traumatic experiences and alleviate sympto- matic suffering;

2. to maintain functional ties with the military framework and prevent discharge;

3. to maintain social, occupational, and family functioning;

4. to prevent hospitalization and the crystallization of a chronic psychiatric disability.

The organization of the installation is expressive of its basic duality. On the one hand it is a military unit that serves the army by helping to maintain traumatized soldiers in service, whereas on the other it is a hospital-like treatment centre. The first aspect is manifested by the hierarchic military structure, which maintains the routines and regime of army life. The soldiers are divided into small groups, and their commanding officers, who are senior men- tal health professionals on reserve duty, are also their therapists and group facilitators. As in front-line installations, there is a strong expectation of improvement and an attitude of normalizing symptomatic manifestations of distress by framing them as natural consequences of exposure to extreme situational stress. All physi- cal, social, and therapeutic activities are structured in order to augment the suggestive effects that this milieu creates, including the push for rapid re-exposure of the men to the military stimuli that they normally try to avoid after their traumatic experiences. Hence, firing range practice is an important part of the routine, and although participation is not forced, group pressure and therapeu- tic suggestions push the soldiers to perform. The idea is that exposure will gradually reduce anxieties and counter the perni- cious effects of avoidance behaviour, which tends to spread into all domains of life. The staff partake in this routine and are expected to provide a personal example. Their mobilization is part of the war effort, and naturally they identify with the fighting men and are highly motivated to help. On duty, the staff share the same uncomfortable military accommodation, wear uniform, carry guns, are subjected to military discipline, and stay on camp around the clock.

Notwithstanding this military environment, it is clear that the Rear Care Installation is primarily an intensive residential treatment centre. Indeed, in comparison with front-line care, its psychosocial therapeutic functions are much more pronounced. The major emphasis is on working through traumatic experiences and their meanings, and the one-month period of stay provides the time for doing so. It is like a moratorium from regular life: a rest period devoted to recuperation. The patients are shielded from the stresses and hassles of daily life. For the larger group of reservists this has to do with their family and occupational roles, whilst for enlisted men it mainly consists of dealing with army bureaucracy and their reintegration into new rear-line units. The impact of this protected time-out period is augmented by the daily routine of individual and group sessions. The therapeutic milieu that is thereby established promotes cathartic sharing and intensive preoccupation with the processing of military traumas.

Front-line experience has indicated that the integration of military and therapeutic roles is facilitated when the staff does not experience a conflict between mental health considerations and military manpower interests. Professionals who worked in the second level of front-line care reported that the maintenance of a demanding yet individually responsive military framework promoted functioning abilities and reduced the potentially regressive effects of the in-patient environment (Levy & Neumann, 1984). The military environment facilitated the successful application of Salmon's treatment principles by pushing and supporting the soldiers' return to combat, while the unsuccessful cases were promptly moved to the rear. The Rear Care Installation, however, is a different case, existing in a twilight zone between the military and the civilian. Its cases are the most severely distressed, lowest in functioning, and with the poorest prognosis (Rabinowitz et al., 1990). Most of them are likely to suffer later from PTSD and will require prolonged outpatient therapy, and a few might even be referred to regular psychiatric hospitals. The central concerns of this group of patients are different from the traditional domain of military psychiatry, belonging in fact more to the field of civilian rehabilitation. Are these concerns best treated in a military residential centre that has been established according to front-line experience and hospital-based practice? The formulation of this question was a central milestone in a differentiation process that was closely connected to the development of my work in the installation.

Establishing a family-oriented programme

The unfolding of inside consultation in the Rear Care Installation will be described in the form of a personal account in order to elucidate how the consultation has been intertwined with the process of self-differentiation. First, some background about my personal history in the medical corps' mental health department: I have been a reservist in the department for almost twenty years, during which I was assigned a variety of projects and have come to know most of its personnel. After the 1982 Lebanon War, I was a member of a commission that carried out a critical appraisal of the mental health department's functioning during the war. Later I was on the PTSD follow-up research team and also served as supervisor of the IDF's family clinic. In addition to these regular reserve duties I was assigned five years ago to the Rear Care Installation. This would be my role during an actual war, while in peacetime the staff meets a few days every year in order to train.

At first, I was one of the installation's junior officers, and my energies were invested in adapting to this new milieu and learning its ways of treatment. My acceptance into this high-level professional group was enriching, but at the same time I had uneasy feelings with regard to the organization of our work. In particular, I was concerned that the patients were isolated from their families and communities and, consequently, that our work with problems of civilian rehabilitation would be less effective by virtue of its being limited to individually oriented interventions. Furthermore, we were depriving our treatment programme of important ecological resources that could significantly add to its effectiveness. Some of these feelings were apparently shared by the installation's senior officers, and they arranged for staff training with a family therapist who came as an outside consultant to teach family crisis therapy. But though family therapy gained acceptance as a kind of "loculated" therapy that may be indicated in some cases, it was not integrated into the overall framework of the organization. This was a frustrating *déjà vu* kind of experience for me. I had just finished writing the results of long-term follow-ups of hospitalized cases and was again faced with defeated attempts to integrate family therapy and family training within the treatment programme. It seemed to be the rule that an accommodating institutional context is required for the rooting of systems work, and while attempts to introduce family therapy and family training could have a temporary impact, the effect of organizational patterns proved to be stronger in the long run (Elizur & Minuchin, 1989). However, as a junior member of the group I could do no more than make my objections known and was in no position to change the organization.

Two years ago, I was asked to assume a new role, as the installation's family supervisor. I should probably have been less surprised since, after all, I had made my position clear with respect to the need for developing family-based care within our installation and was also known as supervisor of the army's family clinic. Consequently, it was difficult for me to decline the promotion even though the new role was in addition to continuing with my regular responsibilities as an officer/therapist, and this meant spending more days on reserve duty. Moreover, I agreed with the director Shlomo Shoham's idea that the integration of family training into our programme would be accelerated by creating this new staff position of family supervisor/consultant. There was an individually oriented chief supervisor working in the installation, and both men thought it best to promote one of the staff members to this position instead of trying to bring in a new outside family consultant—someone who would not only be responsible for family training, but also represent the family viewpoint during all of the senior officers' meetings, most of which were not directly concerned with family care.

The repositioning within the organizational hierarchy proved to be a turning point, and gradually I experienced a profound change in my own perspective with respect to the installation. It was like moving from a child to a parent position and, consequently, gaining a broader understanding of the needs of the family and sharing responsibility for maintenance and development. Even though officially I remained a junior officer, and on training days that were not devoted to family issues I functioned under the direct command of one of the senior officers, my new responsibility forced me to go beyond the rhetoric of family therapy. I had to think in practical terms how to proceed and what to expect.

I began my new role by planning with the senior officers a series of training experiences for the staff. Our objectives were to create a better understanding of family needs and to teach basic skills of family diagnosis and interventions. Real cases that had been treated by the department were used to prepare a variety of simulations that were played in small groups. These experiences were later used to highlight major issues of working with families and to analyse our snag points. On the whole, the workshops were well received, yet I felt dissatisfied—even worried—about the consequences of family training. As a result of our experience, I realized that traditional forms of family therapy training would be contra-indicated for us at this point for the following reasons:

1. The organizational context of the installation does not support family therapy. The installation is located in a military camp that is too far for most families to come for regular sessions. Moreover, the allocation of staff time provides for three to four meetings with each family at best, and even that would be difficult to attain with most families.

2. Family therapy training does not basically fit with staff motivations. Most of our reservists are experienced individually oriented clinicians who feel comfortable in applying their own therapeutic orientations to combat-stress reaction and are highly sensitive towards any apparent attempt to "convert" them into family therapy.

3. The highly stressed families who would come to the installation could open up rather quickly during their first session, particu-

larly when they meet with experienced therapists who are used to long-term commitment and tend to explore dysfunctional processes. However, the simulations demonstrated that there was little time afterwards to work through the complex family issues that were unveiled. The high expectations that usually follow self-disclosure in this crisis situation were consequently frustrated, and the working alliance was disrupted.

Evidently, I needed to re-evaluate my basic directions or risk getting mired in the same type of impasse that only a few years earlier had thwarted the work of the outside family consultant. With hindsight, the reintroduction of family training made it necessary for the senior officers' group to face basic organizational issues that had previously been avoided. The integration of family orientation within all human-service institutions—and our installation was not exempt—is not only a function of staff training and supervision, but depends to a large degree on the creation of a family-friendly organizational context (see Elizur, 1993). This meant a commitment to making some major changes, and at that point I needed to navigate carefully my way between Scylla and Charybdis. On the one hand, I needed to accept the limitations of my role without becoming overly accommodating—that is, to design a more modest family-oriented model of work that would fit our organizational constraints and the different professional orientations of the staff. On the other hand, it was also necessary to challenge the system: I needed to modify some of the installation's basic beliefs and work patterns. As an inside consultant, I experienced the latter task to be the more difficult one of the two.

At this critical juncture, there occurred an unexpected turn of events that was to empower my position and to serve as a catalyst to organizational development. A year ago, our chief supervisor retired from reserve service, and the commander asked me to take his place. As once before, I was not obliged to accept this promotion: it was a personal decision to assume a role that has time-consuming obligations and responsibilities but would also enable me to introduce organizational changes. Up to this point, the installation's basic framework has been like an immutable given, and, though criticisms of basic tenets were occasionally voiced during training days, they did not lead to a serious deliberation of viable alternatives. However, as a chief supervisor I would be in a position to engage our senior officers' group and perhaps even some of the higher officers within the mental health department in a discussion of basic goals, methods, and organizational structure. It is a top position in the installation as the chief supervisor is responsible for all professional functions, and in this capacity he is second in command. It is not an executive position, in that the chief supervisor is not directly responsible for the organization of staff work. His main task during peace times is to elaborate the installation's treatment doctrine and to organize, together with the senior officers' group, the few days that are allocated each year by the army for staff training. However, a chief supervisor who believes that organizational change should be intertwined with training can initiate an organizational reappraisal. In that sense, the supervisor can also serve as a systems consultant (McDaniel, Wynne, & Weber, 1986).

The first task I set for myself was to make our programme family-oriented, in line with the lessons that had been learned in the previous simulations. It was suggested that families would gain the most benefit from an information and support programme that would provide guidelines for PTSD management, teach problem-solving skills, and connect the patient and the family with supporting services in the community. These conclusions were ratified by the senior officers, and it was decided to establish a psycho-educational family programme that would be focused on enhancing family strengths. Furthermore, staff training was to emphasize the creation of working alliance with families by using guidelines that had been delineated previously by the ICE model (Elizur, 1996). Briefly, this model proposes that the working relations between families and provider staff develop in three phases, each of which is defined by a major transactional pattern that is negotiated at the time:

1. *involvement*—establishing basic bonding and communication channels;

2. *collaboration*—partnership based on the recognition of common goals, methods, and threats;

3. *empowerment*—sharing of power and responsibility.

These phases unfold sequentially in that the working through of prior issues lays the foundation for successful coping with later issues.

The ICE model was first applied in an intensive four-day training period that was carried out in the actual camp setting and included full-scale simulations. The staff was engaged in creating the new psycho-educational programme by writing informational handouts that would be given to families during the initial meeting, during the middle phase of the work, and towards the programme's termination. There were role plays of family group meetings and individual family sessions, with an emphasis on supporting families who are expected to be frightened and disoriented by an unfamiliar crisis. The basic therapeutic orientation was to relate to families as allies, partners, and consultants, not as patients, in order to identify common goals that could be shared by staff and families and to promote their achievement by mobilizing family strengths and resources. Subsequently, this approach was supported by making some necessary adaptations in the installation's work organization. It is now mandated that shortly after a new soldier arrives, the staff will make contact with his family and invite them to the installation. They are to participate in an organized families' day that will introduce them to the psycho-educational programme and then to construct with the staff a schedule of meetings that would fit their unique needs and possibilities.

The application of the ICE model to the Rear Care Installation was the first time that it has been used in a service-provider organization for adults. Previous experience has indicated that it is a useful general framework that does not alienate professionals of different schools. The adoption of the model by the installation's staff was found to reinforce a sense of partnership with families and helped to create a more empathic and contextual understanding of their dynamics with an emphasis on strengths. The staff has gained a clearer view of the basic tasks for working with families, and there is the freedom of using different professional methods to achieve our shared goals.

The experience with the psycho-educational programme helped us to create a family-oriented in-patient programme, but it also increased my reservations concerning the in-patient emphasis of our work. The four-day experience with the time-extended simulations strengthened my convictions that this emphasis was still isolating the soldiers from their families and communities. I was concerned that the time-extended moratorium in a protected environment would make it more difficult for the soldiers to make the transition back home. Perhaps our approach towards intractable combat-stress reaction was mistaken in that we were trying to do more of the same by supplementing the two levels of front-line care with a whole month of military exercises, intensive discussions of war experiences, and sport activities. Should not the men be encouraged to resume their work and home functioning more quickly? Could such a month in a mental health installation actually induce a regressive effect which would make the homecoming more difficult? Was it therapeutically correct at this point to put a heavy emphasis on the resumption of military functioning? As I pondered these questions, I felt a need to become clearer in my own thinking about the installation and to develop a more differentiated perspective with respect to my new role as chief supervisor.

An organizational re-evaluation: consultation through self-differentiation

Since embarking on the process of "inside consultation", the concept of differentiation has become increasingly meaningful for me. I did not use this concept before in my work as an outside consultant, probably because my separate identity on entering new organizations was more clearly defined, but at this point it became most helpful for charting a way out of my confusion. "Differentiation is a product of a way of thinking that translates into a way of being" (Kerr & Bowen, 1988, p. 108). It is not a technique but a way of looking at the dialectics of personal and interpersonal growth as a process that involves two intertwined developments: (1) in the ability to contain emotions and to relate to emotionally charged issues in a balanced, non-reactive way, and (2) in the capacity to be in relation without losing one's autonomy and self-defined identity. The concept of differentiation has been usefully applied not only to family systems, but also to military, business, educational, and other types of organizations. Friedman's work in such settings indicated that the quality of organizational leadership greatly affects the functioning of its members. Consequently, he developed an approach called "leadership through self-differentiation" (Friedman, 1985). The basic proposition is that the personal definition of people in positions of leadership is necessary for their ability to take a stand and to be initiators more than reactors. Differentiation, which is expressed in the non-anxious and connected presence of effective leaders, has a systemic effect on the organizational field.

During my one year as the installation's family supervisor, I experienced a sense of differentiation that was related to my greater experience with families. I could provide a vision, felt comfortable in my role as a trainer, and developed working relationships with the senior officers. My superiors were becoming my colleagues during a process in which I was actually working more like an outside consultant who had been solicited by the organization because of a specific expertise. Upon my promotion to chief supervisor, they accepted my lead in introducing family-related organizational changes, but I was beginning to hear squeaks that seemed related to the shift from a subordinate to a superior professional position. While I needed to learn new ways of collaborating with the senior officers, I also found out that some of them had wished to get the promotion to chief supervisor and at that point needed to come to terms with their loss. There were some stormy moments, but on the whole the friendly ties between people, the collaborative spirit and mutual respect that characterizes this senior professional group, and the leadership of our commander supported us in negotiating this transition.

Upon the resolution of this group process and the establishment of our family-oriented programme, I thought that the time had come to apply the experience of working with severe disorders to the organization of care in the installation. This experience has consistently underlined the need for a comprehensive community programme on the one hand, and the dearth of such public services in Israel on the other (Elizur, 1994a, 1994b; Kaffman, Nitzan, & Elizur, 1996). Obviously, our work could not be expected to change decades of neglect in the area of community mental health. Yet it was an opportunity to think again about the needs of soldiers with intractable combat-stress reaction and how to use the resources of our installation to organize better community care for veterans. At that point, I felt challenged to invest myself in a personal/professional process of self-differentiation. I have been working with the mental health department for many years, and my education in military psychology was deeply affected by its professional culture. How could I step outside my own cultural frame and reconsider basic assumptions concerning our approach to combat-stress reaction and PTSD?

I perceived two avenues that could help me to establish a more distant and objective position:

1. gaining a contextual understanding of the installation by learning about the historical and wider social forces that have shaped its structure and function;

2. reviewing the rapidly growing research that is concerned with the course and treatment of combat-stress reaction and PTSD.

It is interesting to note that these two ways that I have taken are parallel with the basic teachings of extended family systems therapy. Clients are coached to attain a more objective view of their family's emotional process by collecting information from multiple sources about the larger family and its multi-generational patterns. In the following section I describe the findings of this search and the way that it has affected my approach to the installation's therapeutic programme. Like all families, the military system can be characterized by a variety of patterns that can be discerned as one studies its historical context and organizational structure. The following analysis will of necessity be limited to a focus on one major pattern—that of denial—which I found to be most relevant for the development of my work.

Acute and post-traumatic combat-stress disorders: a history of denial

The most fundamental and persistent historical pattern that I have encountered since the beginning of this personal investigation has been the resistance of the military to acknowledge the lasting psychological damage that is inflicted by war. There is no one simple explanation for this astounding phenomenon, and yet the history of mental health during the last hundred years reveals that it is not unique to Israel or even to the military domain. The study of trauma has waxed and waned during the twentieth century, and it was influenced by powerful cultural and political forces that induced an attitude of denial towards the long-term psychological sequelae of all traumas. In fact, the recurrence of "episodic amnesias" appears to be the rule rather than the exception, and it is manifested in social and professional attitudes towards different kinds of psychic traumas that afflict men and women alike, on the battle front as well as on the family front (Herman, 1992). In Israel, this phenomenon is all the more striking since the country was established under the shadow of the Holocaust, came into being in the War of Independence, and has been involved with wars ever since. Could there really be a denial of war traumas in such a national context?

Recent historical studies of the development of military psychiatry in Israel showed that basic information concerning the prevalence and detrimental effects of combat-stress reaction was shelved and denied by the army and Israeli society at large for a quarter of a century during which five wars were fought (Levy, Witztum, Granek, & Kotler, 1990; Witztum, Levy, Solomon, & Kotler, 1991). The effects of this denial were most deleterious: lessons that had been learned in previous wars were not applied and seem to have been forgotten again and again, there was no systematic training of army mental health workers, and the organized structures that are necessary for treating soldiers during war times were not established. Two powerful cultural forces will be identified in order throw some light on this intriguing historical process:

1. The traditional tendency to minimize the prevalence of combat-stress reaction, and if possible to avoid facing this subject, reflects a common attitude that used to be held by army officers during times of peace as well. There was an almost magical belief that by colluding to avoid seeing, hearing, and speaking about emotional disorders in the military, the problem will be contained (see Witztum et al., 1991). Many officers believed that

the official acknowledgement of psychiatric injuries is likely to lead to an increase in their overall frequency and to trigger episodes of emotional contagion. Behind this view, there often was a deeply held belief that soldiers who break down are consciously or unconsciously using the psychiatric path to flee the battlefield. The combat-stress reaction victims who were observed under this blaming light were framed as cowards, weaklings, or impostors. This attitude reappeared in the area of compensation, where combat-stress reaction veterans experienced considerable difficulties in proving their disabilities and their disability ratings were much lower, in sharp contrast to the "silver-platter" treatment of physical casualties (Solomon, 1993).

2. Trauma disrupts our basic assumptions about self and the world and breaks down the denial of vulnerability (Janoff-Bulman, 1992). It is painful and difficult for people to let go of their comforting illusions and be confronted with fundamental threats to their identity, and men at war, who also feel responsible for protecting their nation, have a particularly hard time in facing their human frailty. Common masculine standards emphasize expressions of strength and virility, and Israeli men in particular have adopted an attitude of proving themselves in the military realm (Rolbant, 1971). The experience of growing up in the shadow of the Holocaust and under a constant threat to Israel's survival have reinforced these expectations. In this context, any form of mental breakdown during combat becomes a public admission of weakness, which has not only been shameful for individual soldiers but also for the IDF. This point was expressed most poignantly by Solomon (1993): "The idea that participation in combat might leave a searing imprint clashed with the image of the Israeli supermen so assiduously cultivated by Israel's founders and pioneers and so eagerly adopted by subsequent generations" (p. 51)

The ethos of a small and brave army that cannot be defeated because the men are united in fighting with their backs against the wall was shattered by the surprising shock of the 1973 Yom Kippur War. The large number of psychiatric casualties overwhelmed the understaffed and unprepared IDF mental health department. The battle-front denial of combat-stress reaction was broken, and following the Yom Kippur War there was a conspicuous expansion in the size and power of the department. Subsequently, there was an organized front-line treatment of combat reaction in the 1982 Lebanon War, and attention was turned to the long-term sequelae of this disorder. The issues that were deliberated were crucial for defining the principles of rear-line treatment, especially since there were different professional opinions concerning what military functioning should be expected of combat-stress reaction in combat veterans. Obviously, the delineation of realistic, research-based expectations was a necessary step. The staff in the Rear Care Installation needed such a baseline for their formulation of treatment objectives and to prepare the men and their families for the future. Furthermore, a professional opinion on this issue that is based on hard research evidence would also have important implications for the army's manpower policies.

Large-scale studies of traumatized war veterans were initiated by the department after the Lebanon War. These studies revealed that participation in combat often left a searing and irreversible imprint that appeared to spread into different domains of the combatants' personal and family lives and to make them more vulnerable to future stress (Solomon, 1993). Indeed, 59% of the soldiers who were diagnosed during the war as suffering from combat-stress reaction were suffering from full-blown diagnosable PTSD one year later. Three years after the war, the figure was 43%. These rates are astonishingly high considering that nearly all the combat-stress reaction casualties had been intensively treated. These soldiers were compared with a "normal" control group of veterans who had served in the same military units during the war but had never been diagnosed with combat-stress reaction nor had sought treatment for PTSD; one year after the war, 16% of these veterans were also found to be suffering from diagnosable PTSD, and after three years the figure was 9%. These studies were supplemented by a wave of reports from mental health workers who were describing a multiplicity of PTSD symptoms among war veterans. Most troubling were the difficult-to-cure cases, in whom the disorder became crystallized in a rigid and chronic form. PTSD became the centre of these men's lives. They complained of continuous suffering, lost much of their functioning capabilities, and became more and more dependent on their families and the Defence Ministry's disability pension. The considerable body of research data and clinical experience that had accumulated by that time broke through denials concerning the prevalence and severity of PTSD. It became clear that the military establishment, as well as the Defence Ministry and the public at large, would need to make a fuller acknowledgement of this disorder.

These conclusions have been repeatedly underlined during the last decade by professionals from different countries who have been studying PTSD. Clinical work with both civilian and military cases, and long-term follow-ups of combat veterans, has clearly indicated that PTSD can become a lifetime disorder for some people, that it affects both mental and physical health, and that it exists even when people are not officially recognized as having the disability and provided with disability pensions (Beal, 1995; Kulka et al., 1990; Lee, Vaillant, Torrey, & Elder, 1995; Miller, 1994). The wives and children of combatants with stress disorder were also found to be affected by "secondary traumatization" (Rosenheck, 1986; Solomon et al., 1992b). They exhibited traumatic stress symptoms, increased levels of psychopathology and social dysfunctions, and a heightened vulnerability to future stressful experiences. Beyond these effects on individual family members, the disruptive impact of combat trauma was found to reverberate throughout the life cycle, affecting family structure and function (Kulka et al., 1990; Scaturo, 1992). These families have to cope with life transitions burdened by more problems and a higher level of family stress, their marital and parent–child relationships are more often dysfunctional, and the accommodations that need to be made in response to PTSD members warp their organization and construction of reality.

The Koach project

As the long-term course of combat-stress reaction became obvious in both military and civilian circles, there was a return to the most basic questions: What should be the objectives of treatment? Can we cure PTSD, or should our objectives be more modestly oriented to the alleviation of symptoms, the prevention of loss spirals (Hobfoll, Dunahoo, & Monnier, 1995), and psychosocial rehabilitation? Historically, the Koach project was the most significant attempt to answer these questions. Koach is a Hebrew acronym of two words indicating fitness and reinforcement, as well as a word that means strength. The project was initiated in 1986 by the mental health department, four years after the Lebanon War had erupted. In some way, it was a response to the disappointing results of the rear-echelon treatment centre that was established during the Lebanon War. Though this latter installation was named Combat Fitness Retraining Unit, the soldiers' combat potential was subsequently found to be very low (Rabinowitz et al., 1990). It was learned that most of them had civilian and military adjustment problems before the war; those who continued to serve in the army had problems of military adjustment, and many of them eventually suffered from chronic PTSD.

Koach's main objectives were therefore to do more for these men in order to reduce the prevalence and severity of PTSD and to improve military and civilian functioning. Based on prior experience with rear-line treatment, it was carefully planned as a one-month residential programme, located in an army installation, that combined *in vivo* exposure to military routines and practices with an assortment of behavioural/cognitive and group approaches. The veterans were also helped to establish and maintain self-help groups which continued to meet after their discharge. It was an unprecedented investment of resources, much was at stake, and expectations were high. The personal involvement of the staff was considerable, while the department saw Koach as a milestone that signified a change in the IDF's attitudes towards soldiers who had left in "disgrace". The success of Koach would have meant that "properly" treated PTSD veterans, who would receive more and better of the same rear-echelon treatment, could become functional again and rejoin the ranks. It would have also justified the traditional therapeutic principles of the installation that put an emphasis on exposure and help professionals to reaffirm their belief in the more optimistic stress-resolution model rather than face the long-term vulnerability of combat-stress reaction soldiers.

The Koach project became a model evaluation study. The hypotheses were that most or all objectives of the intensive treatment would be met by the end of the residential phase, and/or during the following period of community care. These objectives were: (1) reduction in the prevalence and severity of PTSD, (2) reduction in the prevalence and severity of the accompanying psychiatric symptomatology, (3) improvement of family, social, and occupational functioning, and (4) improvement of military functioning. Results were studied from several perspectives, and assessment continued up to two years after the residential phase. The measures included subjective reactions of the veterans and their therapists, a large battery of self-report measures, and a telephone survey. The 40-member treatment group, which was chosen for their motivation and fitness out of 107 veterans who were interviewed, was compared with a matched control group of 40 combat-stress reaction veterans.

Despite all expectations and the great and sincere effort of Koach professionals, the outcome was most disappointing, and none of the study's hypotheses was confirmed (Solomon et al., 1992a). On the one hand, the subjective reports and anthropological observation of the programme indicated success in bringing the veterans out of their isolation and alienation, engaging them in intense and meaningful interpersonal encounters, and instilling positive expectations for curing PTSD. But on the other hand, the standardized measures of emotional distress and psychiatric symptomatology indicated that Koach's patients actually fared worse than untreated controls. Perceived self-efficacy in combat was the only measure that showed improvement, but it did not prove to be clinically or militarily significant, in that the participants were still too anxious to return to reserve duty.

Professionals in Israel have yet to come to terms with these findings. Parallel attempts in other countries have also indicated that a change towards more modest outcome expectations needs to be made in many quarters. For example, one in-patient programme used "helicopter-ride therapy" with PTSD Vietnam veterans. Though some desensitization to helicopters was achieved, the therapy was found to increase the veterans' level of distress (Scurfield, Wong, & Zeerocah, 1992). Apparently, PTSD is a multidimensional phenomenon that creates neurobiological imprints that are not erased by therapy (Kolb, 1993). The old adage of jumping back on the horse after a painful fall to prevent subsequent fear of riding may be helpful to some—perhaps the majority—of soldiers who receive front-line treatment, but harmful to others: probably a great many of those who fail to improve in front-line care are subsequently referred to the Rear Care Installation. Some riders are apparently more vulnerable to the effects of falling, and some falls are so bad that the safest and most humane solution is to accept that there may well be irreversible traumatic effects. Therapy in such cases should be focused on furthering the victims' adjustment to major life areas, while supporting their decision to avoid horse riding altogether.

Rear-line care: back to the blueprints

The historical and scientific research laid the foundations for the deconstruction of beliefs, myths, and ideologies that were deeply ingrained in the professional culture in which I had grown. As a member, my vision of the installation was broadened, and consequently I was able to conceptualize more clearly the basic issues that I face as an inside consultant. At this point, I could place before my colleagues the pivotal question that had consolidated in my mind: "Are the needs of our severely traumatized cases best treated in a military residential centre that has been established according to front-line experience and hospital-based practice?" The question, which was presented with supporting arguments, was immediately identified as a challenge of the installation's basic premises. It was a disconcerting turn that affected the group like a bolt out of the blue. There were some jocular remarks about the overheating of a fevered mind, but overall the senior officers expressed a keen interest in the ideas and decided to continue the discussion of basic issues concerning the installation.

My basic contention is that we all need to face up to the complex and often debilitating condition of PTSD in order to fulfil our first obligation, not to do harm. In facing up to this, we will be helping our clients and society at large to come to terms with the consequences of trauma. Military psychiatry, which has tended to construct intensive intramural programs that emphasize active coping, needs to expand in two rather underdeveloped directions: (1) accepting the losses inflicted by severe combat stress, and supporting PTSD veterans and their families' attempts to find the most adaptive way of living with continuing symptoms; (2) developing collaborative long-term support services that are focused on the family–community interface and can mobilize the ecological resources that are necessary for promoting a stable and healthy adjustment. A main lesson to be learned from a history of denial is that combat-stress reaction and PTSD can develop into an intractable multidimensional disorder that will not be cured by a quick and simple panacea. A comprehensive and continuous service-delivery system is necessary, and professionals can play an important role in helping the emotionally injured veterans receive the social acknowledgement, institutional benefits, and mental health care that they rightfully deserve.

The installation can play a significant role in the lives of its patients, provided that the staff is aware of the wider sequence of care and makes careful preparations for maximizing the long-term impact of crisis intervention. Essentially, my proposal was to make two fundamental changes in our programme: (1) drastically decrease the emphasis on repairing military functioning by the use of exposure-based therapy, and, in its place, promote psychological functioning as the major goal; (2) make the programme less residential and more connected and continuous with the home environment in order to facilitate a functional reintegration into civilian life. These directions follow the main conclusions that came out of the Koach experience (Bleich, Shalev, Shoham, Solomon, & Kotler, 1992), which until this point has not been applied to the organization of treatment in the installation. Consequently, I have proposed to the senior command of the installation and the mental health department to shorten the one-month residential programme into a one-week period and to add an intensive community-oriented component to our programme. The purpose of such home-based work would be to accompany and support the transition into civilian functioning and to ensure continuity of care by connecting the family with supporting local services. In such an organization, the direct therapeutic role of the staff would be reduced. Instead, they would become more involved in outreach and the provision of support and consultation to those people in the ecosystem who are expected to remain significantly involved with the veteran for the long term.

These suggestions entail a drastic change of the installation's primary functions and the role identity of our staff. The creation of a therapeutic and military milieu would be de-emphasized, and the work would instead focus on the military–civilian interface. The principal functions of the installation would be more tightly defined. During war, it would be a crisis centre that provides for comprehensive biopsychosocial diagnoses, brief and intensive crisis interventions with soldiers and their ecological network, and referrals that are accompanied by home-based follow-up in order to follow-through the crisis intervention into this transitional period and to ensure continuity of care. In peacetime, the installation's staff will not only be engaged in training itself, but also serve as an organizing and training centre for Israeli professionals with respect to acute and posttraumatic stress disorders. The staff would be split into regional groups that will be charged with the establishment, training, and maintaining of groups of civilian professionals who are not on reserve duty, mostly female and/or older colleagues. These community networks would provide a pool of volunteers that could be activated during national crises, a time in which Israelis have always been highly willing to volunteer and to support casualties. Their role would be to accompany veterans and their families on a personal and semi-professional level, providing the installation's staff with an easily accessible, local, and long-term support system that can be used to make contact with the community and to coordinate services.

At the time of writing, the installation's senior officers group has become engaged in discussing the above proposals. It was decided to continue with our regular training programme in order to maintain the stability of our organization and, at the same time, devote time to a re-evaluation of goals, methods, and organizational structure. This chapter was written during this process and was presented to the group, in the hope that it will play a stimulating role in the discussion, much in the way that it has helped the author to clarify and articulate his thinking. Already, we have been joined by our participation in this evolving process. We are involved in creating an organization that none of us ever wants actually to see in operation, and yet we have all been challenged and enriched by playing our respective parts in this evolutionary process.

Summary

The development of consultation in the Rear Care Installation demonstrated the extent to which organizational leadership is intertwined with the self-differentiation of the consultant. It is suggested that differentiation is particularly important when the consultant comes from inside the organization and has been working there for a long time. Inside consultants who seek to develop a broader and more distant perspective for their work need to go through a re-examination of basic assumptions in their professional culture. The tendency to internalize and identify with one's institutional culture, and the bonds of loyalty that are often developed with colleagues over the years, can make the working through of this process most difficult. In the case of the Rear Care Installation, these obstacles were resolved by exploring the installation's sociocultural and historical context, and studying current research about the course and treatment of traumatic disorders. Consequently, there was a discontinuous jump in the consultation that stimulated a re-evaluation of goals, methods, and organizational structure. While these effects demonstrate the usefulness of these processes for increasing differentiation, it is recognized that in consultation, as in therapy, there is more than one road leading to Rome.

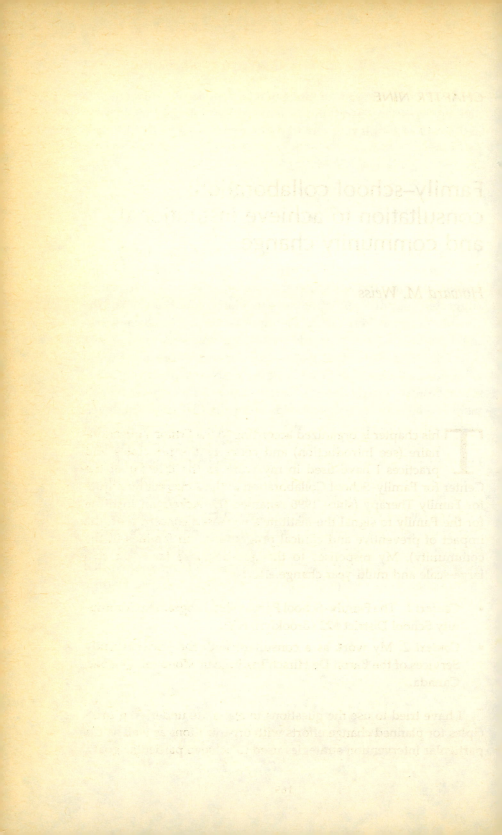

CHAPTER NINE

Family–school collaboration: consultation to achieve institutional and community change

Howard M. Weiss

This chapter is organized according to the Editor's question-naire (see Introduction) and concerns the principles and practices I have used in my work as the director of the Center for Family–School Collaboration at the Ackerman Institute for Family Therapy (since 1996 renamed the Ackerman Institute for the Family to signal the institute's increased concern with the impact of preventive and clinical programmes on families in the community). My responses to the questionnaire focus on two large-scale and multi-year change efforts:

- *Context 1.* The Family–School Partnership Program in Commu-nity School District #22 (Brooklyn, NY).
- *Context 2.* My work as a consultant with the Jewish Family Services of the Baron De Hirsch Institute in Montreal, Quebec, Canada.

I have tried to use the questions to elaborate underlying prin-ciples for planned change efforts with organizations as well as the particular intervention strategies used to achieve particular goals.

The theoretical and practice context

The Ackerman Institute's Center for Family–School Collaboration, founded in 1981 as the Family–School Collaboration Project, aimed to change the nature of family–school relationships from those characterized by alienated and adversarial interactions to ones that were collaborative and mutually supportive. Our conception was that the school could function as a genuine partner to the families of each school child. Our primary target of change was the organization of specific schools, though even from the beginning our "secret" grandiose goal was to change the nature of family-school relations in the New York City public schools—a system with 1,100 schools serving approximately one million children. The important thing to emphasize is that right from the beginning our goals were to generate changes at the level of the organization. If successful, we would see changes in classroom, school-wide, and school district practices and policies regarding interactions with children and their families around learning.

Although parental involvement is now fully accepted as a critical factor in educational reform by federal, state, and local mandates, two obstacles prevent family–school collaboration from making a real difference in children's day-to-day school lives. First, in the current political and economic climate, family involvement efforts are viewed as add-ons, peripheral to the real business of educating children. Consequently, they are often cut back in favour of more apparently instructional programmes. The link between parental involvement and classroom instruction is at best a vague truism to most parents and educators.

Second, parental involvement programmes frequently fail to address parents' and educators' real concerns about how well children are progressing academically and developmentally and about each other. Consequently, these programmes attract relatively few participants. Recent research (Immerwahr, 1994; Johnson & Immerwahr, 1994) indicates that educators, parents of school-aged children, and the general public perceive one another as having broken a sacred contract to support public education. Citizens believe that educators have not met their basic obligation to provide safe, orderly schools that teach fundamental skills. Educators believe that many parents have abnegated their responsibility to instil in their children the values and behaviour necessary for school achievement. As a result, fundamental questions confront any effort at parent involvement:

1. *What do parents want of educators?* Do parents see their children valued as precious human beings by the school? Can parents trust educators to prepare their children to find a meaningful role in society?

2. *What do educators want from parents?* Can parents promote and reinforce the importance and benefits of learning and the activities of school life? Can educators experience parents as educational resources to the classroom and their children?

3. *What do families and educators need to believe and do in order to work collaboratively together?* Can families and schools build a supportive and trusting relationship around the child? Can educators adopt the attitudes and learn the skills necessary to establish collaborative relationships with families and use these skills routinely in their practice?

If educators want to create collaborative relationships with the families of the children they teach as a critical component of school reform programmes, then they will have to acknowledge and address these underlying issues. Only then will they be able to begin to maximize the potential contributions that families can make to their children's learning.

The Center for Family–School Collaboration at the Ackerman Institute for the Family is a vital resource for confronting and overcoming current barriers to successful collaboration. Center programmes help schools make families an integral part of children's learning and create a school climate that dramatically alters the way parents, school staff, and children experience each other. Over the last fifteen years, we have helped more than 100 schools in some of New York City's most impoverished neighbourhoods as well as in suburban communities. School staffs have impressively transformed their relationships with families and discovered that they are in fact on the same team, working on the task of ensuring the success of all students.

We know from experience that family–school collaboration can and should be central to any vision of educational reform. It can connect the two key systems in a child's life—the home and the school—in ways that restore hope and re-energize a shared commitment to children's learning. For example, when teachers create a collaborative learning experience in science in which they interact together with their students and their parents, all have an opportunity to experience the excitement of grappling with ideas to create a hypothesis. Parents enjoy the process of their own children's learning and recognize how they can contribute. Children sense the mutual validation that both their parents and their teachers offer for their positive efforts. When there is no opportunity for collaboration, parents often do not perceive their children's school work as a domain in which they can enhance family relationships as well as contribute to their child's development.

What makes our model unique? Having worked in the most difficult circumstances in New York City elementary and secondary schools, we have identified five factors that are critical for successful family–school collaboration:

1. *Schools build relationships with all parents whether they can come to the school or not.* The school must communicate a genuine interest in connecting with the parents of all of its students to ensure the children's success. This message must make clear how parents' active participation in their children's educational experience will directly enhance their achievement and development. When parents believe that their involvement can make a difference for their children, they invest in the school. Some parents may not be able to come to the school because of work or family demands. We can signal our belief that they still care deeply about their children's learning by providing them with the means to understand and keep up with what is happening in school (e.g. summary letters describing an event they missed, regular newsletters, and homework assignments to create links to the home and back to school again). Maintaining a dialogue about learning and about the school's interest in each child builds connections between home and school that last.

2. *All family–school activities are planned to maximize learning.* Rather

than simply trying to "get parents involved", school staff use the family–school relationship to meet specific educational goals, solve problems, and celebrate the children and their achievement. Family–school interactions involving the children are embedded in orientations, classroom instruction, homework routines, celebrations, presentations of new curriculum, transitions to new grade levels and programmes, procedures for home–school communication and for resolving difficulties.

3. *The child is an active participant in virtually all family–school interactions.* Involvement in a series of family–school collaborative activities throughout the student's school career offers multiple educational opportunities. For example, children of all ages are taught to function as active participants in "family–teacher" meetings. Since it is their life at school which is to be discussed, they come to such meetings as "experts on themselves" who must be there to describe their own experience, thoughts, and feelings. Another example is situations in which the teacher and students together provide parents with an orientation to specific curriculum programmes. Children gain confidence and a sense of efficacy as they contribute to the solution of problems and the improvement of their own school experience.

4. *New collaborative interactions transform the way families and schools experience each other.* A shared vested interest in the child brings the family and school together. Staff learn to build on the strengths of parents and children and to block blame from undermining the collaborative process. When each person feels known, understood, and cared about by the others, a sense of community and common purpose unites the classroom and school with the families of school-age children.

5. *School staffs feel ownership of the change process.* Educators must see the change process and its outcomes as directly beneficial to them in the short and long run. Work must begin where the staff is. Rather than assume that they are ready for yet another training programme, initial on-site consultation helps them understand and use family–school collaboration to enhance their daily classroom and school lives. Over time, staff gain the

skills and experience necessary to utilize the collaboration model on their own to deal with new concerns. The approach becomes a routine way that the school does business. We work systematically with schools to help them develop programmes that incorporate these elements. This approach is unique in the United States for its depth of engagement with families (i.e. all families are the target of connection) and its inclusion of children. It offers a model for creating a dialogue between families and schools that can reinvigorate parents' and teachers' commitment to children's learning. Working with us, schools create experiences that link parents directly to their own child's learning. Family–school collaboration becomes central to the life and calendar of a school. As we help families and schools collaborate, we ensure for each child a network of caring adults who will support their learning and help them solve problems when they occur.

Few schools have been designed to collaborate with families. Establishing a climate of collaboration between families and schools requires overcoming the legacies of past adversarial and alienated relationships. The Center work engages schools at the level of their current philosophy and practice. Educators will show willingness to consider a more collaborative relationship with parents and the inclusion of children in family–school activities only if the difficulties of their work are acknowledged and respected, and if they experience the approach as directly helpful to what they are seeking to achieve. Our emphasis in introducing our model is on looking at how they do what they already do rather than on asking them to add to their already difficult work load. We work to help them implement initial "climate-building activities" (Weiss & Edwards, 1992) which restructure events (including the child as an active participant) that they are already going to do (e.g. parent–teacher meetings). Increased willingness to implement family–school collaboration strategies further comes after experiencing the initial events. Teachers are invariably hooked by the substantial increases in parental participation and by their own positive reactions to the experience of being connected meaningfully as professionals to the students' parents.

The implementation context

> QUESTION 1.   Think of one or two contexts in which you have been involved in changing an institution/organization: (a) as an invited consultant to either the organization or to a specific task.

Context 1.   One context in which our project was involved was with Community School District #22 in Brooklyn, NY. We had already implemented our family–school collaboration model with a cluster of six schools in 1988–1990. This initial consultant relationship with these six schools followed a year or two of informal interventions with two of the district schools which functioned to establish our reputation as effective change agents in generating a different climate of family–school interaction.

We developed the programme with the first cluster of six schools so that the district would have to define the programme as a district-level initiative rather than a pilot programme in one school. Like a pilot-light on a gas stove, a pilot programme in one school can too easily be blown out, for reasons having nothing to do with the programme itself. Since we had already demonstrated positive outcomes in a few schools, we proposed working with a six-school "cluster" next to achieve the budgetary benefits that accrue from a programme of sufficient scale. We made a specific proposal including specific goals and projected outcomes and negotiated a budget that made it financially feasible for the district to go ahead with the programme.

The deputy superintendent coordinating our work with the district viewed our two-year effort with this six-school cluster as quite successful in fostering a new set of expectations and specific routine collaborative "climate-building activities". As a result of this work, the district superintendent and deputy superintendent asked us to write a proposal with them for a federal "family–school partnership" grant to use to bring our programme to three district schools serving poor minority (predominantly African–American) communities. These schools had a long history of having the lowest performance scores on standardized reading and mathematics tests compared to other schools in the district.

We wrote the grant proposal in collaboration with the district deputy superintendent and her grant writer. This context, then, was defined by the proposal we had written which aimed to implement our family–school collaboration programme using three major levels of intervention: (1) staff development training in our model; (2) parent-to-parent skills training (i.e. training parents to train other parents to help their children learn critical skills and attitudes for academic success) using an existing programme called "MegaSkills" developed by Dorothy Rich (1988) of the Home-School Institute in Washington, DC, as the content base; and (3) a multi-session, collaborative, family reading curriculum, which we designed with district reading staff and teachers to engage teachers, parents, and children in each school together.

Context 2. The second context is the Jewish Family Services (JFS) of the Baron de Hirsch Institute in Montreal, Canada. This context is particularly interesting because it reflects the level of complexity that our programme has grown to address. In this case, we were asked to consult to JFS because their supervisor of school support services had recognized in our preventive and collaborative approaches in schools a model for the kinds of therapeutic community-connection building that JFS sought to bind together the diverse Jewish community in Montreal. The supervisor had seen a presentation about our work that we gave at an American Orthopsychiatry Association conference.

In this context, I was asked by the JFS executive director and the school service supervisor to work with them and their staff of fifty social workers to develop a change strategy for encouraging family–school collaboration in approximately forty Jewish schools. The most general goal was to use the Ackerman Family–School Collaboration model as a common focus for Jewish schools in Montreal that would build a general climate of partnership and connection across the wider community. Briefly put, the goal was to use the schools as the entry point for a change effort targeted for general community impact.

QUESTION 2. Consider the structure of the organization, its objectives, and its ways of functioning and define these briefly. In what ways do you believe the dominant culture or other culture or ethnic factors have organized the structure and/or goals of that organization?

Context 1. Community School District #22 is one of thirty-two "decentralized" districts of the New York City Board of Education. The community district superintendent oversees approximately thirty elementary and junior-high schools (pre-kindergarten through eighth grade), and he is overseen by an elected community district school board. Most New York City school districts are themselves as large as small cities in scale. Management at the level of the school is guided by a school principal and increasingly by a school-based management committee of teachers and parents. The structures of the district and each individual school are hierarchically defined, with boundaries, rules, and routines codified by the New York City Board of Education and contractual rights and obligations negotiated with the United Federation of Teachers (teachers' union). On general and specific levels, the school district and individual schools seek to provide the means and opportunities for state and locally defined objectives for appropriate academic and social/emotional development of children. Within broad parameters, school principals and teachers can define how they will reach the broadly defined objectives, with the results of their efforts measured by standardized test scores and teachers' evaluations of student performance. Most important for our purposes is the typical definition of the relationship between family and school. While in recent years there has been an increasing recognition of the importance of "parental involvement" in education, in practice this involvement is defined in quite traditional terms in which the parents/family members are typically a passive audience to school events unless called by school personnel to resolve a problem that their child is having at school.

The structure of family–school relations is defined by generations of history in which these two primary socializing systems for children operate in parallel to one another. Each system delegates certain educational and socializing tasks to one another, but the

school and family rarely operate as genuine partners in support of
children. Schools and families are viewed as linked to a larger
social contract that prescribes each system's role in preparing
future citizens. Unfortunately, the participants in each of these
systems and the society at large increasingly seem to fear that the
general contract has been broken. Results from national (Johnson
& Immerwahr, 1994) and Connecticut state (Immerwahr, 1994)
surveys done by the Public Agenda Foundation indicate that
school personnel and parents see each other as not adequately
performing their assigned tasks to prepare children to lead productive lives. In large urban school systems like that of New York
City, the dominant culture increasingly views the public schools as
failing to educate the present school population. As the urban
public school population is increasingly made up of minority
and immigrant children, the dominant culture often blames the
children's families—and implicitly (sometimes explicitly) their
culture/race—for the students' lack of academic success and for
declining academic standards in general. This ascription of blame
stands as a barrier to a more collaborative approach to finding
successful educational strategies for today's state-school children.
The perception that state schools exist for the education of other
people's children as opposed to their functioning as the foundation
of democratic society also explains the general difficulty of funding state schools adequately.

Context 2.   In the Montreal work, I have been working with an
organization (the Baron de Hirsch Institute) which has been a
major organizing force and service provider for the Jewish community for more than a hundred years. The executive director of
JFS defines her objectives in terms of Reform, Conservative, and
Orthodox communities, as well as different ethnic (e.g. recent Rus-
sian immigrants) and language communities, all of which generate
different types of demands. The fact that the Montreal Jewish community is itself viewed as an "ethnic" or minority community in a
wider conflictual community (i.e. English- and French-speaking
Quebec) defines some common needs.

QUESTION 3.   Define the overall and specific tasks that are the *raison d'être* of that organization and institution. In what ways do you think that the particular "human structures" (variously called Institutions and Organizations) developed as responses to the particular human tasks: child care, education, mental health care, social order, social/community provisions, manufacturing and marketing, financial services, group and professional identities.

Context 1.   The *raison d'être* of the schools and school districts is to educate, train, and socialize children to become fully functioning members of the community. Specific tasks of child care, and of transmitting community norms and values, serve broader community-building goals. To the degree that subgroups of the population are not able to build functional relationship connections with their children's schools, they are less able to envision hopeful pathways for family success and their children's future.

Context 2.   The JFS provides broad-based mental-health and social services support for the Montreal Jewish community. The Baron de Hirsch Institute has a long history as an umbrella agency for diverse organizations serving and supporting the Montreal Jewish community in areas including mental health, child care, community education, and identity.

QUESTION 3 (*continued*).   To what extent do you think that the particular "human structures" developed in response to factors other than the primary human tasks of that organization (political/economic factors, survival of the identity of a particular organization, philosophical religious or "power" factors, etc.)?

Context 1.   The structure of the community school districts in New York City, particularly the "decentralized" school board which hires the superintendent and sets policy, is a direct result of a teacher strike in 1967 which pitted the African–American community against a centralized bureaucracy associated with unionized teachers. This subtext still underlies the politically loaded relationship contexts of the central Board of Education and thirty-two community school districts, as well as the hostility of the New York City mayor towards the New York City Schools chancellor and the central Board of Education, whose budget he cannot control. Therefore, the organizational structures (both city-wide and local) that run the more than one thousand New York City schools are products of many historical political power struggles. Important consequences of this situation include: local schools boards controlled by a very small electorate turning out for elections; rigid budgeting procedures necessitated by complex systems for fiscal and educational accountability at the central and local district levels; vague quality standards for educational outcomes. The New York City mayor makes the school system his target for fiscal inefficiencies and waste and for poor educational outcomes. He seeks full control of the school system's budget.

Context 2. The Baron de Hirsch Institute was the legacy of a wealthy Jewish philanthropist in the 1860s. Its functions are shaped by the need to preserve and protect the Montreal Jewish community as a minority religious/ethnic entity in a larger community.

QUESTION 4.   Give a hypothesis about why that particular structure of organization might be the response to those particular needs or tasks. Include in your hypothesis the relevant cultural and ethnic influences that you believe may have organized that institution to be structured and operate in that particular way. What do you believe was the kind of thinking or "logic" that was inherent in the choice of each particular structure as a response to that particular task, and the forces that prescribed that choice in the face of alternatives?

Context 1. The particular organizational structure that is relevant to consider here is the way that schools are typically organized in relation to the parents/families of schoolchildren. The model of American schools that still shapes present relationships is that which emerged in the late nineteenth and early twentieth century, in which the public schools were seen as inducting the children of immigrants into "American culture". From this perspective, the schools wanted to establish rigid boundaries between themselves and the home so as to reduce the cultural impact of the home and to increase the schools' socializing influence in producing "American citizens". Parents were conceived as having the role of encouraging their child's compliance with a school's socializing and academic demands. The emphasis of parental involvement until very recently has been as an adjunct support for the school's programme, together with "effective parenting" to make children "ready" for school and achievement. Inculcating values has been seen as the domain of the family. Coleman's classic study (Coleman & Hoffer, 1987) of the American private and state high-school systems emphasizes that performance has always been best in environments in which parents and school personnel perceive each other as sharing a similar set of values. In other words, the families and the school view themselves as extensions of each other.

Context 2. My impression is that the Baron De Hirsch Institute functions as a central clearinghouse and resource centre for the diverse elements of the Jewish community and for their joint needs in relation to the larger non-Jewish community. JFS is one important component of the Baron de Hirsch Institute which offers a school support and various mental health programmes. My work began with a subcomponent of the JFS which provides social work and psychological services to various Jewish schools. By providing a centralized organizational structure for support services, this organization makes it possible for small schools to afford services that they would otherwise be unable to have. The supervisor of this school-support unit initially sought consultation from the Center because she hoped to increase the social influence of her social workers in their schools settings, particularly in terms of creating an enhanced climate for family–school relations. Because the social workers come to the school from another organization, they can more easily be introduced to alternative modes of thinking about family–school relations or mental health services in schools through their primary organizational affiliation than through the school. JFS supervisors wanted their social workers to function not only as clinicians but also as change agents who could form alliances with the principals and staff to change the climate of family–school relationships within schools. They also wanted their change efforts to have continuity across the schools so that their social workers could have the support necessary from their supervisors and each other to sustain long-term change efforts.

The head administrators of the school-support section of JFS first decided that if they trained their social workers and psychologists in the Ackerman Family–School Collaboration model, these workers could introduce the model into their respective schools. In particular, they assumed that they could offer this special expertise to the school principals and then form a more powerful alliance with them to change specific family—school relationships and to build a more collaborative overall school climate.

QUESTION 5.   On reflection, could you think of better or more rational (in your terms) structures or ways of operating such an organization, or can you define a totally different organization that you think would have been more appropriate?

Context 1.   The primary focus of the Center for Family–School Collaboration is to help schools and school districts develop different ways of operating as organizations such that a general climate of family–school collaboration fosters increased academic achievement and enhanced social/emotional growth for children. To operate in this way, the relationships between child and teacher, between parent and child, and between parent, child, and teacher are viewed as critical levers for enhanced educational outcomes. We train the staff in the skills and strategies necessary to self-consciously build a collaborative family–school climate (Weiss & Edwards, 1992). These include how to block blame as a pattern of interaction or explanation of events; how to ask questions that encourage meaningful responses from children and parents; how to lead family–teacher meetings (i.e. student, parent, teacher); how to lead family–school problem-solving meetings including with staff, the children, parents, and significant others; and how to plan and implement family–school collaborative "climate-building activities". Readiness and willingness to build a collaborative family–school climate and to work with parents as genuine partners requires school staff (teachers and administrators) to change their mind sets about parental involvement in schools, as well as their routine classroom and school-wide practices.

Changing the nature of family–school relations from those characterized by alienating and/or adversarial interactions to those that are collaborative and mutually enhancing requires engaging staff, children, and parents in sets of experiences in which they can experience each other as genuine partners (Weiss, 1996; Weiss & Edwards, 1992). For example, early in the school year all schools can use their initial orientation programmes as opportunities to engage staff, students, and parents in interactive activities that send very clear messages about how they do business. For example, they would want to communicate that they value parents' input and intend to engage them in collaborative programmes throughout the year. The student is involved actively in these events so that all participating families come away stimulated by direct experiences of interactive learning with their own children. They have direct discussions with their own children about their individual and mutual goals for learning and social growth during the school year. The central ideas from these family discussions are then shared among the participating students, parents, and teachers. The participants typically experience a sense of community, with a shared sense of mission and purposes. The collaborative elements of this activity are then experienced again in subsequent activities like student–family–staff discussion forums or curriculum-based shared learning events. Only after they develop a sense of normative expectations about each other as collaborative partners do they project these expectations routinely into other joint interactions.

My aim in responding to this question is not to describe the whole sequence of strategies we use to generate an organizational change. I think that it is important to emphasize that the "better way of organizational functioning" we help schools to develop is one in which staff naturally, consciously, and routinely create opportunities for students, parents, and staff members to collaborate together. These events should occur within activities that the staff are already doing or in new situations in which family–school collaboration becomes the means for dealing with specific issues or concerns (e.g. a family–school asthma workshop aimed at reducing unnecessary absences). As staff and parents experience the mutual benefits of including students in collaborative family–school events, family–school collaboration becomes the school's "way of doing business" in general. Whenever they are planning large or small events, or planning to deal with particular concerns, they come to consider routinely how the situation offers an opportunity for collaboration between family and school.

In its work with schools and school districts, the Center for Family–School Collaboration offers a model for establishing school structures and processes that produce a general school climate of collaborative family–school relations in support of children's learning. Rather than viewing the family and school as two significant primary systems operating in parallel to one another, we suggest that collaborative relationships between these two systems can be fostered self-consciously to maximize resources for children's learning and development. Our approach views all aspects of the school experience (curriculum, administrative and communication procedures, special programmes, after-school activities, assessment and evaluation procedures, health programmes, etc.) as potentially offering opportunities for parents/family, students, and school staff to collaborate with one another in planning, decision-making, and problem-solving and in specific learning-related activities. We help school staffs learn to create sets of experiences throughout the school year in which students, their parents and other family members, and staff routinely collaborate together. We start with a core set of three activities that can connect with events that are always part of any school's calendar (Weiss & Edwards, 1992):

1. *Family–teacher meetings.* A restructured version of the parent–teacher meeting in which the child is included as an active participant. Children are prepared ("trained") to discuss with their parents and teacher their school experiences, achievements, and areas in need of improvement. The meeting is one to which parents are invited by the teacher and the children to learn about classroom life.

2. *Orientations.* These are events in which the school introduces itself or critical components of its programme. Typical orientations included in most school calendars are "meet the teacher events", "open-school day or night", orientations to

specific curriculum components, and initial programmes for new students and families entering the school. All of these activities provide opportunities to communicate critical messages about "how the school does business". Such messages are sent not only by the content of the programme but also by how the programme is done. For example, to send the message that the school wants to engage families actively in learning activities, the staff would create situations in which students and parents can interact directly around important issues with staff (e.g. what the central goals are for the year).

3. *Family–school problem-solving or planning meetings.* These are meetings convened because of a concern about a specific child or family–school relationship. Participants include all of those who are part of the systemic context of the presenting problem. These might include students, parents, other family members (e.g. siblings in the same school), extended-family members, teachers involved presently or in the past with the child, guidance counsellor or social worker, principal, and sometimes persons from the larger community (e.g. physicians, neighbours). These meetings follow a specific meeting flow sequence in order to establish a non-blaming, collaborative context for family–school problem-solving. The steps include:

  a. overview (defining purpose and ground-rules of meeting);

  b. "finding facts" (what are participants primary concerns);

  c. "blocking blame" (maintaining focus on understanding issues and problem-solving);

  d. checking for consensus (tracking and highlighting areas of agreement within the group);

  e. "determining a decision" (establishing the issues to decide about);

  f. "arriving at action" (who is going to do what, when, where, and how, and how to follow-up).

Usually, an initial and a follow-up session are held. These meetings are meant to be therapeutic, not therapy (which connotes blame to the family).

These core activities are so loaded with associations from the past for students, parents, and teachers that the restructuring into a collaborative activity sends a message of difference in powerful ways. We use these memory-loaded routine school activities to create the first school-wide experiences of family–school collaboration because of their power in overcoming the "legacies of the past"—expectations of adversarial and alienated relations between school and home.

Usually, once a school has implemented these three core activities, they have learned the process and basic strategies of collaborative family–school interaction and they make this collaborative process a permanent element (particularly the inclusion of the child) of these events in the future. They then plan "elective" family–school collaborative activities to address the specific needs or concerns of their own schools (e.g. underachievement, drug abuse or pregnancy prevention, health concerns like asthma, mainstreaming learning-disabled children, ethnic or racial conflict, introducing new curricula, assessment, incorporating new immigrant families, etc.). Thus, our implementation model includes generic components that are implemented in all schools and specific components that address the unique needs and concerns of each school community. This is a very important feature for achieving organizational and institutional change, since each school and district is particularly sensitive about having its uniqueness recognized explicitly. School administrators and teachers insist that any proposed change programme specifically address what they are most concerned about. Their willingness and commitment to engage in a meaningful change process over time requires that they see the potential for finding concrete answers to specific problems. We do not suggest a "one size fits all approach" but, rather, design applications of family–school collaboration that address each school's specific concerns. Unless they can see us in that way, we cannot act as effective change agents.

The Center consultants train and consult with school staff to enable them to plan and implement these climate-building activities. The initial aim is to get schools to enact the core activities so that they will experience the difference between collaborative family–school climate-building events and their typical parent–school activities. The consultants then help the staff to generalize from their initial experiences with core activities to deal with their own critical concerns.

Of course, resistance is an aspect of any change process. We deal with resistance in particular ways at different stages of our intervention process: readiness, transformation, and ownership (Weiss, 1996). In the readiness phase, we must often deal with teachers' and administrators' feelings of hopelessness or frustration, as well as the difficulty of effectively joining with school staff (due to time constraints). To do this, we have developed an on-site preparation stage. We join school staff in their daily activities and help them see the potential benefits of our approach for them and their school. This phase begins the essential process of restoring hope and experiencing collaboration first-hand through their relationship with us.

The transformation phase may overlap with the readiness phase. Self-consciously and systematically over time, schools, parents, and children participate in new experiences with each other. In this phase, the school redesigns existing parent–teacher activities into the set of three collaborative family—school core activities related to learning: family–teacher meetings, orientations, and family–school problem-solving meetings. Participation in a number of family–school collaborative events provides several significant opportunities to create a more constructive and supportive climate. Our interventions with schools create concrete opportunities to build trust. As families and schools interact in new ways, they come to see each other as resources who can do more for the child working together than they can struggling on their own.

In the third stage, the ownership phase, school personnel increasingly take responsibility for maintaining core activities. Their resistance lessens considerably as they initiate ideas for elective activities designed to address critical issues such as increasing academic achievement, dealing with potential hold-overs, reducing absenteeism among asthmatic children, validating families' cultures, and creating homework-help networks for recent immigrant groups.

Most of the schools we work with come to see family–school partnerships as a central organizing principle. After two to three years of work with us, the school staff are able to maintain and expand this work on their own.

There are particular structural elements that are basic to establishing a system ready to implement our model:

1. a principal who is committed to the idea that the family has an important role to play in a child's school achievement and who has an interest in enhancing the family–school relationship;

2. designation of a family–school coordinator, a staff member who takes on the responsibilities of liaison to the Center and facilitator among his or her colleagues of collaborative programmes with families and children;

3. commitments of time for staff development training as well as team planning, implementation, and evaluation of climate-building activities.

Resistance is also overcome and willingness to try new procedures increased by modelling a collaborative stance, being consistently respectful of educators' and parents' skills and resources, and validating all constructive efforts. The consultants continually "plant seeds" for understanding how issues can be engaged collaboratively. They regularly offer examples of how issues being faced by the school can be handled using the model. In doing so, they are careful to draw on the school's previous positive experiences implementing climate–building activities.

Our programme offers schools the conceptual models, planning and action strategies, and specific intervention skills to self-consciously create sets of experiences in which all constituencies of the school community can genuinely experience each other as partners in support of learning (Weiss, 1996). After two or three years, schools may have family–school collaborative activities woven throughout each month of the school year. They routinely seek opportunities to engage students (elementary school through high school) in planning, decision-making, problem-solving, and curriculum-based learning activities in which they interact directly with their parents (and other family members) and teachers. When children have these experiences numerous times throughout each year, they can be viewed as a set of skill-building activities that are as much a part of the school's curriculum as are more typical classroom activities. These sets of experiences in different home and school situations build up a history of shared satisfaction images as collaborative partners that can be drawn on to deal with new community situations.

In the beginning of our work, our consultants worked with staffs to gradually induce them to try out our model. Their willingness was initially engaged by their interest in having us lead family–school problem-solving meetings to deal with particularly problematic children or families. Our reputation for effectiveness and the legitimacy of our model has grown over the years. We have therefore been increasingly able to insist that the preconditions necessary for success must be met before we will work with schools.

Context 2.   The ways of operating schools and the strategies for fostering collaborative family–school climates described above for Context 1 also have relevance for the current context. In this, a community seeks to build a collaborative context incorporating its schools and community organizations. Consistently in my consultations with the JFS, I advised their supervisors to seek means for including all stakeholders in the change process. Self-consciously building family–school collaboration across the community was proposed as a task requiring input and involvement of all segments of the Jewish community and their schools. The JFS not only sought to have its own staff learn the family–school collaboration model, but also to convene the leadership of other organizations and schools to try to establish a shared community mission and purpose. Taking this perspective, the leadership of JFS now saw themselves as facilitating a community-wide systemic change, as opposed to supporting a more narrow service-delivery mission in specific schools. They have enlarged their vision to include fostering collaboration across city agencies in support of children's learning as well as community integration.

> QUESTION 6.   What is your hypothesis about why the current structure of the organization developed rather than the one you had subsequently proposed?

Context 1.   The culture of "educational expertise" creates a boundary around the school which communicates to parents that they should entrust their children's learning to the school. The school looks to the family to prepare the children with values and patterns of behaviour that will help them succeed in the culture of the school. When there is a mismatch between expectations and norms of the home culture and that of the school, then the student is likely to have difficulty. The school typically assumes that the student and family must accommodate to the demands of the school. It is not unusual for the school to be rather vague about how the student and family can best meet the demands of the school. It is most unusual for the school to start with the assumption that it is the responsibility of the professionals to "join" the families in ways that will create home–school relationships likely to ensure academic success.

Context 2. The Baron de Hirsch Institute in Montreal stands as a symbol of commitment to support the Jewish community. The JFS school-support programme at the Institute defined its primary mission and purposes as the provision of mental health and social-work support services to children in Jewish schools. From this perspective, each of their social workers placed in schools was on the receiving end of individual referrals. They had a circumscribed relationship with the principals of each school. Not surprisingly, the schools defined the possible contribution of JFS very narrowly—that is, as the placement of a social worker. When the programme redefined its purposes to include fostering the creation of collaborative family–school climates in the wider Jewish community, its possibilities for influence increased. The programme now also includes purposes that cut across all the schools and which their staff as a collective group unite in accomplishing. To be successful, the supervisors now recognize that they must work together with the school principals and with other community groups to set collective goals for the community. The programme's purposes have increasingly taken on the tasks of community building, with JFS supervisors functioning as community facilitators and convenors.

QUESTION 7.   If one wanted to move from the current organization to the structure that you proposed, what ideas do you have about what would be needed to happen for that to be achieved?

The model that I have developed in the work of the Center for Family–School Collaboration is shown in Figure 9.1. Premises that distinguish family–school collaboration from other views of parental involvement are also described diagrammatically in Figures 9.2 to 9.4.

Figure 9.2 shows the five central factors that are essential for building a culture of family–school collaboration in schools. These factors build on the basic premise that families and schools have (or should have) a shared vested interest in the success of the children. When parents, students, and educators are engaged with one another in meaningful learning tasks, they discover ways in which they are uniquely valuable to each other. Such activities include writing and reading stories about their own experience;

INPUT	PROCESS		OUTCOMES
	Staff Development and Consultation		
		CORE Orientations Family-Teacher Conferences Family-School Problem Solving Meetings	*Collaborative School Climate as reflected in:*
Existing School Climate + *Issues Facing the School and its Community*	**Climate Building Activities**		Increased Parent Involvement Staff Skills Classroom Practices School Policies Physical Environment Shared Values and Beliefs
		ELECTIVE (Examples) Adolescent Family-School Forum Asthma Workshop Series Multicultural Programs Family Reading/Math Curricula Multi-Family Group Problem Solving Meetings	
	Organisational Components	Committed Principal School Coordinating Committee Family-School Coordinator	*Student Outcomes*
	Guiding Principles	Blocking Blame Building on Strengths Defining Common Goals Including Child as Active Partner Maximizing Learning	Increased Academic Achievement Increased Attendance Decreased Behaviour Problems Decreased Referrals to Special Education

(NEEDS ASSESSMENT runs vertically along the Process section.)

FIGURE 9.1

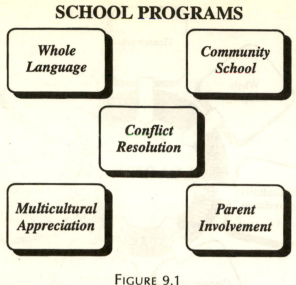

SCHOOL PROGRAMS

Whole Language	**Community School**

Conflict Resolution

Multicultural Appreciation	**Parent Involvement**

FIGURE 9.1

Parent involvement is one of the many programmes
that schools implement

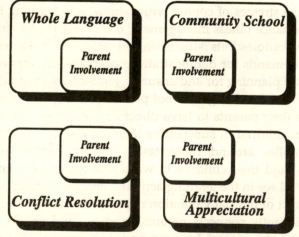

SCHOOL PROGRAMS

Whole Language / *Parent Involvement*	**Community School** / *Parent Involvement*
Parent Involvement / **Conflict Resolution**	*Parent Involvement* / **Multicultural Appreciation**

FIGURE 9.1

Parent involvement is a component of each school programme

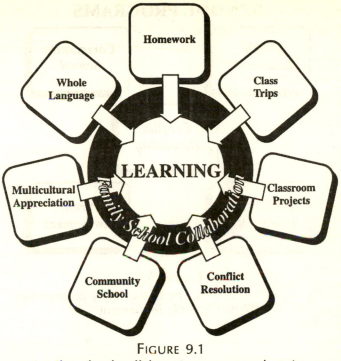

FIGURE 9.1
Family–school collaboration promotes learning
in all school endeavors

sharing the stresses of coping with asthma, and learning together how to enhance illness management; discussing the tensions generated by adolescents' increasing desires for autonomy and parents' demands for demonstrations of increased responsibility-taking; and planning for and ensuring high-school graduation and preparedness for college. School personnel design such activities to enable their parents to have direct opportunities to work with their own children in substantive learning tasks, to interact with other families around those tasks, and to interact with the teacher(s) and their children in ways that reflect the importance that they all see in the learning activities and the children's efforts. This context of mutual validation not only motivates the children, but significantly connects parents, teachers, and children in the important enterprise of learning and development. Teachers receive the kind of validation from families that make them feel quite special in their role of educator.

QUESTION 8.   In which of the three above roles (invited consultant, member, or manager/leader) were you in, in the work you have described? If you were in a role that is not covered by these definitions, can you define it? What do you believe principally activated you to take on your particular role as an agent of change: interest, altruism, money, power, belief systems, etc.?

In my work with the Center for Family–School Collaboration, I am most typically in the role of invited consultant. In situations in which we are working as partners with a school district or in a coalition of organizations supporting a change effort in support of schools, I may function as a member of a change team.

My own personal, political, and professional interests have always been shaped by my altruistic values and interests in contributing to effective social-change efforts aimed at increased justice and equality of opportunity for all. My own Jewish upbringing has also emphasized the importance of one's contribution to the community. In the United States, these issues are centrally crosscut concerns for achieving racial equality and harmony. I purposely sought out graduate training that blended social and clinical psychology with a focus on being a skilled change agent who could operate at individual, group, organizational, and community levels (Lippitt, Watson, & Westley, 1958). Understanding family structure, dynamics, and intervention strategies has always interested me, not only in their own right but also as building blocks for interventions to change societal systems and communities in which they are embedded. My focus on families and schools is driven by the centrality of these two systems as building blocks for community and society. If we are to have better-functioning community systems, then we must achieve changes at a level and scale that one family at a time in therapy will not achieve. So my focus over the last ten years has moved emphatically toward building contexts for families which are themselves therapeutic and can function in preventive, strength-enhancing ways.

QUESTION 9. If you were there as an invited consultant, who authorized you to act, and how would you define that person's level of power/influence/authority in relation to that organization or the people to whom it is responsible?

Context 1. The deputy superintendent of three elementary schools in Community School District #22 asked me to write a proposal for a federal grant with the District to work with three schools in poor, predominantly African–American and recent immigrant communities. She had supposedly sought the interest of the principals of the three schools, but I later found that they had taken offence at the way the criteria for the federal grant proposal labelled them. They were insulted that their school community and children were always described in terms of the deficits of their poor community (e.g. low standardized maths and reading test scores, high minority population, high incidence of single-parent families, and poverty) rather than their efforts to cope with extraordinary demands. When the district was awarded the grant, we were invited to start the programme with the three schools. The superintendent and deputy superintendent had the legitimate authority and power to provide the programme for the schools. However, each principal had the power and influence with his staff to determine if the programme would be accepted and be successful. We made clear in our initial meetings with the principals and their staff that the descriptions of the schools in the federal grant application were written to respond to specific requirements. We had to demonstrate in our relationships with them, and in our strategies, that we focused on strengths and aimed to validate and celebrate the achievements of their students, parents, staff, and community.

Our interventions included training of leadership teams from the three schools together, and I assigned a project consultant from Ackerman to each school. It was the responsibility of the Ackerman consultant to establish a working relationship with the principal, project coordinator, staff, and parents on-site. The staffs at the three schools, like any New York City schools, took a "show-me" attitude. They only really joined the change effort earnestly after they experienced how our core climate-building activities in fact changed the interactional patterns of staff and parents and increased the involvement of the families enormously. In these three schools, the principals decided which grade levels we would work with first. They all tested out the impact with two or three grade levels and then expanded the approach to the remaining grades. We routinely used the influence that teachers have with one another to influence the change effort. First, one group of teachers who have had success with the approach share their experience with others. They describe the application in ways that emphasize issues that their colleagues also value (e.g. the response of the children, ways in which they prepared, reaction of parents to their work). Once they have tried the approach in the series of core activities, they have confidence that families and children will be responsive. They then use family–school collaboration to address other purposes—for example, to deal with children who were in danger of being held back a grade if their work did not markedly improve.

Context 2.   I was invited by the executive director and school support supervisor to introduce my family–school collaboration model in Montreal. In consultation with them we planned a series of workshops to introduce the work systematically to the entire community over time. They began with those staff who had full authority to engage with their own social work staff (50 persons). Our focus was to increase this group's level of skill in family–school collaboration strategies and techniques so that they could use the approach in their regular work. Once they had introduced the ideas to their school principals, we convened teams of principals, teachers, and parents from forty Jewish schools for a workshop. The reputation of the Baron de Hirsch Institute and that of the Ackerman invitation made the offering initially quite attractive. However, the community-wide conception of enhancing family–school relations had the further attraction of binding the overall community together around a common purpose. The Jewish community takes pride in the centrality of family and learning in its culture. To promote these connections as a point of common purpose built on fundamental shared values. It also enabled the community to emphasize similarity within itself in the face of external stresses fostered by a campaign in Quebec to secede from Canada and establish a French-speaking, independent country.

During the same visits, the JFS leadership at Baron de Hirsch Institute invited the community leadership to presentations to engage them in this community effort. For example, we invited the community leadership of the secular and religious school community to a presentation on family–school collaboration so that they could consider how this programme could best be used in their own schools.

Following the team training, the principals of the schools requested a separate training session for themselves so that they could feel comfortable that they could implement the strategies and skills before involving their staff and school communities. This session for the principals only galvanized a sense of common purpose across the schools. It was not until that meeting that the principals began to have a sense of a common purpose across the schools and a shared confidence that they could provide effective leadership in implementing the approach in their schools.

Another strand of the community-wide work derived from consultations I had with the JFS executive director and her schools supervisor. To make a truly community-wide effort, they recognized that the other major city-wide Jewish organizations also had to become collaborating partners in this change effort. Through telephone consultations, I coached the JFS leaders on how they might engage these other large organizations (which heretofore were frequent competitors with one another) in a shared project. While I am not certain what motivated these organizations to move from competition to collaboration, I believe that they all saw the task of connecting families and schools in support of children's learning as a community-level goal to which they all had special resources to contribute. Such a project could be more readily accepted as one to which they all would be valuable contributors, as opposed to being the domain of only one group.

After a period of initial cross-organization discussion, they established the "Family–School Collaboration Consortium", giving their coalition a name so as to signal their intent to work on the effort together over the long term. They then recruited a few schools as their pilot exemplars to showcase how they have implemented the model since the training workshops. An interesting aspect of the consortium's efforts to be inclusive was its effort to get the Jewish teachers' union to become a part of the consortium.

This effort first raised significant tensions among the union leadership because they did not want to be put in the position of having to agree as consortium partners to do specific things in relation to parents and the community. Such decisions might have to be considered as ᵖᵃʳᵗ of contract negotiations. It was clear that the union as an organization would always have to protect its ability to take independent positions in relation to school management. Therefore, rather than trying to engage them as members of the Family–School Collaboration Consortium, it was more appropriate to seek their interest and willingness to contribute to the project as an essential non-member stakeholder interested in achieving common goals. Representatives of the teachers' union were invited to attend discussion and planning meetings as participant observers of the consortium so that they would be informed about the group's purposes and plans. The consortium made clear that implementing the family–school collaboration model would strongly validate the work and contributions of teachers to the community. The teachers' union could only support the consortium's efforts when their representatives perceived that the consortium respected teachers as professionals and recognized them as essential contributors to the accomplishment of shared community purposes. When the consortium leaders accomplished this task, the union demonstrated increased openness to collaborate to achieve the overall goals.

QUESTION 10.   On reflection how would you define your role, task, and goals that you had set yourself in this piece of work (change, consultation, etc.)? In what ways are your own answers organized by your own cultural/ethnic influences?

Context 1.   My role as the director of the Family–School Collaboration Project (now called the Center for Family–School Collaboration) involved developing and maintaining relationships with the superintendent and deputy superintendents of Community School District #22 as well as with principals of schools we had worked with in seven schools. When this intervention began with the three chapter-I schools (poverty-level communities), my role was also to coordinate the efforts of each of the three consultants whom I assigned to work on-site with one of these three schools. I was also the head trainer for the series of cross-school training workshops.

The goal of this three-school programme, called the Family–School Partnership Program, was to implement our family–school collaboration model with the three schools as the basis for a whole-district application. This programme included the staff-training component, the development and implementation of a family-reading curriculum component in which family–school collaboration activities were embedded, as well as a parent-to-parent training component using a pre-existing programme called Mega-Skills (Rich, 1988) as the content base. The latter programme involved training a group of parent-trainers to teach other parents in a set of prescribed workshops how to impart critical values (e.g. cooperation, perseverance, etc.) essential for school and life achievement to their children. The implementation of this entire programme aimed at establishing a stable climate of family–school collaboration in which children would be routinely active participants in all family–school activities. The shift in climate was measured by changes in school policy, classroom and school-wide activities, increased parental involvement in school activities, changes in teacher and parent attitudes towards cooperative educational efforts, and increased attendance and academic achievement by the students.

These definitions of roles, tasks, and goals are certainly shaped by a set of values that define society and large institutions like schools as improvable through planned change efforts (Lippitt et al., 1958). I accept as a basic premise that all children can learn and that professionals must find the educational, developmental, and psychological support practices that will insure children's academic and socio-emotional development.

Context 2.   With the Jewish Family Services of the Baron de Hirsch Institute in Montreal, my role was that of organizational consultant, trainer, and change agent. My tasks were to provide the JFS leadership with a sense of how they might envision a collaborative and systemic community-building mission in their work with schools as well as to their staff and teams of school staff and parents to achieve specific goals and purposes. To accomplish these tasks, I had to increase the willingness and motivation of the various community stakeholders to build collaborative relationships between families and schools. I also had to provide supervisors, social workers, and the teams of school staff and parents with concrete skills to implement specific climate-building activities so they would be able to experience the transforming power of collaborative family–school relations. I consistently provided ongoing support (by telephone) for the JFS supervisor coordinating the whole programme so that she felt able to continue the change process in spite of predictable resistances.

I was particularly challenged in this context because the goals, purposes, and hoped-for outcomes of the work were defined from the beginning at the community level. While family–school collaboration is implemented in schools and school districts, I conceive its importance and ultimate purpose as community building. My own emphasis on making professional contributions—an emphasis that is certainly grounded in my own Jewish values—has a positive impact on children and families as well as a community-level impact. Imparting the importance of learning and of community participation to children as a legacy of family life is a critical belief for me.

QUESTION 11.   What were the forces acting on you that led you to choose this course of action and to define yourself in this way (your own skill base, beliefs, ethical position, financial reward, cultural influences, or pressure from others, managers, bosses, colleagues, allegiances, etc. or particular ambitions of success, fame, etc.)?

My discussions of both the Family–School Partnership Program and JFS reflect the fact that I have always been interested in large-scale community-level change. I very self-consciously sought an intensive multidisciplinary graduate training that would give me the clinical, organizational, and social planning skills to competently implement planned change efforts. Founding and directing the Family–School Collaboration Project (and later the Center) represents a convergence of many personal, professional, and political strands in my life (including 1960s experiences in civil rights efforts and the Vietnam anti-war movement, experiences working in the Hong Kong resettlement areas as one of a few Caucasians among hundreds of thousands of Chinese, teaching secondary school in California and Kentucky in African–American communities, working as a consultant in a low-income housing project, and founding and leading the Yonkers Fair Housing Council to counter city-wide resistance to federal court–ordered racial desegregation in housing and schools). As a person and a professional, I see myself operating in the "connecting" and community-building business. My clinical work as a family therapist provides me with a range of practised interpersonal and intervention skills and a systemic focus that forms a basis for these connecting efforts.

I suppose that my Jewish background also contributes to my strong sense of obligation to be a constructive force in my community. My strengths in envisioning large-scale goals and conceiving how to achieve them include the courage to be grandiose in conception and practical-minded in intervention skills. My own ambitions are driven by a desire to make large-scale contributions to improve life for myself and others. I have always been drawn to contexts and issues involving changes to achieve racial harmony and justice.

QUESTION 12.   If you reflect on the components of this piece of work that were successful or those that were failures, how would you link those forces with those successes or failures? Specifically, what influences from your own current and past experiences, both personal and professional, have effected how those choices were made?

Most important in my choices to focus my energies towards large-scale organizational change that can directly affect ongoing institutional (i.e. school) experiences of children and families has been my range of personal and professional experiences (listed above) and the interdisciplinary graduate training in applied social psychology I sought out to become an effective change agent. Successful social change efforts require conceptual, strategic, and logistical planning and the perseverance to stick with the work over the long term (Liggett, 1980). My personal and professional experiences have enabled me to recognize how the small events in proximal time are also manifestations or building blocks for long-term organizational change. The most critical choices have been the selection of a staff that is excited by the clinical work at the micro level and the organizational interventions at the macro level. It takes dedication to collaboration as a central way of working as a colleague and consultant to model it over the long term, with multiple levels of an organization. Training a large enough cadre of interested professionals to carry on this work and implement it widely is a task that needs doing. In the first context, I trained a group of skilled colleagues to work in the programme. They provided the on-site consultant support for each school while I focused on the large-scale training presentations and the administrative and supervisory functions. In the second context, I was the only consultant. I have made choices to be an interventionist for most of my professional life. Now I am focusing much more on the pathways for training different types of professionals and graduate students in systemic consultation skills. Success in these endeavours on the community or societal scale requires the committed involvement of many skilled professionals over the long term. Finding ways to support such an undertaking is still a question to be answered.

REFERENCES

Ackoff, R. L. (1960). Systems, organizations and interdisciplinary research. In: F. E. Emery (Ed.), *Systems Thinking* (pp. 330–347). Harmondsworth, Middlesex: Penguin/Allen Lane.

Ainsworth, M. D. S., Blehar, M. C., Waters, E., & Wall, S. (1978). *Patterns of Attachment: Assessed in the Strange Situation and at Home.* Hillsdale, NJ: Lawrence Erlbaum.

Allport, G. (1954). *The Nature of Prejudice.* New York: Doubleday.

Andersen, T. (Ed.) (1991). *The Reflecting Team: Dialogues and Dialogues about the Dialogues.* New York: W. W. Norton.

Andersen, T. (1995). Reflecting processes: acts of informing and forming: You can borrow my eyes, but you must not take them away from me. In S. Friedman (Ed.), *The Reflecting Team in Action: Collaborative Practice in Theory* (pp. 11–37). New York: Guilford Press.

Anderson, H. (1990). Opening the door for change through continuing the conversation. In T. Todd & M. Selekman (Eds.), *Family Therapy Approaches with Adolescent Substance Abuse.* Needham, MA: Allyn & Bacon.

Anderson, H. (1994). "Therapy as Mutual Inquiry: Combining the Clients' Expertise on Themselves and the Therapist's Expertise on a Process." Paper presented to the meeting of the Realities and Relationships: Social Construction in Therapy and Organization Development Conference, Taos, New Mexico (2 April).

203

Anderson, H. (1995). Collaborative language systems: Toward a post-modern therapy. In R. Mikesell, D. O. Lusterman, & S. McDaniel (Eds.), *Integrating Family Therapy: Family Psychology and Systems Therapy*. Washington, DC: American Psychological Association.

Anderson, H. (1997). *Conversation, Language and Possibilities: A Postmodern Approach to Therapy*. New York: Basic Books.

Anderson, H., & Goolishian, H. (1988). Human systems as linguistic systems: preliminary and evolving ideas about the implications for clinical theory. *Family Process, 27* (4): 371–393.

Anderson, H., & Goolishian, H. (1990). Beyond cybernetics: comments on Atkinson and Heath's "Further Thoughts on Second Order Family". *Family Process, 29*: 157–163.

Anderson, H., & Goolishian, H. (1991). Thinking about multi-agency work with substance abusers and their families. *Journal of Strategic and Systemic Therapies, 10*: 20–35.

Anderson, H., & Goolishian, H. (1992). The client is the expert: a not-knowing approach to therapy. In S. McNamee & K. J. Gergen (Eds.), *Constructing Therapy: Social Construction and the Therapeutic Process*. London: Sage.

Anderson, H., Goolishian, A., & Windermand, L. (1986). Problem-determined systems: towards transformation in family therapy. *Journal of Strategic and Systemic Therapies, 5*: 1–13.

Anderson, H., & Rambo, A. (1988). An experiment in systemic family therapy training: a trainer and trainee perspective. *Journal of Strategic and Systemic Therapies, 7*: 54–70.

Anderson, H., & Swim, S. (1995). Supervision as collaborative conversation: connecting the voices of supervisor and supervisee. *Journal of Systemic Therapies, 14* (2): 1–13.

Audit Commission (1989). *The Probation Service: Promoting Value for Money*. London: HMSO.

Barzun, J. (1965). *Race: A Study of Superstition*. New York: Harper & Row.

Bateson, G. (1972). *Steps to an Ecology of Mind*. New York: Ballantine Books.

Bateson, G., Jackson, D. D., Haley, J., & Weakland, J. H. (1956). Toward a theory of schizophrenia. *Behavioral Science, 1* (4): 251–264.

Beal, A. L. (1995). Post-traumatic stress disorder in prisoners of war and combat veterans of the Dieppe Raid: a 50-year follow-up. *Canadian Journal of Psychiatry, 40* (5): 177–184.

Ben-Tovim, G., Gabriel, J., Law, I., & Stredder, K. (1986). *The Local Politics of Race*. Basingstoke: Macmillan.

Bion, W. R. (1961). *Experiences in Groups*. London: Tavistock Publications.

Bleich, A., Shalev, A., Shoham, S., Solomon, Z., & Kotler, M. (1992). PTSD: Theoretical and practical consideration as reflected through Koach—an innovative treatment project. *Journal of Traumatic Stress, 5* (2): 265–271.

Borwick, E. (1978). *The Truncated Pyramid*. Brussels: Borwick Publications.

Borwick, E. (1986). The family therapist as business consultant. In: L. C. Wynne, S. H. McDaniel, & T. T. Weber (Eds.), *Systems Consultation: A New Perspective*. New York: Guilford Press.

Boscolo, L., Cecchin, G., Hoffman, L., & Penn, P. (1987). *Milan Systemic Family Therapy*. New York: Basic Books.

Boszormeny-Nagy, I., & Spark, G. M. (1973). *Invisible Loyalties: Reciprocity in Intergenerational Family Therapy*. New York: Harper & Row.

Bottoms, A. E., & McWilliams, W. (1979). A non-treatment paradigm for probation practice. *British Journal of Social Work, 9* (2): 159–202.

Bowlby, J. (1969). *Attachment and Loss, Vol. 1: Attachment*. London: Hogarth.

Bowlby, J. (1973). *Attachment and Loss, Vol. 2: Separation, Anxiety, and Anger*. London: Hogarth.

Bowlby, J. (1980). *Attachment and Loss, Vol. 3: Loss*. London: Hogarth.

Burr, V. (1995). *An Introduction to Social Constructionism*. London: Routledge.

Campbell, D. (1995). *Learning Consultation: A Systemic Framework*. London: Karnac Books.

Campbell, D., Coldicott, T., & Kinsella, K. (1994). *Systemic Work with Organizations*. London: Karnac Books.

Campbell, D., Draper, R., & Huffington, C. (1990). *Systemic Approach to Consultation*. London: Karnac Books.

Cecchin, G. (1987). Hypothesizing–circularity–neutrality revisited: an invitation to curiosity. *Family Process, 26* (4): 405–413.

Cecchin, G., Lane D., & Ray, W. (1992). *Irreverence: A Strategy for Therapists' Survival*. London: Karnac Books.

Cleese, J. (1991). "Stress at Work." Presentation to inaugural meeting of Organisation Stress Service, Institute of Family Therapy, London.

Coleman, J. S., & Hoffer, T. (1987). *Public and Private High Schools: The Impact of Communities*. New York: Basic Books.

Coleman Report (1989). Home Office Circular.

Cooklin, A., & Gorell Barnes, G. (1988). Sexuality, intimacy, partners and the workplace. Published as "Sessualità e Intimità, Coppia e Lavoro", in M. Andolfi, C. Angelo, & C. Saccu (Eds.), *La Coppia in Crisi*. Roma: I.T.F.

Cooklin, A., & Gorell Barnes, G. (1991). Taboo and social order: new encounters for family and therapist. In E. Imber Black (Ed.), *Secrets in Families and Family Therapy*. New York/London: W.W. Norton.

Cooper, T. A. (1981). *The Individual in a Bureaucratic Organisation: Victim or Participant? Management and the Concept of Self*. Monograph, Group for the Advancement of Psychodynamics and Psychotherapy in Social Work (1 April).

Department of Health/Home Office (1994). *Race, Gender and Equal Opportunities. Review of Health and Social Services for Mentally Disordered Offenders and Others Requiring Similar Services, Vol. 6*. London: HMSO.

Derrida, J. (1978). *Writing and Difference*, trans A. Bass. Chicago, IL: University of Chicago Press.

De Shazer, S. (1985). *Keys to Solutions in Brief Therapy*. New York: W. W. Norton.

DiNicola, V. (1994). The strange and the familiar: cross-cultural encounters among families, therapists, and consultants. In M. Andolfi & R. Haber (Eds.), *Please Help Me with This Family: Using Consultants as Resources in Family Therapy* (pp. 33–52). New York: Brunner/Mazel.

Drucker, P. (1990). Managing the non-profit organisation. London: Butterworth/Heineman.

Edmunds, I. W., & Thomas, L. K. (1978). The role of the probation officer in court. *The Journal of Legal Practice in Magistrates Court, 4* (3).

Elizur, Y. (1993). Ecosystemic training: conjoining supervision and organizational development. *Family Process, 32* (2): 185–201.

Elizur, Y. (1994a). Community mental health in Israel: anatomy of failure. *Society and Welfare, 14* (2): 103–127 [Hebrew].

Elizur, Y. (1994b). Whose pain is it? Consulting at the interface between families and social-medical systems. In: M. Andolfi & R. Haber (Eds.), *Please Help Me with This Family: Using Consultants as Resources in Family Therapy* (pp. 162–180). New York: Brunner/Mazel.

Elizur, Y. (1996). Involvement, collaboration, and empowerment: a model for consultation with human-service agencies and the development of family-oriented care. *Family Process, 35*: 191–210.

Elizur, Y., & Minuchin, S. (1989). *Institutionalizing Madness: Families, Therapy and Society.* New York: Basic Books.

Emery F., & Trist, E. L. (1965). The causal texture of organisational environments. *Human Relations, 18:* 21–32.

Faulkner, D. E. R. (1989). *Future of the Probation Service: A View from Government.* Home Office Circular (July).

Fernando, S. (1988). *Race and Culture in Psychiatry.* London: Croom Helm [reprinted London: Routledge, 1989].

Fernando, S. (1991). *Mental Health, Race and Culture.* London: Macmillan/MIND.

Ferns, P., & Madden, M. (1995). *Training to Promote Race Equality—in Mental Health in a Multi Ethnic Society,* edited by S. Fernando. London: Routledge.

Fluegelman, A. (1981). *More New Games! and Playful Ideas from the New Games Foundation.* Garden City, NY: Dolphin Books/Doubleday.

Foucault, M. (1972). *The Archeology of Knowledge.* New York: Harper.

Foucault, M. (1980). *Power/Knowledge: Selected Interviews and Other Writings 1972–1977,* edited by C. Gordon. London: Harvester Wheatsheaf; New York: Pantheon.

Fried, M. N., & Fried, M. H. (1980). *Transitions: Four Rituals in Eight Cultures.* New York: W. W. Norton.

Friedman, E. H. (1985). *Generation to Generation: Family Process in Church and Synagogue.* New York: Guilford Press.

Fryer, P. (1984). *Staying Power: The History of Black People in Britain.* London: Pluto Press.

Furman, B. (1990). Glasnost in family therapy. *Family Therapy Networker, 14* (3): 61–63.

Gennep, A. (1969). *Les Rites de Passage.* Paris: Mouton Maison des Sciences de l'Homme.

Gergen, K., & Gergen, M. (1986). Narrative form and the construction of psychological science. In: T. Sarbin (Ed.), *Narrative Psychology: The Storied Nature of Human Conduct.* New York: Praeger.

Gleick, J. (19887). *Chaos: Making of a New Science.* London/New York: Penguin.

Goffman, E. (1959). *The Presentation of Self in Everyday Life.* New York: Anchor Books.

Goolishian, H., & Anderson, H. (1987). Language systems and therapy: an evolving idea. *Journal of Psychotherapy, 24* (3S): 529–538.

Goolishian, H., & Anderson, H. (1988). Human systems: some evolving ideas about the problems they present and our work with them. In L. Reiter, J. Brunner, & S. Reither-Theil (Eds.), *Von der*

Familientherapie zur systemischen Therapie. Heidelberg: Springer-Verlag.

Gorell Barnes, G. (1990). The little woman and the world of work. In: R. Perlberg & A. Miller (Eds.), *Gender and Power in Families.* London: Routledge.

Guba, E. G., & Lincoln, Y. S. (1989). *Fourth Generation Evaluation.* Newbury, CA: Sage.

Hampden-Turner, C. (1990). *Charting the Corporate Mind.* Oxford: Blackwell.

Herman, J. L. (1992). *Trauma and Recovery: The Aftermath of Violence.* New York: Basic Books.

Hirschorn, L., & Gilmore, T. (1980). An application of family concepts to influencing organisational behaviour. *Administrative Science Quarterly, 25*: 18–36.

Hobfoll, S. E., Dunahoo, C. A., & Monnier, J. (1995). Conservation of resources and traumatic stress. In J. R. Freedy & S. E. Hobfoll (Eds.), *Traumatic Stress: From Theory to Practice* (pp. 29–47). New York: Plenum Press.

Holmes, T. (1900). *The London Police Courts.* London: Nelson.

Home Office (1988). *Green Paper: Punishment, Custody and the Community.* Home Office Circular.

Home Office and Central Office of Information (1977). *Racial Discrimination. A Guide to the Race Relations Act 1977.* London: HMSO.

Howe, R., & Von Foerster, H. (1974). Cybernetics at Illinois. *Forum, 6*: 15–17.

Imber-Black, E. (1988). *Families and Larger Systems.* New York: Guilford Press.

Immerwahr, J. (with J. Boese & W. Friedman) (1994). *Broken Contract: Connecticut Citizens Look at Public Education.* New York: Public Agenda.

Janoff-Bulman, R. (1992). *Shattered Assumptions: Toward a New Psychology of Trauma.* New York: Free Press.

Jenkins, H. (1991). When are guests best? East/West links and the development of collaboration in family therapy training programmes: some possible difficulties. *Psychoterapia* [Poland], *1*: 61–69.

Johnson, J., & Immerwahr, J. (1994). *First Things First: What Americans Expect from the Public Schools.* New York: Public Agenda.

Jones, J. S. (1981). How different are human races? *Nature, 293*: 188–190.

Jones, M. (1968). *Social Psychiatry in Practice.* Harmondsworth: Penguin Books.

Kaffman, M., Nitzan, D., & Elizur, Y. (1996). Bridging individual, family, and community care: a comprehensive treatment program for the chronic mentally ill. *Israel Journal of Psychiatry and Related Sciences, 33* (3): 144–157.

Katz, D., & Kahn, R. L. (1966). *The Social Psychology of Organisations.* New York: Wiley.

Keeney, B. P. (1983). *Aesthetics of Change.* New York: Guilford Press.

Kerr, M. E., & Bowen, M. (1988). *Family Evaluation.* New York: W. W. Norton.

Kolb, L. C. (1993). The psychobiology of PTSD: perspectives and reflections on the past, present, and future. *Journal of Traumatic Stress, 6* (3): 293–304.

Kuhn, T. S. (1970). *The Structure of Scientific Revolutions* (2nd ed.). Chicago, IL: University of Chicago Press.

Kulka, R. A., Schlenger, W. E., Fairbank, J. A., Hough, R. L., Jordan, B. K., Marmar, C. R., & Weiss, D. S. (1990). *Trauma and the Vietnam War Generation: Report of Findings from the National Vietnam Veterans Readjustment Study.* New York: Brunner/Mazel.

La Fontaine, J. S. (1985). *Initiation: Ritual Drama and Secret Knowledge across the World.* Harmondsworth: Penguin.

Lee, K. A., Vaillant, G. E., Torrey, W. C., & Elder, G. H. (1995). A 50-year prospective study of the psychological sequelae of World War II combat. *American Journal of Psychiatry, 152* (4): 516–522.

Leff, J. P., Berkowitz R., Shavit, N., Strachan, A., Glass, I. & Vaughan, C. (1990). A trial of family therapy v. a relatives' group for schizophrenia. Two year follow-up. *British Journal of Psychiatry, 150*: 571–577.

Leff, J., Kuipers, L., Berkowitz, R., Eberlein-Vries, R., & Sturgeon, D. (1982). A controlled trial of social intervention in the families of schizophrenic patients. *British Journal of Psychiatry, 141*: 121–134.

Levy, A., & Neumann, M. (1984). The role of suggestion in the treatment of combat reactions within a specific military installation during the war in Lebanon. *Israel Journal of Psychiatry and Related Sciences, 21* (2): 85–91.

Levy, A., Witztum, E., Granek, M., & Kotler, M. (1990). Combat reactions, Israel 1948–1973, Part 4. The 1967 Six Days War. *Sihot-Dialogue: Israel Journal of Psychotherapy, 4* (3): 217–221.

Lewis, G. (1980). *Day of Shining Red.* Cambridge: Cambridge University Press.

Liggett, W. A. (1980). "Unfreezing Behaviour During Social Change: An Empirical Test of Selected Theoretical Propositions." Unpublished Ph.D. dissertation, New York University.

Lippitt, R. L., Watson, J., & Westley, B. (1958). *The Dynamics of Planned Change: A Comparative Study of Principles and Techniques.* New York: Harcourt, Brace & World.

Lyotard, J. F. (1984). *The Post-Modern Condition: A Report on Knowledge.* Minneapolis, MN: University of Minnesota Press.

Main, T. F (1957). The ailment. *British Journal of Medical Psychology, 30:* 129.

Malik, K. (1996). *The Meaning of Race: Race, History and Culture in Western Society.* Basingstoke: Macmillan.

McCaughan, N., & Palmer, B. (1994). *Systems Thinking for Harassed Managers.* London: Karnac Books.

McDaniel, S. H., Wynne, L. C., & Weber, T. T. (1986). The territory of systems consultation. In L. C. Wynne, S. H. McDaniel, & T. T. Weber (Eds.), *Systems Consultation: A New Perspective for Family Therapy* (pp. 16–28). New York: Guilford.

McNamee, S., & Gergen, K. (1992). *Therapy as Social Construction.* London: Sage.

Mental Health Act Commission (1985). *The First Biennial Report of the Mental Health Act Commission 1983–85.* London: HMSO.

Mental Health Act Commission (1987). *The Mental Health Act Commission. Second Biennial Report 1985–87.* London: HMSO.

Mental Health Act Commission (1989). *The Mental Health Act Commission. Third Biennial Report 1987–89.* London: HMSO.

Mental Health Act Commission (1991). *The Mental Health Act Commission. Fourth Biennial Report 1989–91.* London: HMSO.

Mental Health Act Commission (1993). *The Mental Health Act Commission. Fifth Biennial Report 1991–93.* London: HMSO.

Mental Health Act Commission (1995). *The Mental Health Act Commission. Sixth Biennial Report 1993–95.* London: HMSO.

Menzies, I. E. P. (1970). "The Functioning of Social Systems as a Defence against Anxiety." Tavistock Pamphlet No. 3, Centre for Applied Social Research. London: Tavistock Institute of Human Relations.

Menzies Lyth, I. (1988). *Containing Anxiety in Institutions.* London: Free Association Books.

Merkel, W. T., & Carpenter, L. J. (1987). A cautionary note on the application of family therapy principles to organisational consultation. *American Journal of Orthopsychiatry, 57* (1): 111–115.

Miller, E. J. (Ed.) (1976). *Task and Organisation.* London/New York: Wiley.

Miller, E. J. (1989). *The Leicester Model: Experiential Study of Groups and Organisational Processes.* London: Tavistock Publications.

Miller, E. J., & Rice, A. K. (1967). *Systems of Organisation: The Control of Task and Sentient Boundaries*. London: Tavistock Publications.

Miller, L. (1994). Civilian post-traumatic stress disorder: clinical syndromes and psychotherapeutic strategies. *Psychotherapy, 31* (4): 655–664.

National Audit Office (1989). *Home Office: Control and Management of Probation Services in England and Wales*. London: HMSO (May).

Obholzer, A., & Roberts, V. Z. (Eds.) (1994). *The Unconscious at Work: Individual and Organisation Stress in the Human Services*. London: Routledge.

Patten, J. (1988). *Home Office Policy for Probation*. Home Office Circular (April).

Penn, P. (1982). Circular questioning. *Family Process, 21*: 267–280.

Penn, P. (1985). Feed-forward: future questions, future maps. *Family Process, 24*: 299–310.

Rabinowitz, S., Margalit, C., Mark, M., Solomon, Z., & Bleich, A. (1990). Debate reawakened: premorbid factors for soldiers with refractory posttraumatic stress disorder. *Psychological Reports, 67*: 1363–1366.

Ramseyer, U. (1977). Ritual and music in Tenganen Pegeringsingan. In: *The Art and Culture of Bali*. Oxford: Oxford University Press.

Rich, D. (1988). *MegaSkills: How Families Can Help Children Succeed in School and Beyond*. Boston: Houghton-Mifflin.

Richards, A. (1956). *Chisungu: A Girl's Initiation Ceremony Among the Bemba of Zambia*. London: Faber & Faber.

Ricoeur, P. (1983). *Time and Narrative*. Chicago, IL: University of Illinois Press.

Roberts, E. (1991). *Organisational Theory Relevant to Social Work Departments as Organisations*. Research Highlights in Social Work, No. 4. London: Jessica Kingsley.

Rolbant, S. (1971). *The Israeli Soldier: Profile of an Army*. New York: Thomas Yoseloff.

Rorty, R. (1979). *Philosophy and the Mirror of Nature*. Princeton, NJ: Princeton University Press.

Rose, S., Lewontin, R. C., & Kamin, L. (1984). *Not in Our Genes. Biology, Ideology and Human Nature*. Harmondsworth, Middlesex: Penguin.

Rosenheck, R. (1986). Impact of posttraumatic stress disorder of World War II on the next generation. *Journal of Nervous and Mental Disease, 174*: 319–327.

Said, E. W. (1978). *Orientalism*. London: Routledge & Kegan Paul [reprinted Harmondsworth, Middlesex: Penguin, 1985].

Salmon, T. W. (1919). The war neuroses and their lesson. *New York State Journal of Medicine, 51*: 993–994.

Scaturo, D. J. (1992). The impact of combat trauma across the family life cycle: clinical considerations. *Journal of Traumatic Stress, 5* (2): 273–288.

Scurfield, R. M., Wong, L. E., & Zeerocah, E. B. (1992). An evaluation of the impact of "helicopter ride therapy" for in-patient Vietnam veterans with war-related PTSD. *Military Medicine, 157*: 67–73.

Selvini Palazzoli, M. (1986). *The Hidden Games of Organizations*. New York: Pantheon.

Selvini Palazzoli, M., Boscolo, L., Cecchin. G., & Prata, G. (1980a). Hypothesizing–circularity–neutrality: three guidelines for the conductor of the session. *Family Process, 19* (1): 3–12.

Selvini Palazzoli, M., Boscolo, L., Cecchin, G., & Prata, G. (1980b). The problem of the referring person. *Journal of Marital and Family Therapy, 6*: 3–9.

Senge, P. M. (1990). *The Fifth Discipline*. New York: Doubleday.

Shorter Oxford Dictionary (1973). Oxford: Clarendon Press.

Sluzki, C. E. (1992). Transformations: a blueprint for narrative change in therapy. *Family Process, 31*: 217–230.

Sluzki, C. E. (1996). *La Red Social: Frontera de la Terapia Sistemica*. Barcelona: Gedisa [in Spanish]; Rio de Janeiro: Casa do Psicologo [in Portuguese].

Sluzki, C. E., & Veron, E. (1971). The double-bind as a universal pathogenic situation. *Family Process, 10*: 397–410.

Solomon, Z. (1993). *Combat Stress Reaction: The Enduring Toll of War*. New York: Plenum Press.

Solomon, Z., & Benbenishty, R. (1986). The role of proximity, immediacy and expectancy in frontline treatment of combat stress reaction among Israelis in the Lebanon war. *American Journal of Psychiatry, 143*: 613–617.

Solomon, Z., Mikulincer, M., & Benbenishty, R. (1989). Combat stress reactions: clinical manifestations and correlates. *Military Psychology, 1*: 35–47.

Solomon, Z., Shalev, A., Spiro, S. E., Dolev, A., Bleich, A., Waysman, M., & Cooper, S. (1992a). Negative psychometric outcomes: self report measures and a follow-up telephone survey. *Journal of Traumatic Stress, 5* (2): 225–246.

Solomon, Z., Waysman, M., Levy, G., Fried, B., Mikulincer, M., Benbenishty, R., Florian, V., & Bleich, A. (1992b). From front line to home front: a study of secondary traumatization. *Family Process, 31*: 289–301.

St. George, S. (1996). Using "As If" processes in family therapy supervision. *The Family Journal: Counseling and Therapy for Couples and Families, 4* (4): 357–365.

Tomm, K. (1985). Circular interviewing: a multifaceted clinical tool. In: D. Campbell & R. Draper (Eds.), *Applications of Systemic Therapy: The Milan Approach.* London: Grune & Stratton.

Tomm, K. (1987). Interventive interviewing, II. Reflexive questions as a means to enable self healing. *Family Process, 26:* 167–183.

Tomm, K. (1988). Interventive interviewing, III. Intending to ask linear, circular or reflexive questions. *Family Process, 27:* 1–16.

Trist, E. L., & Sofer, C. (1959). *Exploration in Group Relations.* Leicester: Leicester University Press.

Watzlawick, P., Weakland, J. H., & Fisch, R. (1974). *Change: Principles of Problem Formation and Problem Resolution.* New York: W. W. Norton.

Weakland, J. H. (1960). The "double-bind" hypothesis and three-party interaction. In D. D. Jackson (Ed.), *The Etiology of Schizophrenia.* New York: Basic Books.

Weiss, H. M. (1996). "Family–School Collaboration: Opportunities for Systems Consultants." Paper presented at the annual meeting of the American Psychological Association, Toronto, Canada (August).

Weiss, H. M., & Edwards, M. E. (1992). The family–school collaboration project: systemic interventions for school improvement. In: S. L. Christensen & J. C. Conoley (Eds.), *Home–School Collaboration: Enhancing Children's Academic and Social Competence* (pp. 215–243). Silver Spring, MD: National Association of School Psychologists.

Wellman, D. (1977). *Portraits of White Racism.* Cambridge: Cambridge University Press.

White, M. (1995). *Re-Authoring Lives: Interviews and Essays.* Adelaide: Dulwich Centre Publications.

Witztum, E., Levy, A., Solomon, Z., & Kotler, M. (1991). Combat reactions, Israel 1974–1982, Part 6: reorganization. *Sihot-Dialogue: Israel Journal of Psychotherapy, 5* (2): 139–144.

Wynne, L. C., McDaniel, S. H., & Weber, T. T. (Eds.) (1986). *Systems Consultation: A New Perspective for Family Therapy.* New York: Guilford.

INDEX

Coventry University